Baseball in Little Rock

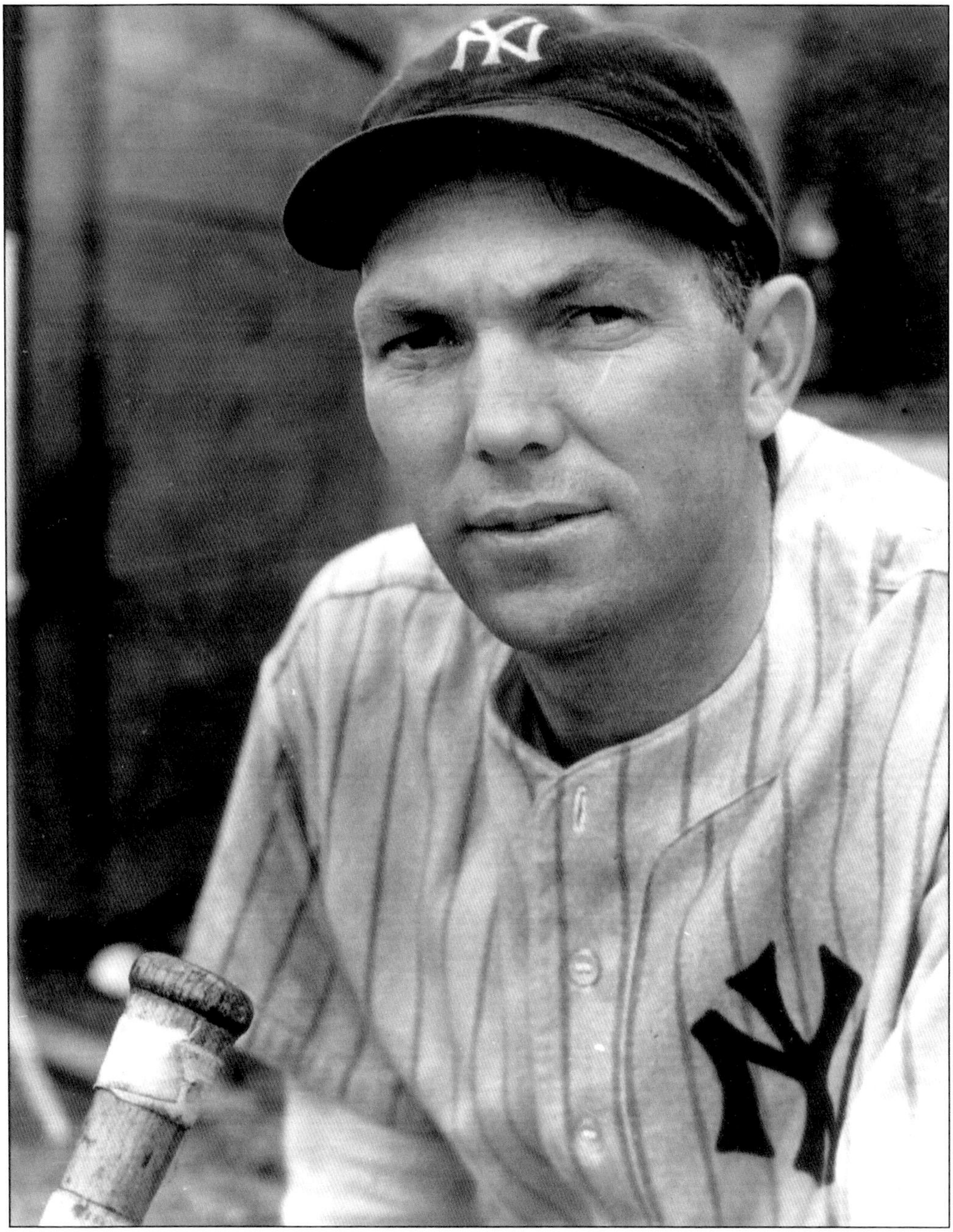

Bill Dickey is the Hall of Fame player most closely identified with the Arkansas Travelers. Born in Bastrop, Louisiana, but raised in Little Rock, he was signed as an 18 year old. In 1926, he played 21 games for Little Rock and batted .375. As the starting catcher for the New York Yankees, his career statistics include a .313 average, 1,209 RBIs, and 202 homers. He was named to the Hall of Fame in 1954 as voters rewarded Dickey's 13 consecutive years of catching 100 or more games. (Courtesy of the National Baseball Hall of Fame Library, Cooperstown, New York.)

BASEBALL IN LITTLE ROCK

Terry Turner

ARCADIA PUBLISHING

ISBN 978-0-7385-3300-1

Published by Arcadia Publishing
Charleston, South Carolina

Printed in the United States of America

Library of Congress Catalog Card Number: 2004107435

For all general information contact Arcadia Publishing at:
Telephone 843-853-2070
Fax 843-853-0044
E-mail sales@arcadiapublishing.com
For customer service and orders:
Toll-Free 1-888-313-2665

Visit us on the Internet at www.arcadiapublishing.com

To Shelby and Sue for a lifetime of love.
To Brenda, my love of a lifetime.

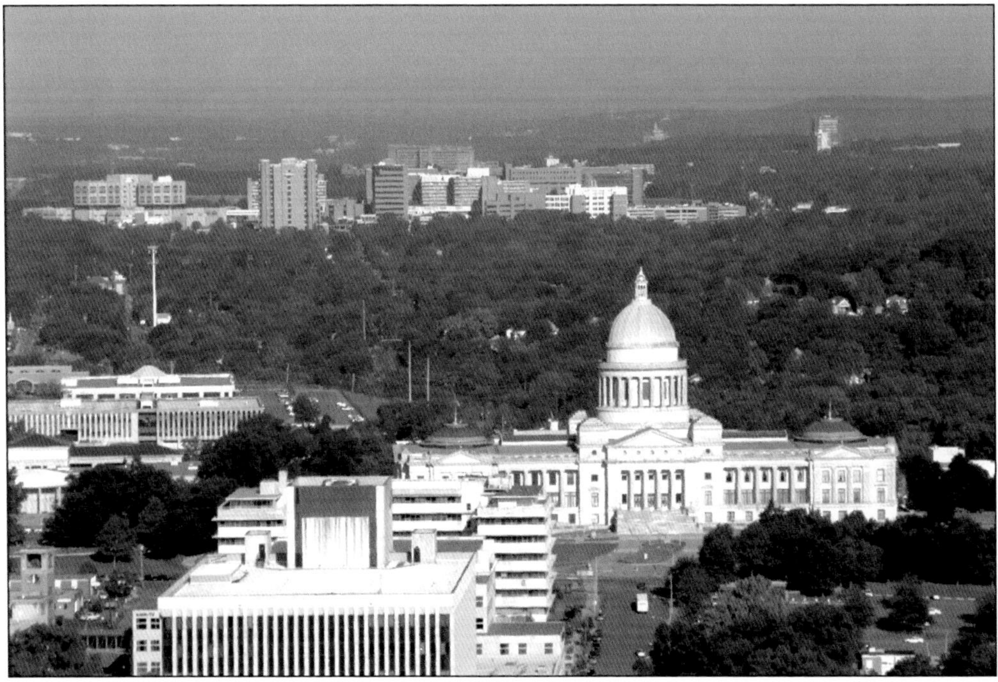

Little Rock, Arkansas, is defined by two main factors: its location on the banks of the Arkansas River and its role as the state's capital city. From downtown looking west toward Ray Winder Field—the mecca for Arkansas baseball fans—both the river and the dome of the Capitol dominate the landscape. The Travelers baseball team is not only a city's team, but a state's team. (Courtesy of Kirk Jordan.)

Contents

ACKNOWLEDGMENTS

This book would not exist without the assistance I received from the Arkansas Travelers Baseball organization. I am very grateful for the access General Manager Bill Valentine afforded me and for the courteous assistance of Phil Elson, Pete Laven, and Troy Russell. Carl Enna spent countless hours on research and photography. Kerry Rodtnick, my own "K-Rod," was a technical wizard in preparing the images. Mark Evans, Jim Bailey, R. C. Otey, Rex Nelson and Jim Rasco provided great historical insights. Louise Atkinson Isgrig, Kathy McQueen, Betty Baird, Don Curdie, and Shirley Rieve all shared material from their private collections. Texas League President Tom Kayser offered images, as well as perspectives, on the Travelers; as did Bill Burdick, manager, Photo Services Department of the National Baseball Hall of Fame and Library, Cooperstown, New York. I appreciate my editor, Jeff Ruetsche, and my publisher, Arcadia Publishing, for the opportunity to write this book. Having two journalists in one family makes for a challenging writing experience. I especially thank my wife Brenda for her help with this book. She's been my editor for over 30 years and remains the only "B" I love better than baseball.

INTRODUCTION

The Arkansas Travelers have played under one name, with one mascot, and on just two fields for parts of three centuries. The team has spent more time in the cellar than in any other place in the standings, but dedicated fans have remained loyal. So dedicated, in fact, that Arkansas became a "fan-owned" team in 1960, with fans purchasing actual stock certificates in the team. The Travelers are not only a city's team, but a state's team. Keeping baseball in the state's capital has always been closer to the hearts of fans than a first place finish.

The team has had five Baseball Hall of Famers on its roster. Several individual stars gained local fame and Arkansas fans followed them in their pro careers. A trio of colorful character—which included a future United States Senator, a livery stable owner, and a former major league umpire—have guided the Travelers' fortunes throughout their history and could be called "saviors" of the team.

Like their namesake, the wandering lawyer of folk song legend, the Travelers are aptly named. The team began in the Southern League in 1895, played 61 years in the Southern Association, spent a season in the International League in 1963, then two years with the Pacific Coast League, and settled in the Texas League in 1966. In all, they've visited over 40 cities. They've traveled to Honolulu, Toronto, Seattle, Salt Lake City, Albuquerque, Buffalo, Syracuse and Lafayette (LA). Among their opening dates were Portland (OR), Denver and Austin.

Little Rock had no affiliation with any major league team until 1939. That year, the Detroit Tigers aligned with them for only one year. In 1946, the Travelers were under the guidance of the Chicago White Sox. Detroit returned to use Little Rock as a farm team off and on from 1948 to 1955. Kansas City, Baltimore and the Philadelphia Phillies all had contracts with the Travelers between 1956 and 1965.

The St. Louis Cardinals, a natural geographical choice, bonded with Arkansas from 1966 through 2000. Now the Anaheim Angels control player movement in Little Rock.

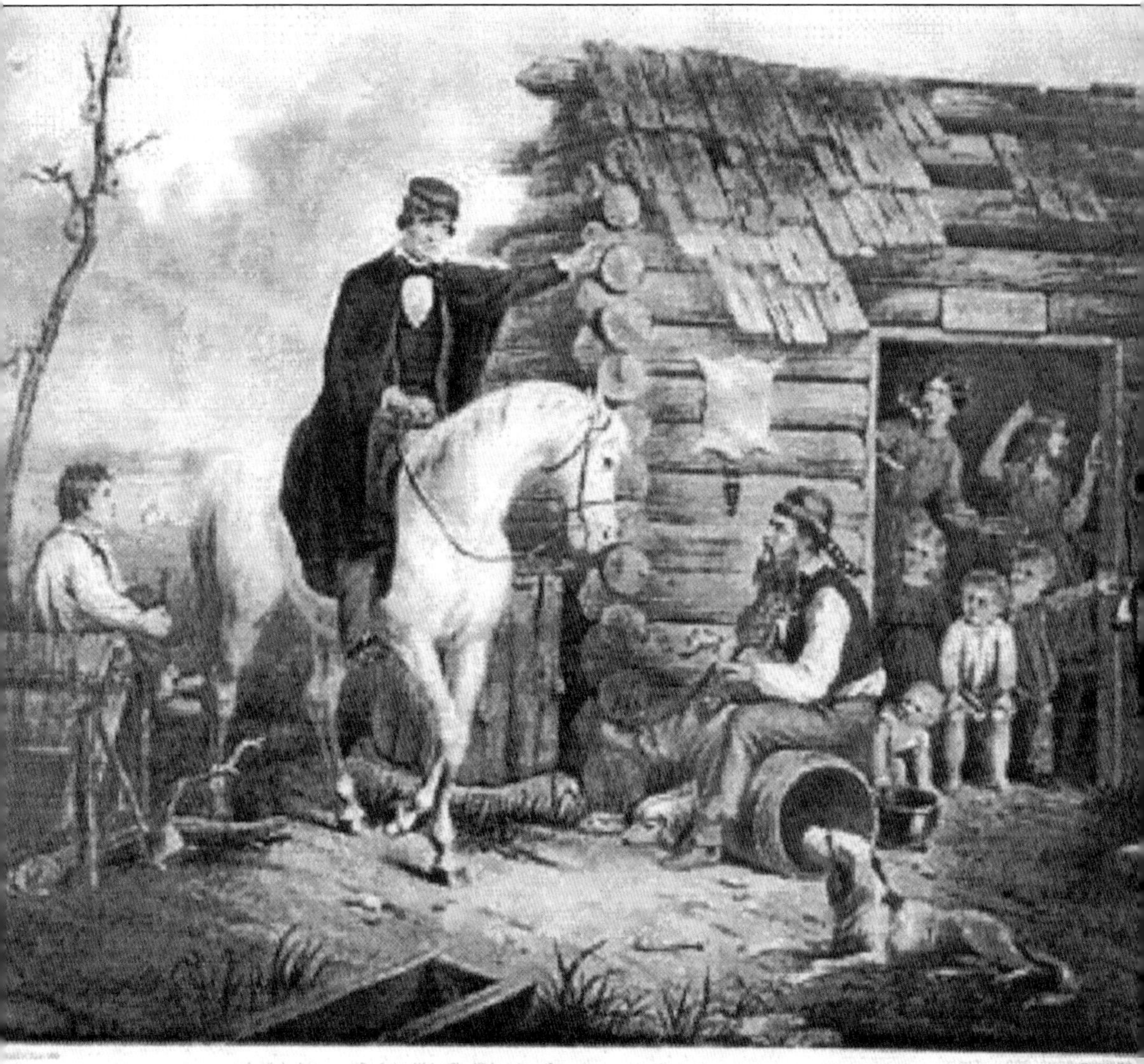

A legendary folk song is the origin for the name of the Little Rock baseball team. A lost traveler happened upon a squatter's cabin, but was offered no hospitality from the stubborn man who continued to play the same verse of a song on his fiddle. The frustrated "Traveler" got off his horse, took over the fiddle, and finished the verses of the song. The grateful squatter, impressed with learning the additional verses, finally offered the weary traveler food and lodging for the night. The song became famous from the Ozarks to the Appalachians. (Courtesy of the Butler Center for Arkansas Studies/ Central Arkansas Library System.)

One

The Early Years 1895–1931

Arkansas' first professional baseball team began life in 1895. The Little Rock Travelers' first season was in the eight-team Southern League. In a precursor of the Travelers' future, they played only 72 games with a 25-47 record, a .347 winning percentage. Future rival Memphis played just 69 games that season. Both teams dropped out of the league, which was not unusual in early professional baseball.

The Southern League had been in existence since 1885. It started with eight teams: Atlanta, Augusta, Nashville, Macon, Memphis, Chattanooga, Columbus and Birmingham, according to Marshall P. Wright, author of *The Southern Association in Baseball 1885-1961*. By the time Little Rock signed up in 1895, only Atlanta, Nashville, Memphis and Chattanooga remained from the original eight. Evansville, New Orleans, and Montgomery joined the Travelers in the pennant chase.

The Travelers' first season set the tone for a topsy-turvy future. Three times they would re-enter the Southern Association. They would eventually be members of four different leagues. Some historians list 1901 as the Travelers' first season, as it was the team's first full season, but 1895 was when Manager Frank Thyne sent out an 18-man team.

It appeared the Travelers did the right thing by sitting out the five seasons between 1896 and 1900. They came back with vengeance in 1901. The New Year brought forth a new name—the Southern Association—and for the first time in Southern baseball history, a professional season was played in its entirety. No members dropped out.

The 1901 Travelers won the first Southern Association pennant with a 76-45 record. Manager Michael Finn's team had some pop. Six batters topped the .300 batting mark. Catcher Ed Lynch hit .367, stole 23 bases and was second on the team with 81 runs scored during the 121-game schedule. First baseman Pat Wright hit .334 with 155 hits. Outfielder John Gilbert led the league with 56 steals, hit .323, and led the team with 105 runs. Home runs and RBI totals were not recorded.

On the mound, league ace Harry Allemang, had a 20-4 record and a league leading .833 winning percentage. Allemang was assisted by John Skopec, who also posted a .833 percentage with a 10-2 record, and William Popp, who finished with a 15-7 record for a .681 mark.

Despite these outstanding accomplishments, league officials overturned the Travelers' first-place finish. In mid-October at a league meeting, several of Nashville's previously negated wins were allowed to stand, which gave the Volunteers just enough wins to capture the league title. Little Rock's woes were just starting. In 1902, the Travelers battled to a second finish again under Finn's leadership and delivered a 75-48 record, but once again, that was six-and a-half games behind Nashville. George Watt, Ted Guese and Allemang each won 19 games. Slugger Jim Delahanty hit .328, tops on the team. Ed Lynch had 17 triples and Gilbert led his teammates with 92 runs. Delahanty was one of five brothers to make the majors. He played 13 years during the Deadball era.

In 1903, Little Rock was again a bridesmaid. Led by league batting champ Delahanty's .383, Finn's Travelers fought to the last game. With a 70-51 record, the team had to idly watch as Memphis finished their season on the last day because of a scheduling oddity. On the mound, Guese went 19-9 and Watt went 17-13. From 1904 through 1909, the Travelers finished sixth, eighth, eighth, fourth, seventh and seventh, respectively. After the 1909 season team officials sold the equipment and players to Chattanooga for $12,000. West End Park was home to no league champions from 1895 through 1909. The Travelers sat out the next five seasons, the team's second long absence from the Southern Association. At that point, they had played nine seasons and missed 10.

Little Rock did not field a team again until 1915. On February 20 of that year, William Marmaduke Kavanaugh, the team's original president, and now Southern Association president, happily announced the team would rejoin the Southern Association. A banquet was held for team presidents and managers. Kavanaugh died the next day of acute indigestion at the age of 49. In his honor, West End Park was renamed Kavanaugh Field later that season. The Travelers finished in last place upon their second entry into southern baseball in 1915.

Little Rock had occasional stars during the 1915–1917 seasons. Pitcher Rube Robinson had an 11-1 record in 1916 and would later be named to the Arkansas Sports Hall of Fame. Ben Tincup pitched a perfect game in 1917.

The Travelers were working their way back to respectability. Little Rock placed second in 1918. In a war-shortened season, they were seven-and-a-half games behind New Orleans. Rube Robinson led the way with an 8-2 record. Thomas Boman was 6-3 and Tim Murchison was 9-5. Little Rock had two .300 hitters in Hamilton Hyatt at .324 and George Distel at .317. The Travelers led the league in homers and runs under the leadership of Kid Elberfield. Elberfield played 14 years in the major leagues. He had a career batting average of .271 and batted over .300 four times. In 1910, as a Washington Senator, he led the American League in fielding with a .943 percentage. While a coach at Montgomery, Elberfield mentored young Casey Stengel and taught him the "inside game."

In 1919, the Travelers crept a little closer to first place. No starter batted over .300, but Dee Walsh and J.S. Frierson were in the .290s. Robinson led the league in wins with a 23-12 mark. Ben Karr paced the league in innings pitched with 336.

Elberfield's squad found the trophy room in 1920 after near misses the previous two years. In late August, the Travelers were in third place. A 14-game winning streak the last two weeks of the season put them two-and-a-half games up on New Orleans. Bing Miller led the league with 19 home runs. He and Joe Connolly (12 in 1922) would be the only Traveler league leaders until Ralph Atkins hit 34 in 1953. League totals had the Travelers as leaders in doubles (219), homers (44), stolen bases (184) and also tops in batting (.269).

Little Rock would slip to fourth place in the next two years. Then they plummeted to eighth place the next six years. This was their Depression. Kavanaugh Field had seen its last champion.

Despite the lack of pennant winners the Travelers did have stars. Harry Harper scored 96 runs and batted .332 in 1921. Guy Tutwiler had 12 home runs. Claude Jonnard won 22 games in a league–leading 58 games and 347 innings. In 1922, Rube Robinson led the league with a 26-22 record. He posted the lowest ERA at 2.03 and pitched the most innings with 327. Robinson was one of the earliest of Arkansas natives to pitch in the big leagues. Born in Floyd in 1889, he pitched for six years in the big leagues between 1911 and 1918 and had a 42-37 record. He also pitched 13 years in the Southern Association and won over 200 games. First baseman Dutch Schleiber led the league with a .354 percentage and 194 hits. Catcher Peter Lapan hit .335, Ike Boone .329, and Joe Connolly .323. Future Hall of Famer Travis Jackson, of Swifton, Arkansas, batted .280 in 147 games. Later that season Jackson started his 15-year career with the New York Giants.

Joe Guyon had a stellar season in 1924. The Travelers outfielder batted .346 and stole 28 bases. In 1925 Travelers' outfielder Thomas Gulley hit .378 and led the team with 17 homers.

Gulley also had 16 triples. John Clancy topped the Travelers with a .340 mark, 15 steals and 28 doubles in 1926. The Little Rock Travelers wandered around the Southern Association: they finished eighth 17 times, seventh nine times and sixth nine times. Thirty-eight times the team was in the second division.

Little Rock did lighten things up a bit in 1930. On June 21, they played the first night game in Southern Association history under newly installed lights at Kavanaugh Field where the Travelers beat Birmingham in 10 innings. Little Rock still finished fifth, but their attendance rose over 20 percent that year.

In 1931, the Travelers drew 113,738 in attendance. It was the second highest attendance figure for the club, topped only by the 1920 championship season. Successful attendance figures or not, the stage was set to move the team to a new location within the city. As 1931 came to an end, the Travelers moved west to brand new Travelers Field.

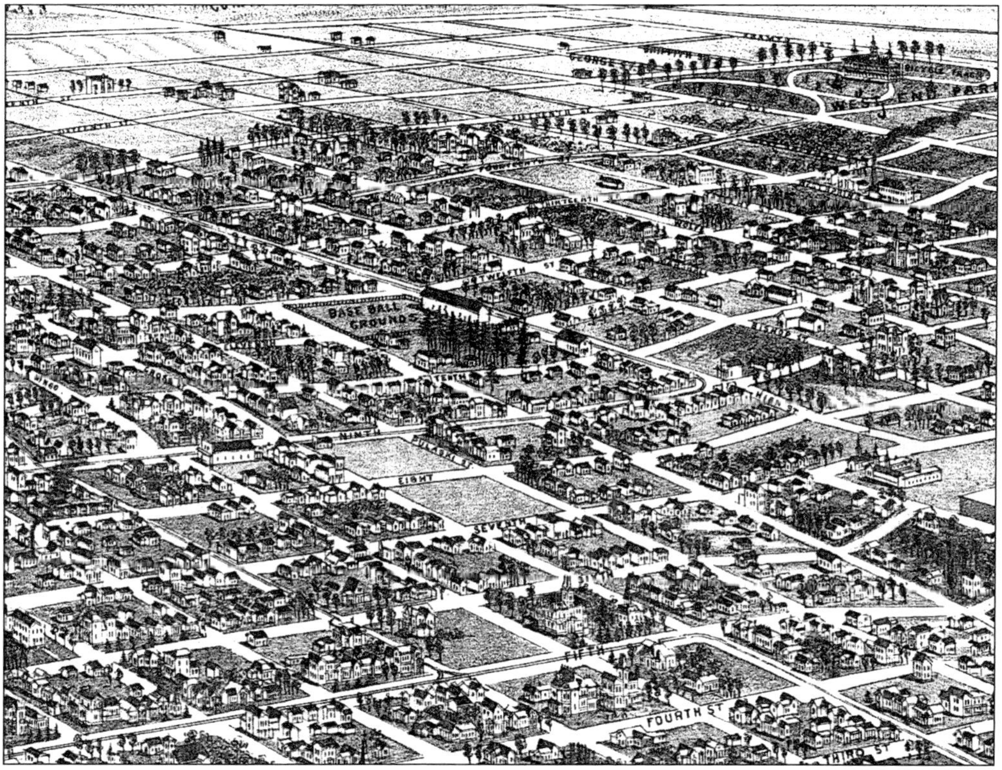

An 1887 map of Little Rock shows the "baseball grounds" at the intersection of High and 12th Streets. At that time, the Travelers were eight years from joining the Southern League. Baseball had grown in popularity since the first major league game had been played in 1875. Because of Reconstruction, the Little Rock population had grown to almost 13,000. By the end of the 19th century, electric lights, telephones and a public water system were introduced. Streetcars began operation and the city grew westward into Little Rock's first suburb, Pulaski Heights. By the early 20th century, Little Rock had nearly 40,000 residents, 170 businesses, six rail lines, one seven-story building, a public library, 75 churches and more than 60 social clubs. (Courtesy of the Butler Center for Arkansas Studies/ Central Arkansas Library System.)

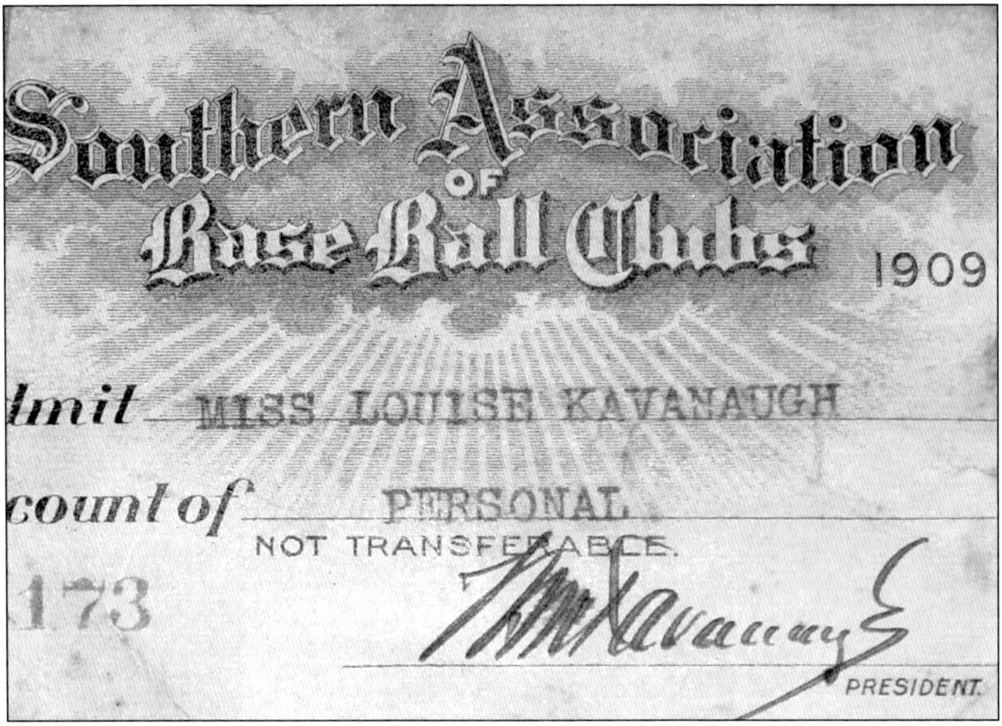

This 1909 season pass belonged to Louise Kavanaugh, Judge Kavanaugh's daughter, who represented her invalid mother at official functions. (Courtesy of Louise Atkinson Isgrig.)

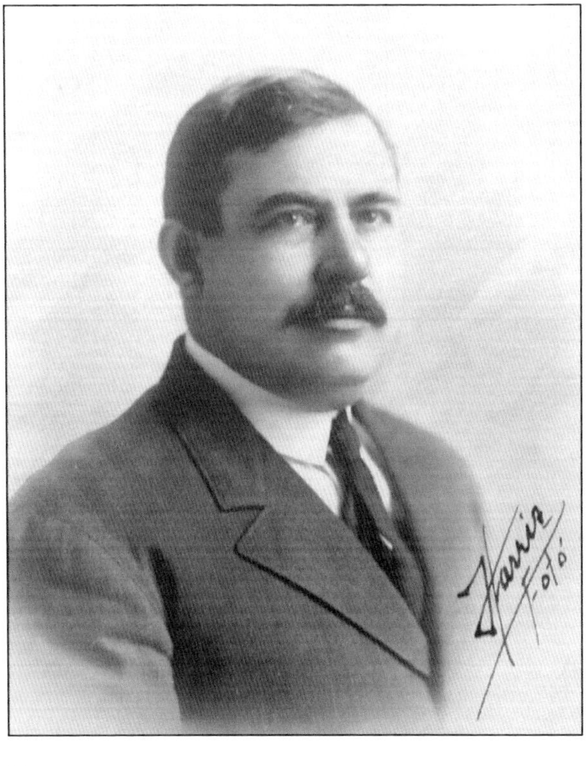

Judge William Marmaduke Kavanaugh was a born leader. He was city editor of the Arkansas Gazette, Pulaski County sheriff, probate judge, and United States Senator. He was the first Little Rock Travelers president in 1895 and he was elected president of the beleaguered Southern Association in 1903. He was also elected to the prestigious National Association of Professional Baseball Clubs. Because of his calming influence on the Southern Association, Kavanaugh was asked to run for the National League presidency. "Baseball is my hobby," he said as he turned down the invitation. He found time to develop Pulaski Heights and built a road there named in his memory—Kavanaugh Boulevard. After his death in 1915, the team renamed West End Park after their late leader. (Courtesy of Louise Atkinson Isgrig.)

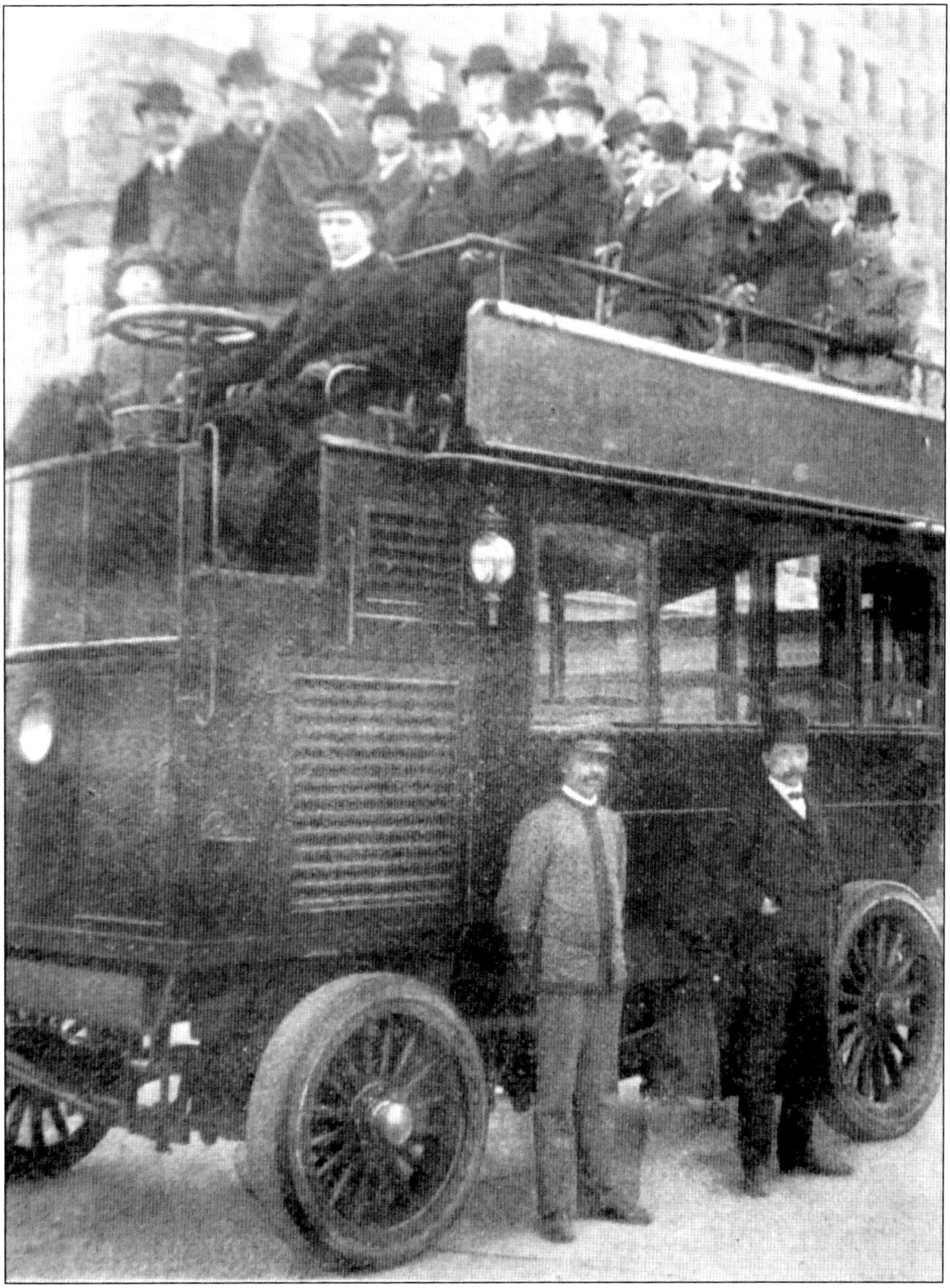

Southern Association President Judge William Kavanaugh visits New York City in 1904. Kavanaugh was elected to the prestigious National Association of Professional Baseball Clubs Board of Directors. Kavanaugh's talent for leadership and organization saved the Southern Association in the early 1900s.

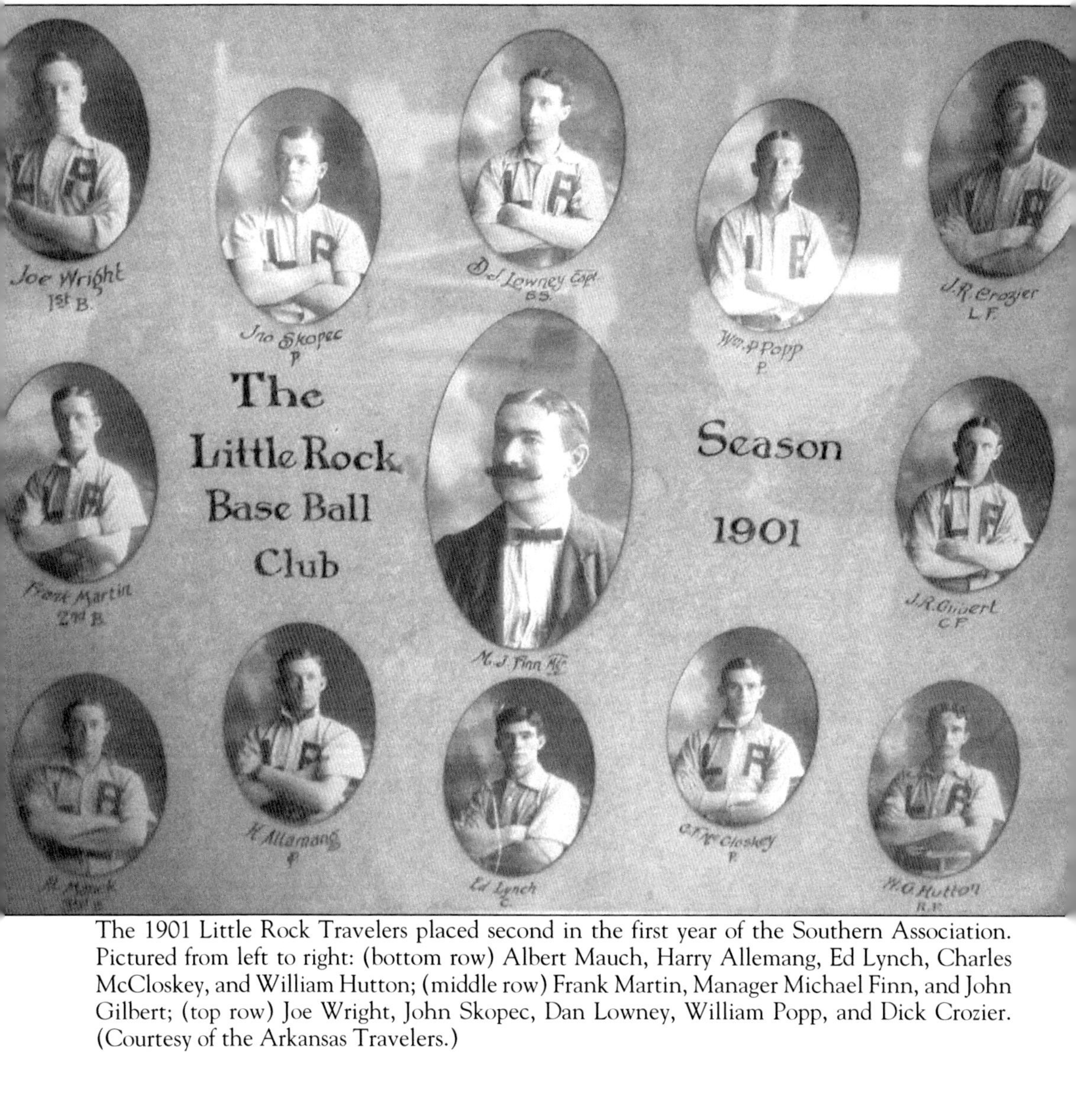

The 1901 Little Rock Travelers placed second in the first year of the Southern Association. Pictured from left to right: (bottom row) Albert Mauch, Harry Allemang, Ed Lynch, Charles McCloskey, and William Hutton; (middle row) Frank Martin, Manager Michael Finn, and John Gilbert; (top row) Joe Wright, John Skopec, Dan Lowney, William Popp, and Dick Crozier. (Courtesy of the Arkansas Travelers.)

The Travelers 1903 pocket schedule lists the team's home and away games. For the third straight year, the Travelers placed second in the Southern Association. The Memphis Chicks edged them by one game. The Travelers would not get near another championship until 1920. In seven of the next nine seasons, they would finish in the second division. They did not field a team from 1910 through 1914. (Courtesy of the Arkansas Travelers.)

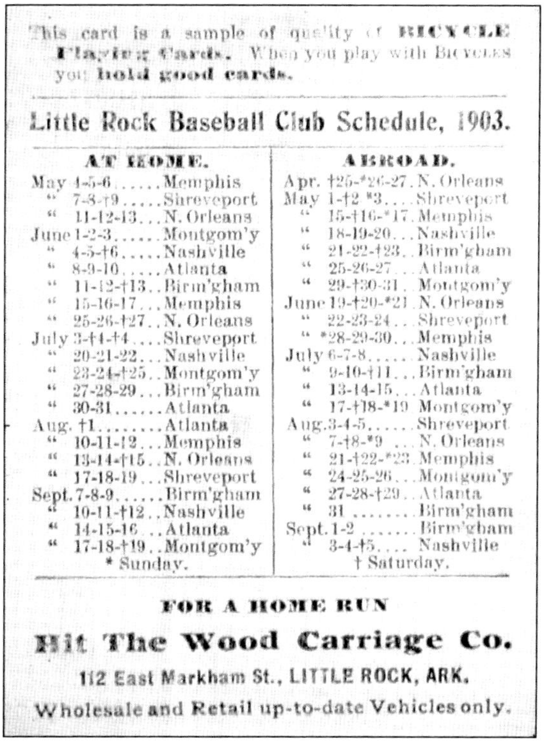

This card is a sample of quality of BICYCLE Playing Cards. When you play with BICYCLES you hold good cards.

Little Rock Baseball Club Schedule, 1903.

AT HOME.		ABROAD.	
May 4-5-6	Memphis	Apr. †25-*26-27	N. Orleans
" 7-8-†9	Shreveport	May 1-†2 *3	Shreveport
" 11-12-13	N. Orleans	" 15-†16-*17	Memphis
June 1-2-3	Montgom'y	" 18-19-20	Nashville
" 4-5-†6	Nashville	" 21-22-†23	Birm'gham
" 8-9-10	Atlanta	" 25-26-27	Atlanta
" 11-12-†13	Birm'gham	" 29-†30-31	Montgom'y
" 15-16-17	Memphis	June 19-†20-*21	N. Orleans
" 25-26-†27	N. Orleans	" 22-23-24	Shreveport
July 3-†4-†4	Shreveport	" *28-29-30	Memphis
" 20-21-22	Nashville	July 6-7-8	Nashville
" 23-24-†25	Montgom'y	" 9-10-†11	Birm'gham
" 27-28-29	Birm'gham	" 13-14-15	Atlanta
" 30-31	Atlanta	" 17-†18-*19	Montgom'y
Aug. †1	Atlanta	Aug. 3-4-5	Shreveport
" 10-11-12	Memphis	" 7-†8-*9	N. Orleans
" 13-14-†15	N. Orleans	" 21-†22-*23	Memphis
" 17-18-19	Shreveport	" 24-25-26	Montgom'y
Sept. 7-8-9	Birm'gham	" 27-28-†29	Atlanta
" 10-11-†12	Nashville	" 31	Birm'gham
" 14-15-16	Atlanta	Sept. 1-2	Birm'gham
" 17-18-†19	Montgom'y	" 3-4-†5	Nashville
* Sunday.		† Saturday.	

FOR A HOME RUN

Hit The Wood Carriage Co.

112 East Markham St., LITTLE ROCK, ARK.

Wholesale and Retail up-to-date Vehicles only.

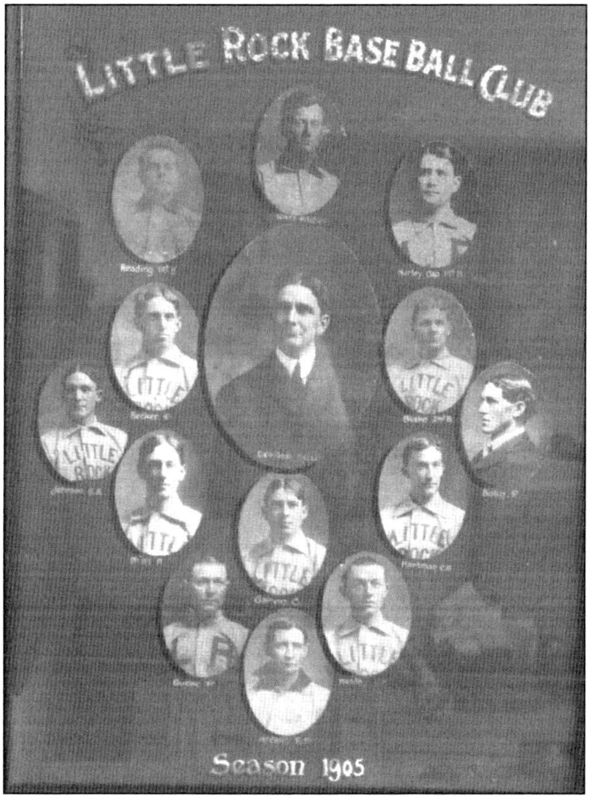

The 1905 Travelers are pictured clockwise from the top: George Watt, William Hurley, William Blake, Bolin, William Hartman, Welday, Mike McCann, Garvin, Ted Guese, Chinn, Otis Johnson, John Bender, and Reading. Manager Dale Gear is pictured in the center. (Courtesy of the Arkansas Travelers.)

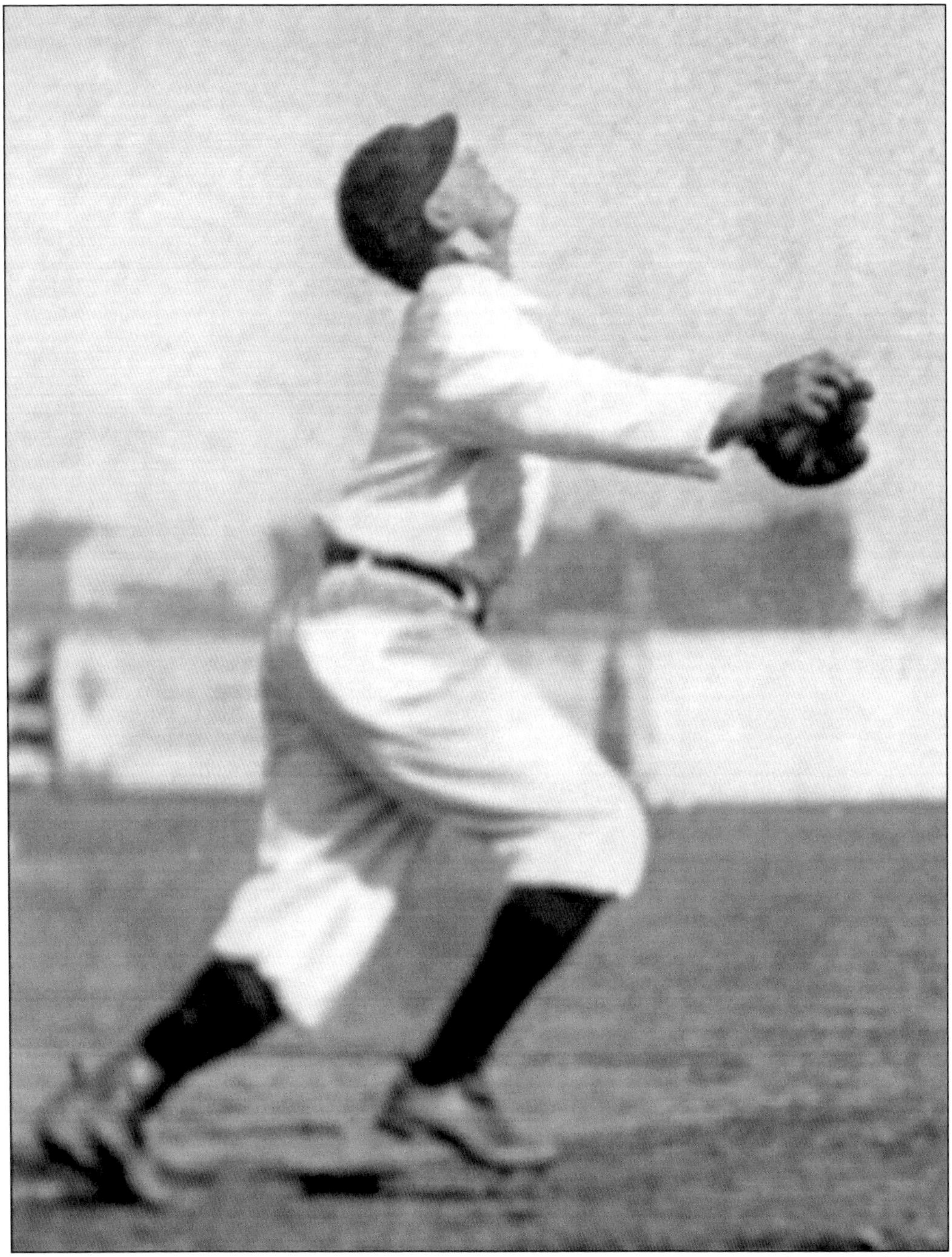

Norman "Kid" Elberfield managed the Travelers for seven seasons. In 1920, he piloted them to their first championship. Elberfield managed Little Rock from 1918 to 1924 and kept them in the first division his first five seasons. Elberfield's 1920 team led the Southern Association in stolen bases and home runs, as well as batting average at .269. He is pictured in action with the 1911 Washington Senators; the previous year he led the American League in fielding percentage with a .943 ledger.

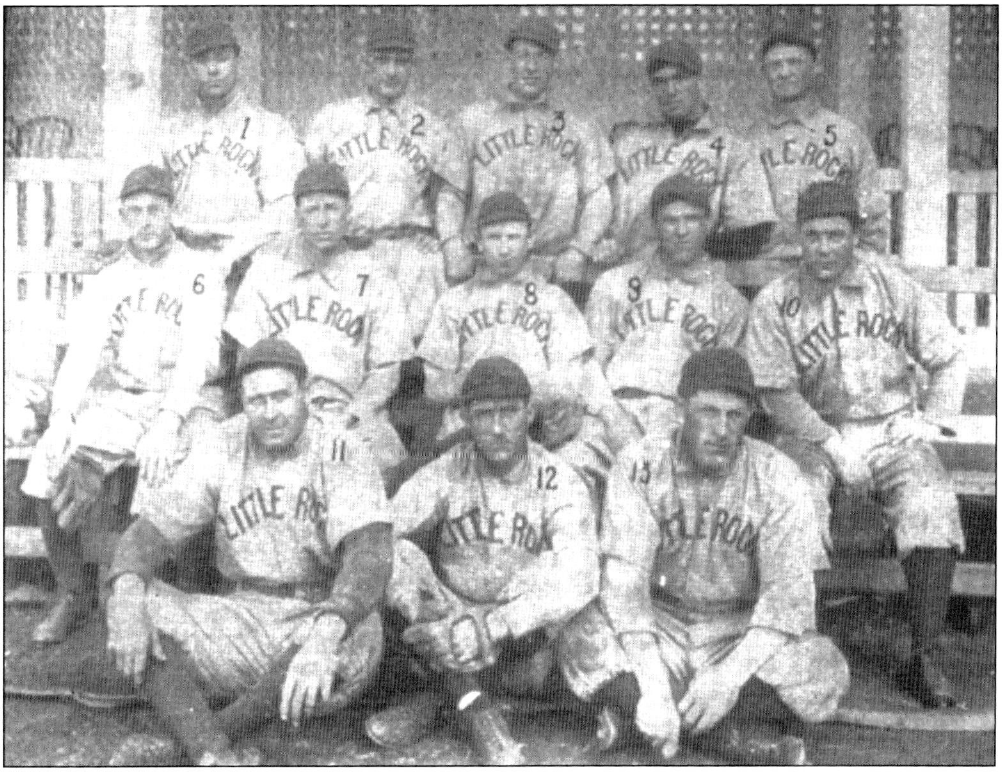

The 1907 Travelers placed fourth—right in the middle of the Southern Association—with a 66-66 record. Mike Finn was the manager. Pictured are McCarty, Elwood Eyler, Hess, Ed Orr, Bill Hart, Billy Page, Jim Buchanan, John Gilbert, Kunkle, Ike Rockenfield, William Douglas, Ben Bowcock, and Dakin Miller.

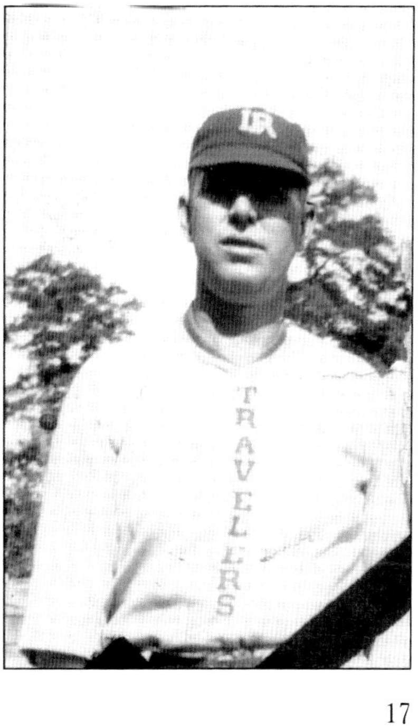

Righthander "Rube" Robinson, a native of Floyd, Arkansas, became a legend in the Southern Association. In 1920, during the Travelers first pennant chase, he won 26 games to lead the league. He won over 200 games in the Southern Association and was later elected to the Arkansas Sports Hall of Fame. (Courtesy of the Arkansas History Commission.)

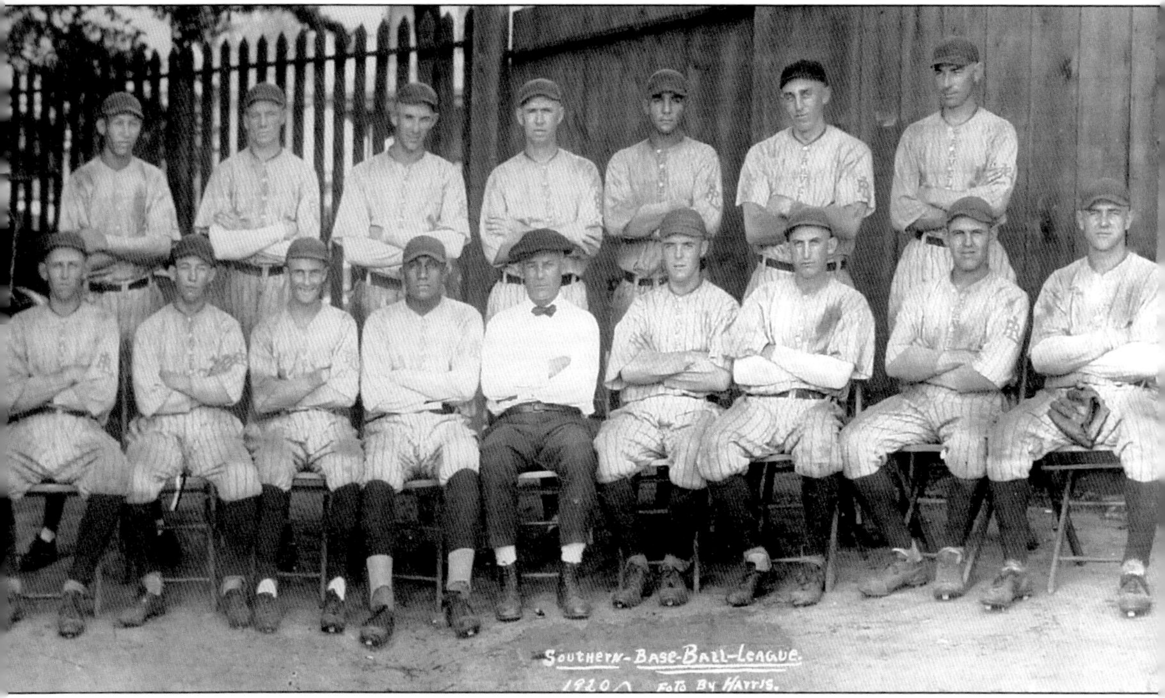

In 1920, the Little Rock Travelers won their first undisputed flag. With a record of 88-59, a .599 winning percentage and a two-and-a-half game lead, Kid Elberfield's team edged the New Orleans Pelicans. The Travelers had five players with 21 or more steals. Pitcher Rube Robinson led the Southern Association with 26 wins and Moses Yellowhorse had 21. Future Athletics star Bing Miller led the Southern Association with 21 triples and 19 homers. Harry Harper's .346 led the league in batting. As the Southern Association's league champion, the Travelers advanced to the first Dixie Series, losing to the Fort Worth Cats. After waiting 15 seasons for a league title, the Travelers would have to wait 17 more years for another. Team members were William Wano, George Distel, George McGinnis, William Moore, Miller, Harper, Tony Brottem, Robinson, Frank Zoellers, Yellowhorse, F.W. Hengeveld, Herb Hunter, and Jacinto Cavo. (Courtesy of the Arkansas Travelers.)

Bing Miller roamed centerfield at Kavanaugh Field. The Iowan hit a league-leading 19 homers for the 1920 season. He was also the leader in triples. His power hitting helped the Travelers to their first Southern Association championship. In a 16-year major league career, Miller batted .311. He was a central figure in the Philadelphia A's dominance of the major league's in 1929, 1930 and 1931. The A's stopped the reign of the Yankees and won the World Series in 1929 and 1930 and took the St. Louis Cardinals to seven games before losing the 1931 Series. (Courtesy of the Arkansas History Commission.)

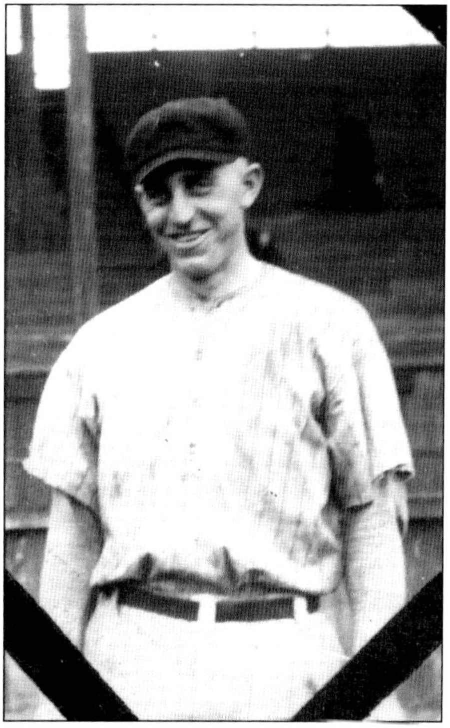

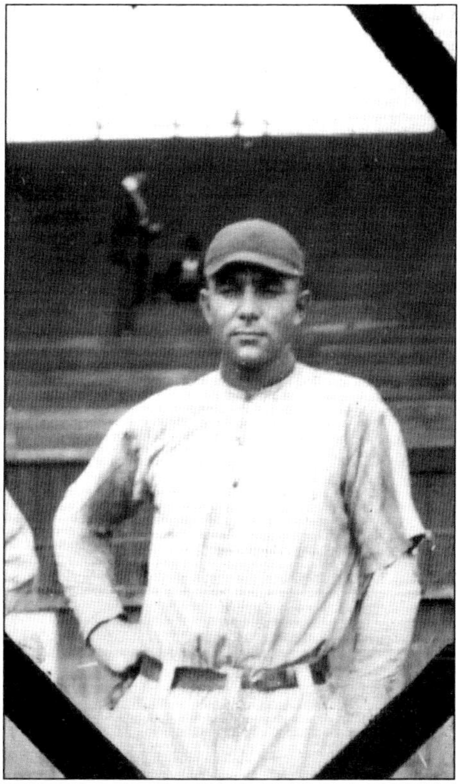

In 1920, right fielder Harry Harper led the Southern Association in hitting with an average of .346. He also topped the league in hits with 196. In addition to his success with the bat, Harper stole 35 bases to contribute to the Travelers' championship year. In 1921, Harper hit .332. (Courtesy of the Arkansas History Commission.)

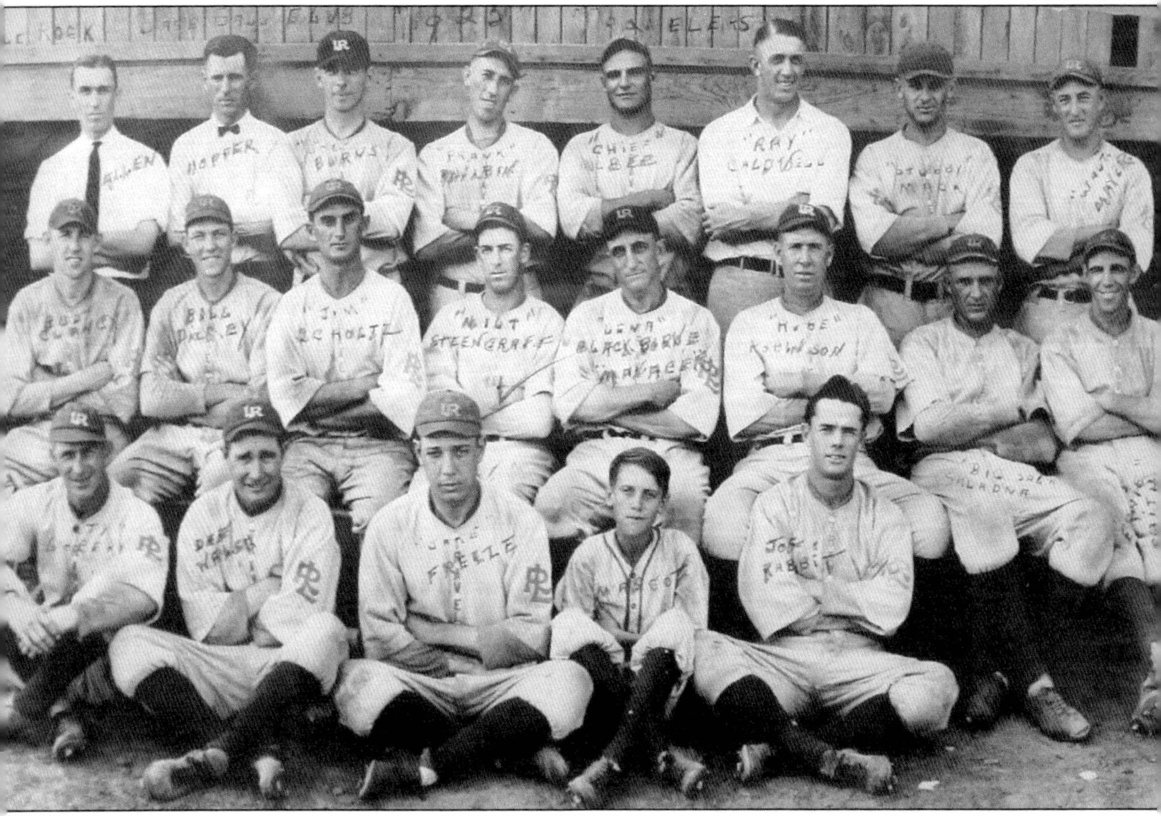

The 1925 Travelers finished in last place. Managed by Lena Blackburne, Little Rock posted a 67-86 record and a .438 winning percentage. They scored the fewest runs and struck out the most. But they did have a fresh-faced catcher who batted .300 (3 for 10). He was Bill Dickey, a beloved player who later called Little Rock home and even managed the Travelers in 1947. As an 18 year old in 1925, he showed Blackburne enough promise to get a short stint behind the plate. It would lead to a Hall of Fame career with the Yankees. Pictured from left to right: (front row) Ty Lober, Dee Walsh, Carl Freeze, mascot, and Joe Rabbitt; (middle row) Bud Clancy, Bill Dickey, Jim Schultz, Milt Steengraffe, Manager Lena Blackburne, Rube Robinson, Sal Saldina, and Ernie Smith; (back row) Allen, Hopper, Joe Burns, Frank Philbin, Chief Imbler, Ray Caldwell, Stubby Mack, and Walt Mayer. (Courtesy of the Arkansas Travelers.)

Two

The Years of Turmoil and Travel 1932–1965

The Little Rock Travelers found themselves in a new home by the season of 1932. The team had been forced from Kavanaugh Field to a newly constructed Travelers Field. In addition to hosting the Travelers baseball team, Kavanaugh Field had been used as a home field by high school baseball and football teams and the University of Arkansas Razorbacks football team.

Due to the growth of Little Rock High School, which had been built in 1927, additional grounds were needed for the school's athletic teams. In 1930, Fordyce High had upset Little Rock High in the first night football game in Arkansas at Kavanaugh Field. Future coaching legend "Bear" Bryant starred for Fordyce. To accommodate football games, the grass outfield section of the ballpark was used. With the school needing the facilities, the Travelers had to move.

The City of Little Rock offered the Travelers land in Fair Park, now known as War Memorial Park. A portion of the land was on state hospital grounds and a portion was on city land. A provision was written that stated that should the Travelers go more than two years without a team, the land would revert to the city. Typically, the land was rocky and uneven, much like the Travelers' past.

The previous year, a group of Little Rock businessmen, headed by Roy L. Thompson, H. Grady Manning, and Al C. Jones, purchased the team from R. G. Allen. The new business manager was a former ticket seller for the Travelers named Ray Winder. Winder had run a few lower classification teams for Allen in the 1920s.

The stage was set for an interesting era in Traveler baseball. The Travelers teased their fans by finishing third their first year at the new Travelers Field, then followed with four straight years in the second division. James Thompson "Doc" Prothro took over the direction of the Travelers in 1935. After the four straight second-division finishes, the Travelers were ready for new heights. Prothro had a five-year career in the majors. He had a career .318 average mostly with the Washington Senators. His Travelers spent two seasons in the middle of the pack before taking off in 1937.

In 1937, Prothro guided the Travelers to their all-time high in wins with 97-55, .638 winning percentage. Stars like Leo Nonnekamp, Lindsay Deal, Al Niemiec, and Jim Tabor led the way. Little Rock led the league with 808 runs scored. They did lead the league in triples and were second in walks, third in stolen bases. The pitching staff was balanced with seven pitchers in double figures. Byron Humphreys was 16-7 and Emerson Dickman was 16-8. Robert Porter was 12-5 for a .706 percentage and a 2.65 ERA.

Just before the season started local fans got a clue just how good the '37 team might be. In consecutive exhibition games, the Travelers beat the World Champion New York Yankees with Lou Gehrig and Bill Dickey and the Cleveland Indians with Bob Feller. With the regular season underway, Little Rock went 97-55 for a .638 winning percentage. They outdistanced big rival Memphis by nine games. They drew 162,503, the second highest total in team history.

The Travelers set what would become a once-a-decade title precedent. Prothro had a collection of 10 players who had or would have major league careers. With a mixture of youth and experience, the Travelers piled up the wins in the summer of '37. Now affiliated with the Boston Red Sox, the Travelers held a double-digit lead in early September and claimed the pennant on September 6. Jim Tabor hit .290 while the team hit only 27 homers, less than half of leader Nashville with 69. From April 25 to May 2, the Travelers played 10 consecutive errorless games, handling 252 putouts and 119 assists.

Prothro's pitching staff was full of aces. All seven had percentages of over .500. Byron Humphreys went 16-7. Emerson Dickman was 16-8. Jennings Poindexter turned in a 15-10 mark. Dick Midkiff and Lee Rogers posted identical 13-8 records. Robert Porter was 12-5 and Kola Sharpe 11-9. The starting batting order listed six hitters with batting averages of .295 or higher. The team led the Southern Association in runs and triples. Top Traveler sluggers were Al Niemiec at .313, Art Graham, .307, and Ray Thompson, an even .300.

Playing in the smallest and westernmost city in the Southern Association, the Travelers had to maximize their pennants. They won four while in the Southern Association, and drew a season attendance of 162,503 during the Depression. It was a count that would not be broken until 1951.

Little Rock's next title came rather quickly. In 1942, Manager Willis Hudlin, a 16-year veteran of pitching wars in the American League, won the pennant in his rookie year. The team won 87, lost 59 and won the pennant by four-and-a-half games over Nashville. The Travelers were next to last in homers at 37, and next to last in runs scored. But seven of their nine pitchers were at .500 or above. Three—Jim Trexler (19-7), Al Moran (17-9) and future Yankee great Ed Lopat (6-4)—were over .500. James Tyack led the league in triples at 19. Robert Fausett hit .334 and Thomas McBride hit .329.

The Travelers 13-game winning streak late in the season put them on top. In the first war summer of 1942, the Travelers pulled in 98,461 fans. But the post-season battles went to Nashville after the Volunteers beat Birmingham 3-1 and blanked the Travelers 4-0. Hudlin had a talented squad: 17 players on the roster could count major league time on their resumes.

The war years of 1942–1945 gave the fans a rare breath of first division air, but the team settled back into second division play in 1945, 1946 and 1947. In 1942, as the War claimed many able-bodied men, the Travelers used just 17 players. As World War II continued in 1945,the roster ballooned to 39 men. A total of 42 players were used in 1946 as the major leagues scrambled to restock their postwar rosters.

Despite an eighth place finish in 1946, one Traveler had a glorious day on July 21. In a doubleheader against Memphis, Lew Flick got nine straight hits in 19-inning loss. In the second game, he got two more hits and raised his average 31 points in one day. He batted .346 for the year. In 1949, Travelers outfielder Pat Haggerty eked out a batting title by .0004 of a point over Thomas Neill of the Nashville Volunteers. Haggerty battled .3464 to Neill's .3460. Haggerty also led the league in walks and stolen bases. The Travelers came in last, seven games behind Chattanooga.

There was no way to foretell it, but a championship awaited the fans in the decade of the '50s. After nine seasons with no pennants, the Travelers in 1951 went 93-60 and attracted 225,780 fans. The attendance set records that and would not be broken for 36 years. Gene DeSautels became the second straight Little Rock rookie manager to win the Southern Association title. It had been 30 years since a team had gone from last to first, when the Detroit farm team won first place without leading the league in a single offensive category. It was the greatest turnaround in Southern Association history. Slugger Hal Simpson led with 121 runs, 23 homers and 83 RBIs.

The Travelers spent most of the season on top, built up a double-digit lead and clinched the crown on September 4 before a crowd of 7,051. Pitchers Al Yaylian and Robert McCall each won 16 games. R.C. Otey scored 110 runs and batted .305. Dave Jaska hit .309.

Americans discovered television and air conditioning in the early 1950s. As the Travelers went back to second division finishes, watching Milton Berle at home became more fun than watching the Travelers at the ballpark. Finishing seventh, seventh, sixth, eighth, eighth, seventh, and sixth in successive seasons would wear out anybody.

Attendance in 1958 dropped to 67,810 fans. It was the second lowest crowd total since the war year of 1945. After the end of the season, Ray Winder and the John P. Baird heirs sold the franchise to Shreveport. It was the first time since 1914 that Little Rock was without a baseball team. Nationally, the minor leagues began to suffer, but the Travelers came up with a system that saved them in 1960. The team became fan-owned; the stockholders never profited from baseball and never intended to. The purpose was to keep baseball solvent in Arkansas.

The team changed its name in 1957 to the Arkansas Travelers. Although many baseball writers still referred to them as Little Rock, the Travelers were thought to be the first professional franchise named after a state.

From 1958 through 1965, the Travelers traveled past the Southern Association through the International League, the Pacific Coast League, and finally came to a halt in the Texas League. The 1964 team was known as the "Boom-Boom" Travelers. They blasted 208 home runs and won the Pacific Coast League Championship. Costen Shockley with 36 homers and Norm Gigon with 30 and Aldolfo Phillips with 29 led the way for the pennant winner. Frank Lucchesi was the manager.

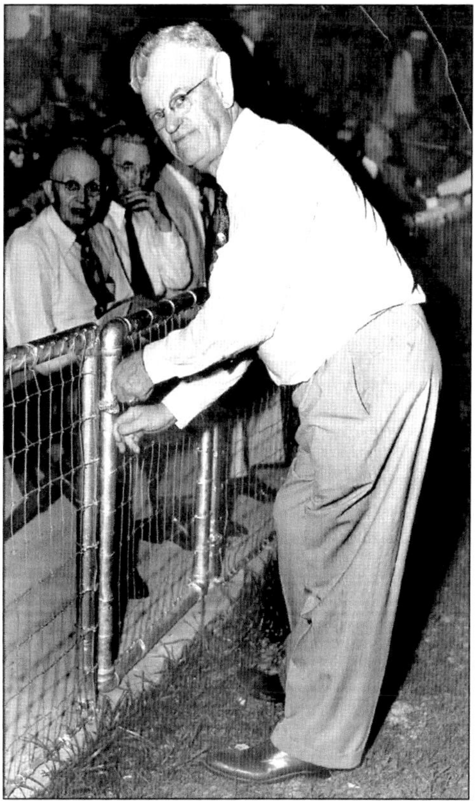

Ray Winder, Travelers General Manager, was the "gatekeeper" for the club. He started as a ticket seller in 1915 and stayed with the team through hard times. His persistence paid off in 1960 when the Travelers received a Southern Association franchise after a one-year absence. He was forced to borrow bats as well as players from other teams. Winder put together a "quilt-like" team that finished third in the league, but won the Southern Association playoffs. (Courtesy of the Arkansas Travelers.)

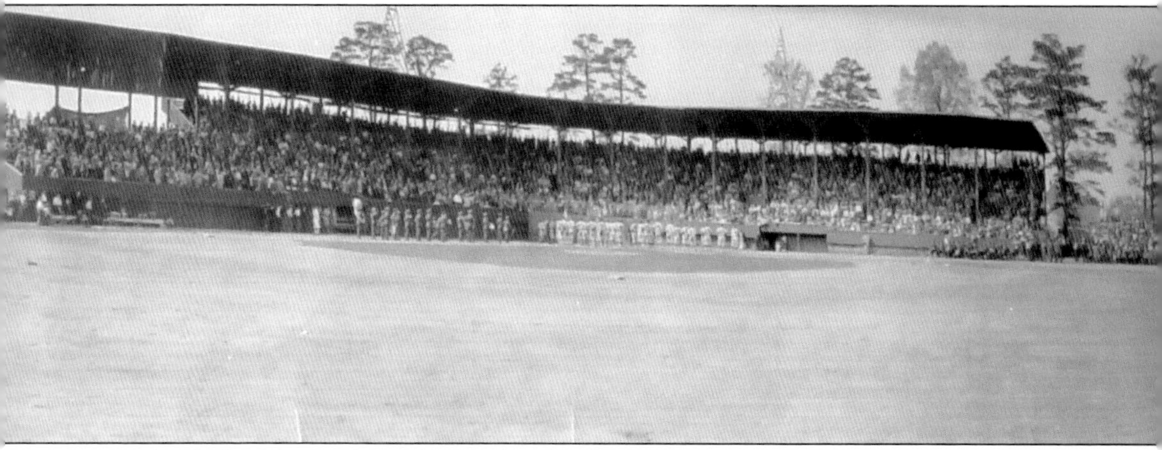

On April 15, 1931, Little Rock played its last home opener at Kavanaugh Field. In their 27th season at the former West End Park, the Travelers drew a season attendance of 113,738. A battling Travelers team placed second in the league. Quigley Stadium, near Little Rock Central High School, stands near the site of the old ballpark. (Courtesy of the Arkansas Travelers.)

Little Rock advertised its new steel and concrete grandstand for the 1932 home opener. The Travelers played 27 years at West End Park/ Kavanaugh Field, but started a new era at Travelers Field. The Memphis Chicks were a natural rival for the Arkansas team. In 1932, Memphis would place second and Little Rock third. (Courtesy of the Arkansas Travelers.)

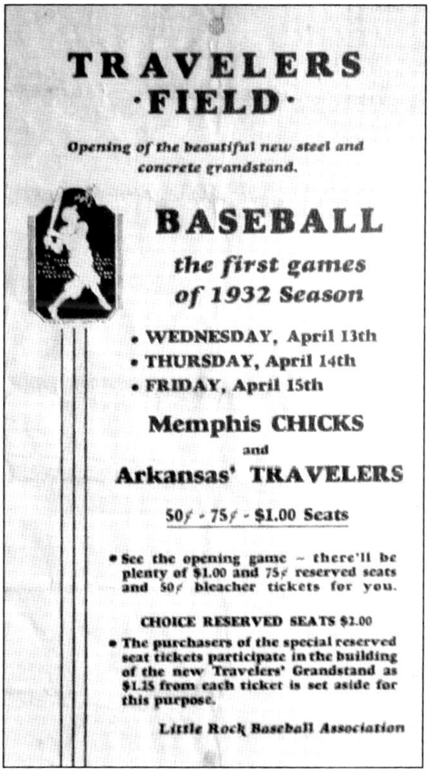

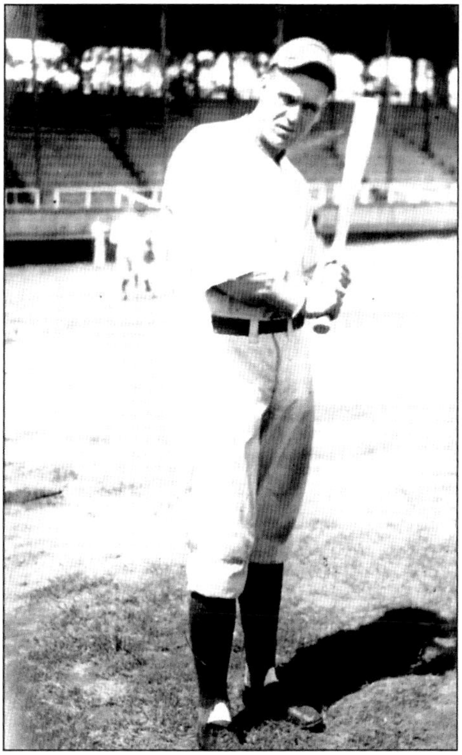

Tom Gulley played five games over two seasons in the big leagues with the Cleveland Indians before coming to Little Rock. Gulley, a right-handed hitter, hit .378 for the last place Travelers in 1925. He lost the batting title by one point, but topped the team in runs produced with 168 in 125 games. In 1926, Gulley played 18 games for the White Sox, batted .229 and was finished as a major leaguer. He returned to the Travelers in 1927, batted .290, hit seven homers and led the team in seven categories. (Courtesy of the Arkansas Travelers.)

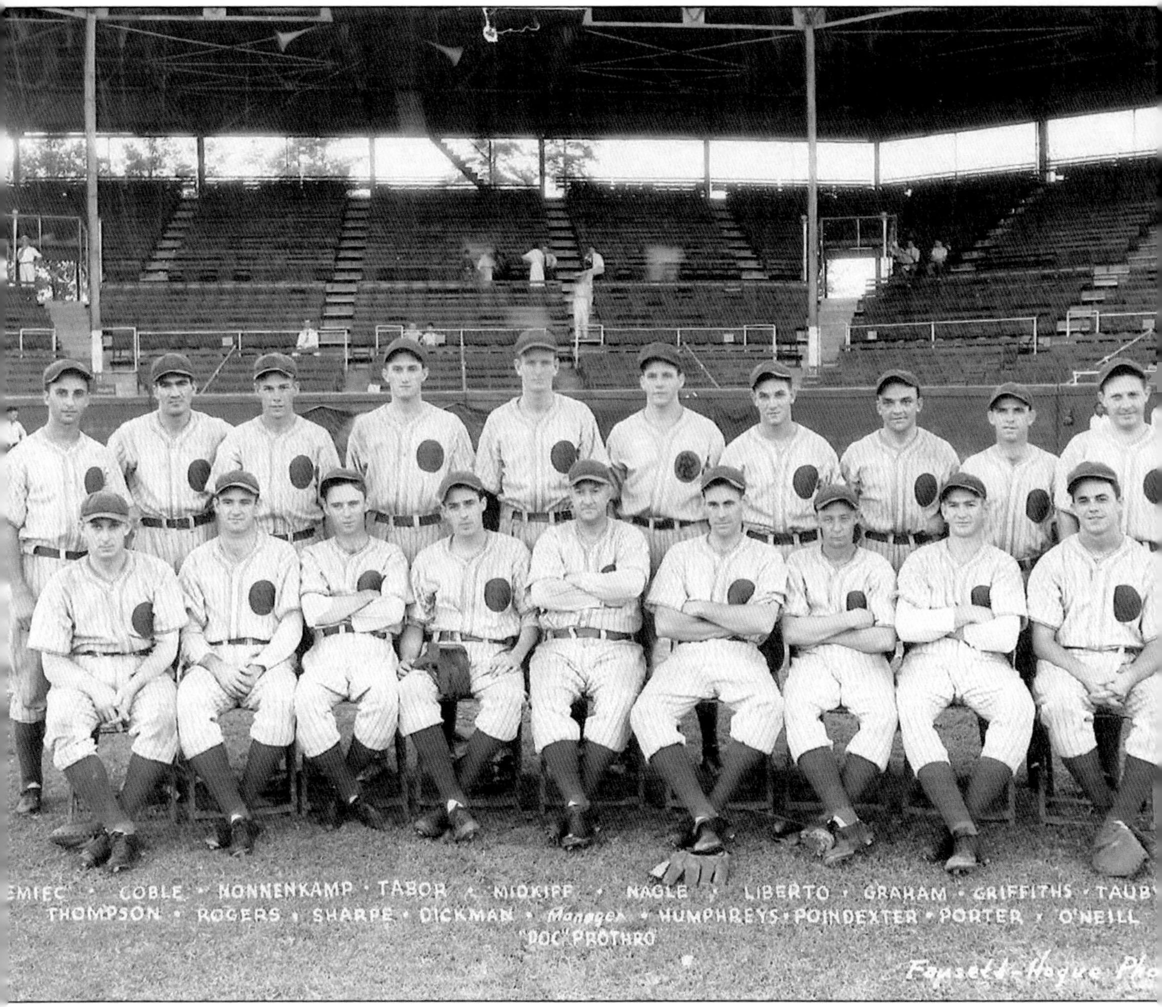

As a Red Sox farm team, the 1937 Travelers used a combination of youngsters and veterans to post a nine-game advantage over the Memphis Chicks. Veteran manager Tommy Prothro made up for years of futility by clinching the flag on September 6, 1937. The Travelers finished 97-55, their all-time high in wins. Leo Nonnenkamp led the league with 145 runs scored and led in walks with 103. Lindsay Deal topped Little Rock with a .340 average. Third baseman Jim Tabor batted .295. Al Niemiec hit .313 as a second baseman. At this point, the Travelers had few stellar seasons and this was a pinnacle. In their sixth year at Travelers Field, the team had won its second pennant in its history. The next would not come until 1942. Pictured are Ray Thompson, Dave Coble, Lee Rogers, Leo Nonnenkamp, Al Niemiec, Kola Sharpe, Emerson Dickman, Jim Tabor, Manager "Doc" Prothro, Byron Humphreys, Jennings Poindexter, Robert Porter, John O'Neill, Sammy Liberto, Art Graham, John Griffiths, Fred Tauby, Dick Midkiff, Bill Nagle, and Lindsay Deal. (Courtesy of the Arkansas Travelers.)

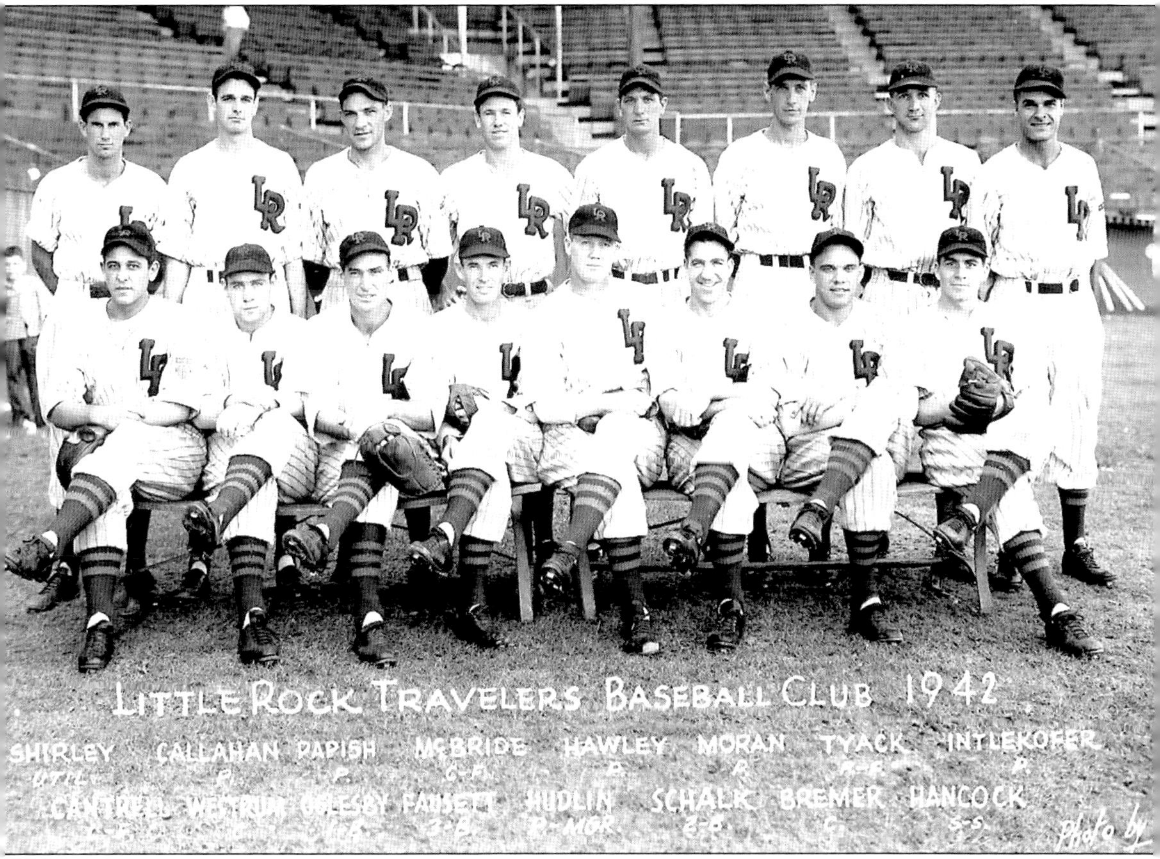

A 13-game winning streak late in the season gave the 1942 Champion Travelers the pennant over Nashville. Veteran major league pitcher Willis Hudlin was the rookie manager for the Little Rock team. The Travelers led the league only in triples while Nashville led in eight offensive categories. However, Little Rock did the have the Southern Association's Most Valuable Player in second baseman Leroy Schalk. Pictured from left to right: (front row) Rosie Cantrell, Wes Westrum, James Oglesby, Robert Fausett, Hudlin, Leroy Schalk, Herb Bremer, and Fred Hancock; (back row) William Shirley, Joseph Callahan, Frank Papish, Thomas McBride, Charles Hawley, Al Moran, James Tyack, and John Intlekofer. (Courtesy of the Arkansas Travelers.)

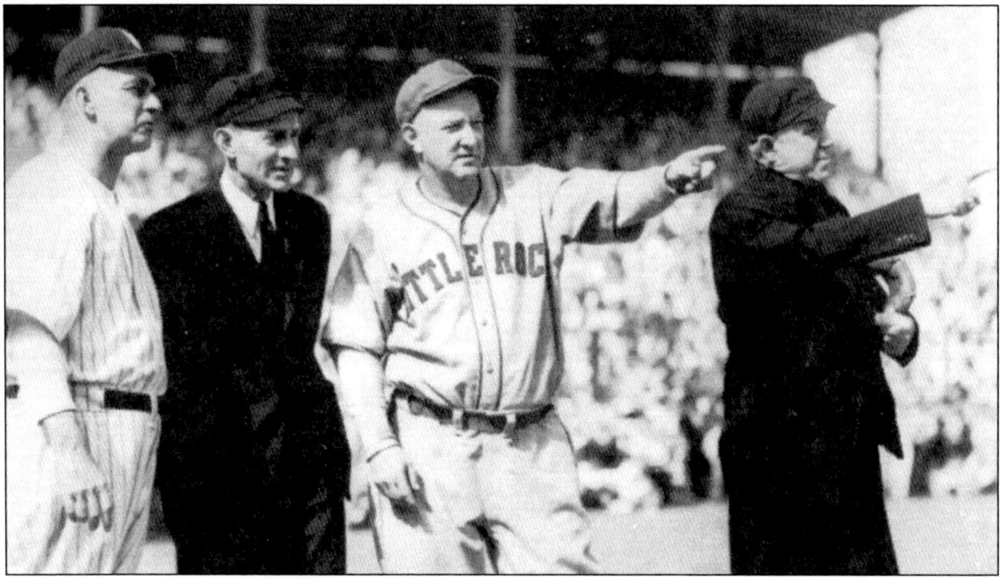

Larry Gilbert (left) and Little Rock's "Doc" Prothro battled each other as Southern Association skippers in the 1930s. Famous umpire Steamboat Johnson is on the far right. Prothro guided the Travs from 1935 through 1938, which included a Southern Association title in 1937. Larry Gilbert guided both the Memphis Chicks and the New Orleans Pelicans. In 1930 and 1933, Prothro put the Memphis Chicks in first place over Gilbert's Pelicans. (Courtesy of the Arkansas Travelers.)

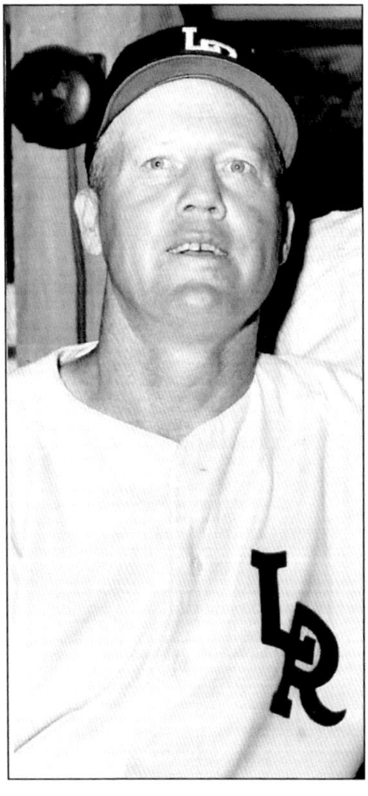

Willis Hudlin managed the Travelers three times in the 1940s and 1950s. His first season was the team's most successful, with an 87-59 record and a .596 winning percentage. A 13-game winning streak near the end of the season salted away the pennant. Hudlin managed the Travelers to consecutive eighth-place finishes in 1945 and 1946. He came back in 1952 for a seventh place finish. (Courtesy of the Arkansas Travelers.)

Rosie Cantrell was a steady outfielder for the Travelers in the 1940s. In his rookie year of 1942 he helped lead the Travelers to a Southern Association championship. Cantrell played 142 of the scheduled 146 games and batted .301. He was second on the team with five homers and 86 RBIs. In 1943, Cantrell drove in 101 runs to lead the team. In 1944, he led Little Rock with 113 runs and six homers. (Courtesy of the Arkansas Travelers.)

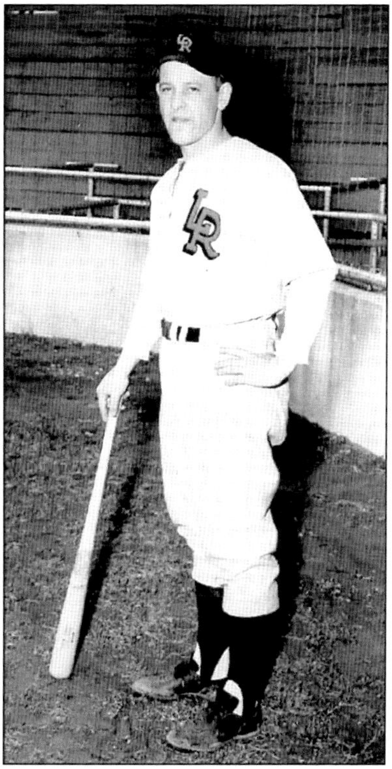

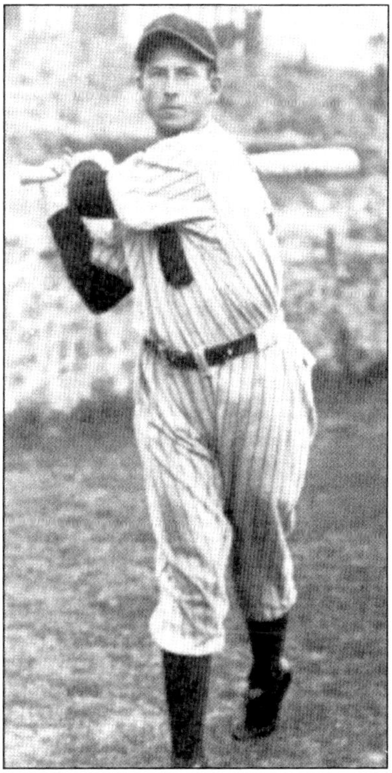

Lindsay Deal was a minor league hitting star of the Southern Association. With stops at Knoxville, Little Rock, Atlanta and Memphis, he batted under .300 only once and that was a .294 average his first year with Knoxville. In his third year with the Travelers in 1937, Deal blossomed. He hit .340 in 72 games, and was a part of the Travelers second league title. Lindsay hit .305, .356, .320, .365, .334 and .327 his remaining six seasons in the Southern Association. His peak year was 1944 with Atlanta, when the outfielder led the circuit in hits, doubles, and RBIs. (Courtesy of the Arkansas Travelers.)

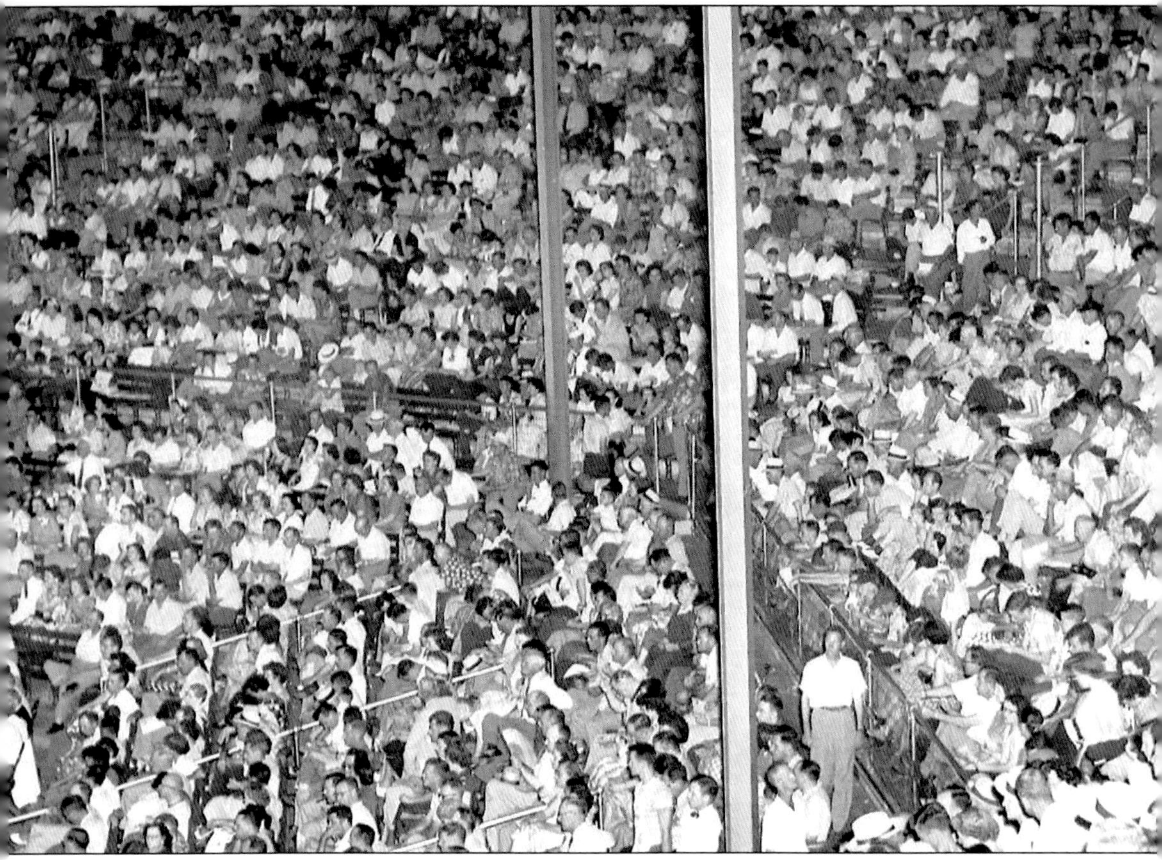

A sellout crowd fills Travelers Field for the 1951 Southern Association All-Star Game. The team attracted large crowds throughout the season and won the Southern Association title that year. (Courtesy of the Arkansas Travelers.)

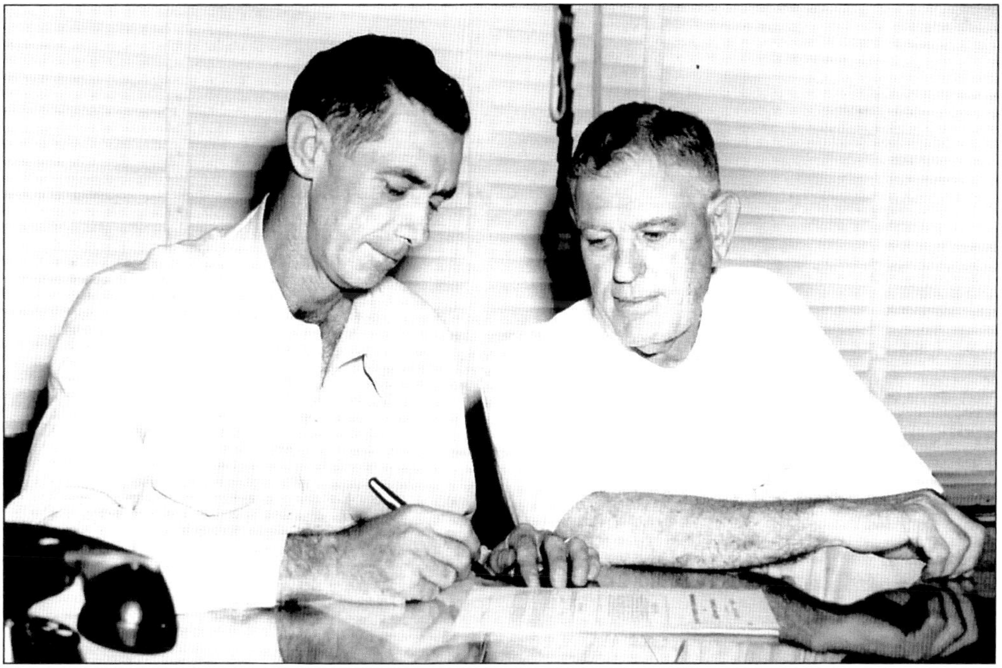

Manager Jack Salzgaver inks another contract for Travelers General Manager Ray Winder. Salzgaver skippered Little Rock in 1948, 1949 and 1950. His best team was in 1949, which placed sixth with a 69-85 record. (Courtesy of the Arkansas Travelers.)

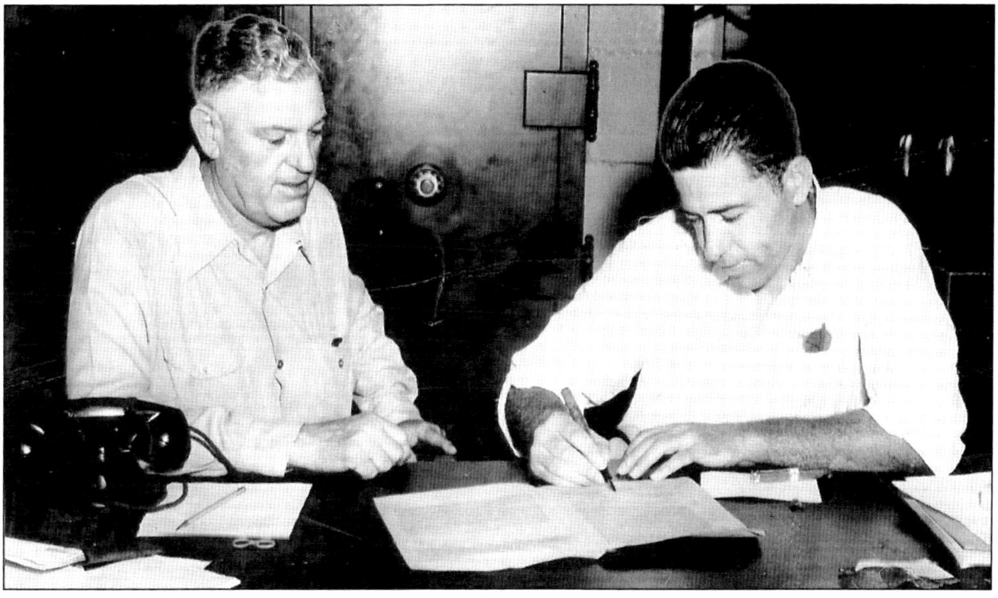

Paul Dee "Daffy" Dean signs a Little Rock Travelers contract in Ray Winder's presence just before the 1944 season. Dean had just finished a nine-year major league career in 1943. As a Traveler, the Lucas, Arkansas, native put together seasons of 5-2 in 1944 and 2-1 in 1946. The younger brother of Hall of Famer "Dizzy" Dean, Paul had two fine seasons with the St. Louis Cardinals in 1934 and 1935 with 19 wins each year. He won two World Series games in 1934 as did "Dizzy." (Courtesy of the Arkansas Travelers.)

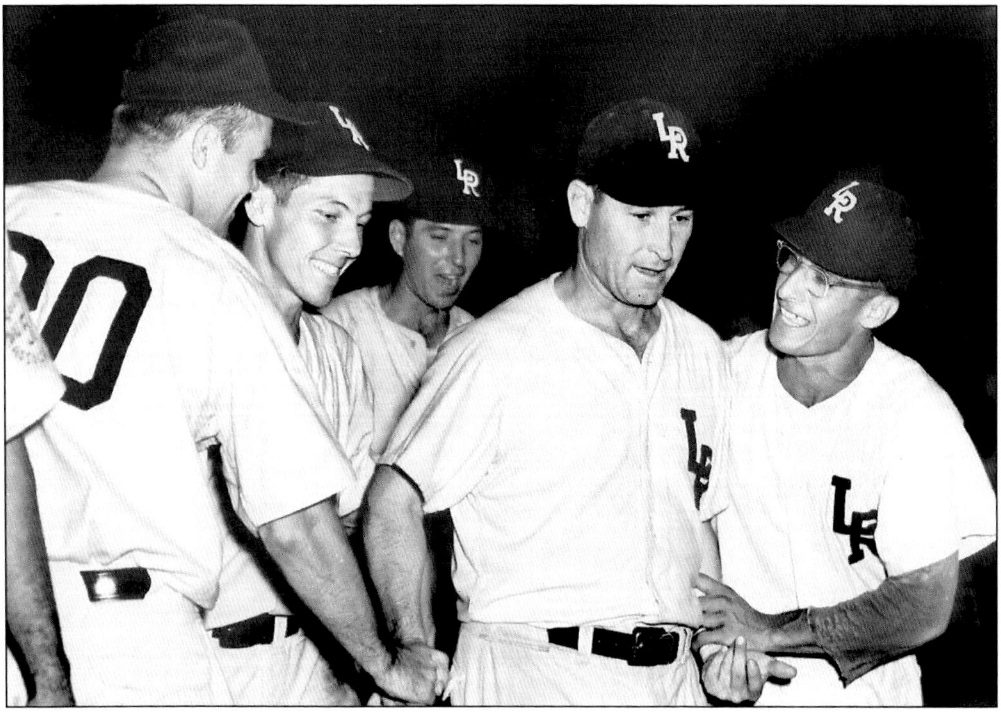

(*above*) Powerful Hal Simpson, the Travelers "Franchise" player in the 1950s, gets a hero's welcome from his teammates. The New Boston, Texas native set homer marks that still stand. Simpson holds the Travelers' record for career home runs with 106 in six seasons. In three seasons, he homered 20 or more times; and in six straight seasons from (1949–1954) he had 10 or more. In 1949, Simpson was a one-man drawing card. His late season home run barrage got the fans out to the park. Despite a sixth-place finish, the Travelers drew 153,812, their biggest attendance in 13 years. (Courtesy of the Arkansas Travelers.)

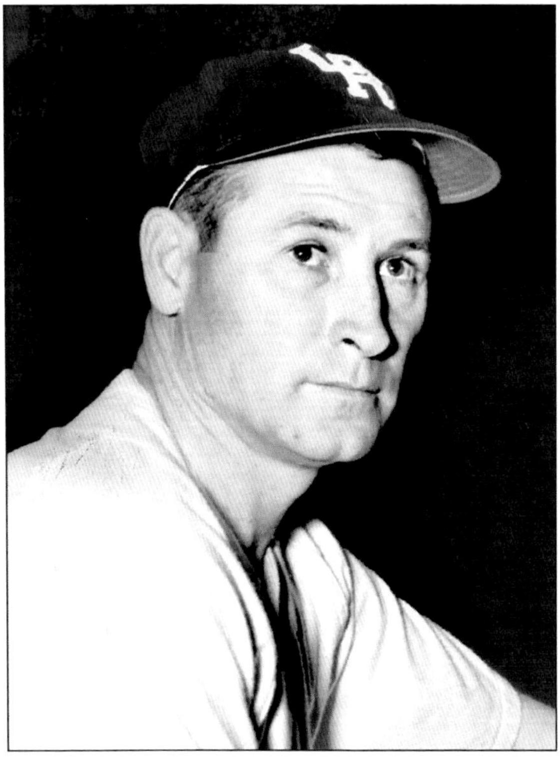

(*left*) Hal Simpson was a major factor in the Travelers' turnaround in 1951. After eighth and sixth place finishes the two years before, the Travelers won the pennant by a whopping 10 1/2 games. In contributing to the pennant win, the outfielder slugged 23 homers. He accounted for a total of 226 runs for his team. Simpson was right around the .300 mark the next three years in Little Rock, batting .288, .311 and .299. (Courtesy of the Arkansas Travelers.)

Ralph Atkins hit 103 homers for the Travelers of the early 1950s. For the 1951 championship team, the left-handed slugger produced 76 runs in just 57 games. As a part-time player, he was third on the team in homers with eight. Atkins's breakout season was 1953. Even though the Travelers placed seventh, Atkins led the league in home runs at 34. He drove in 100 and scored 82. Atkins helped again in 1954 with 31 homers, 108 RBIs and 103 runs. He holds the two-season record at 65 and is second to Costen Shockley for single season homers at 36. (Courtesy of the Arkansas Travelers.)

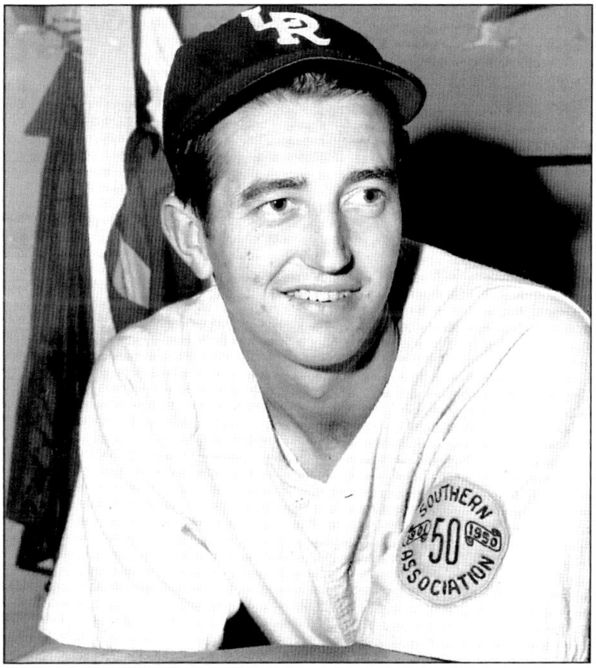

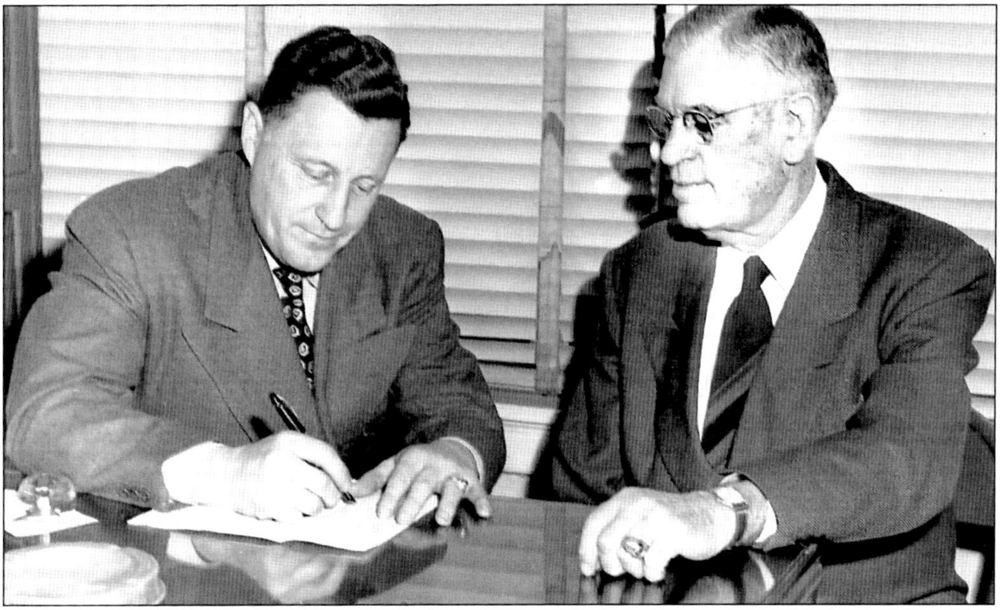

Travelers General Manager Ray Winder witnesses manager Gene Desautels' contract signing. In 1951, Desautels' only year with Little Rock, the team won the league title. The Travelers went 93-60 for a .608 winning percentage and a healthy 10 1/2 game lead over the Birmingham Barons. They won the pennant with the greatest one-season turnaround in Southern Association history. The Travelers had a pair of pitchers with 16 wins. Al Yaylian and Robert McCall tied for the league lead. Hal Simpson batted .311, led the league with 121 runs and was an All Star. R.C. Otey at .305, Ken Humphrey at .304, John Grice at .308 and Dave Jaske at .309 helped put the Travelers at the top of the Southern Association in batting. (Courtesy of the Arkansas Travelers.)

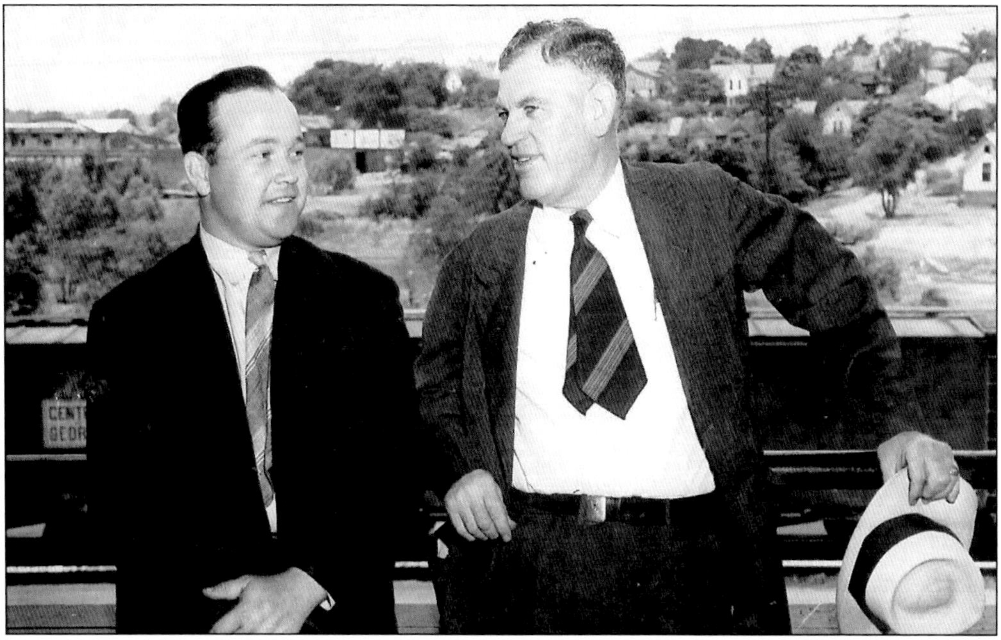

Travelers outfielder Bruce Sloan and General Manager Ray Winder visit at Union Station before a road trip. Sloan played two years for Little Rock. In 1944, he batted .365. As a part-time player for the New York Yankees, Sloan hit .269 in 59 games. (Courtesy of the Arkansas Travelers.)

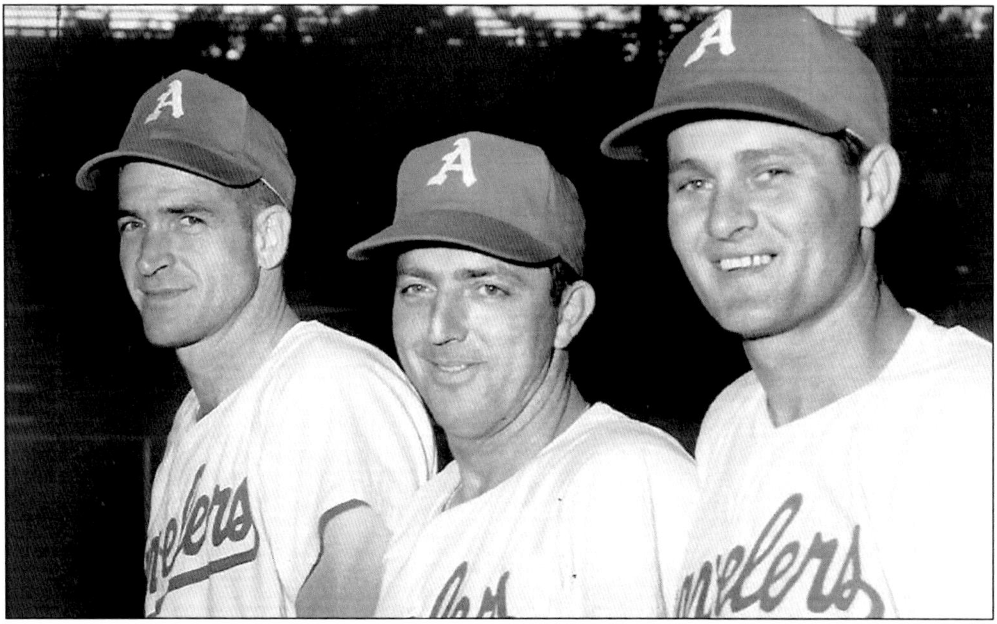

The trio of Bob Thorpe, William "Ace" Reynolds and Bob Hazle (left to right) roamed the outfield at Travelers Field in 1960. The surprising Travs entered the Southern Association one last time and claimed third place. Thorpe had 13 homers, batted in 94 and hit .290. Reynolds led the team with 19 homers and batted .281. Hazle batted .291 and split time with Birmingham. In 1957, he earned the nickname "Hurricane" Hazle as he hit .403 for that year's World Champion Milwaukee Braves in an emergency role. (Courtesy of the Arkansas Travelers.)

William "Ace" Reynolds" toured" the Southern Association while playing for three teams: Atlanta, New Orleans, and Little Rock. He had his best year in 1960 playing for the Travelers. (Courtesy of the Arkansas Travelers.)

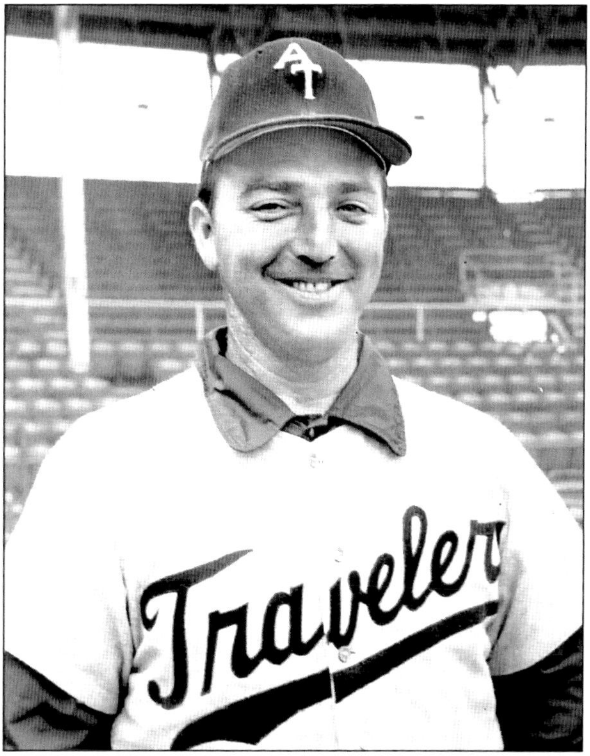

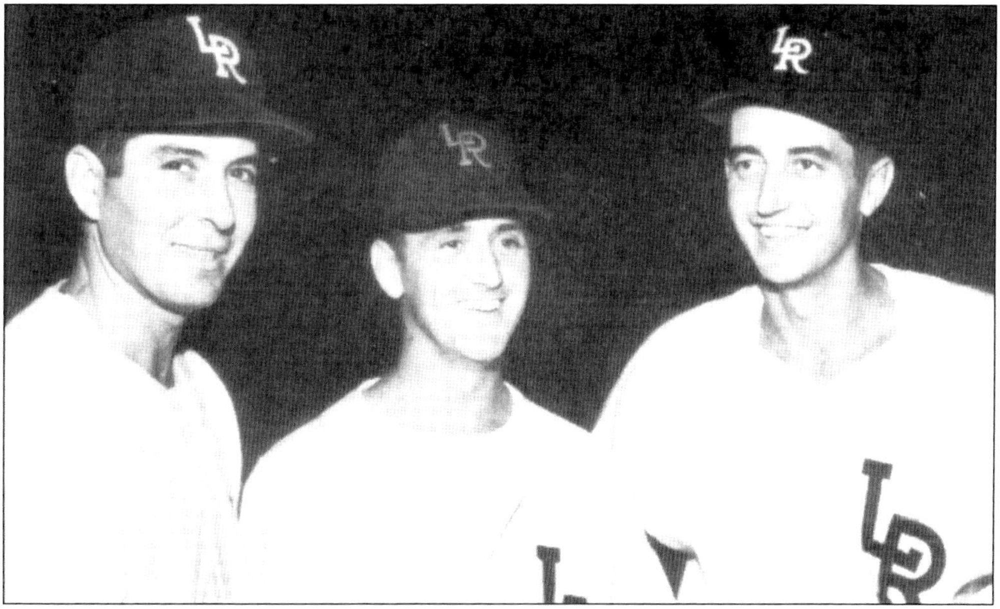

Alex DeLaGarza, R.C. Otey and Ralph Atkins anchored the Little Rock lineup of the early 1950s. DeLaGarza was a steady shortstop starting with the Travelers in 1948. Otey was a solid contributor at second base for 10 years. Atkins was a slugging outfielder who hit 142 homers in the Southern Association, 112 for the Travelers. (Courtesy of the Arkansas Travelers.)

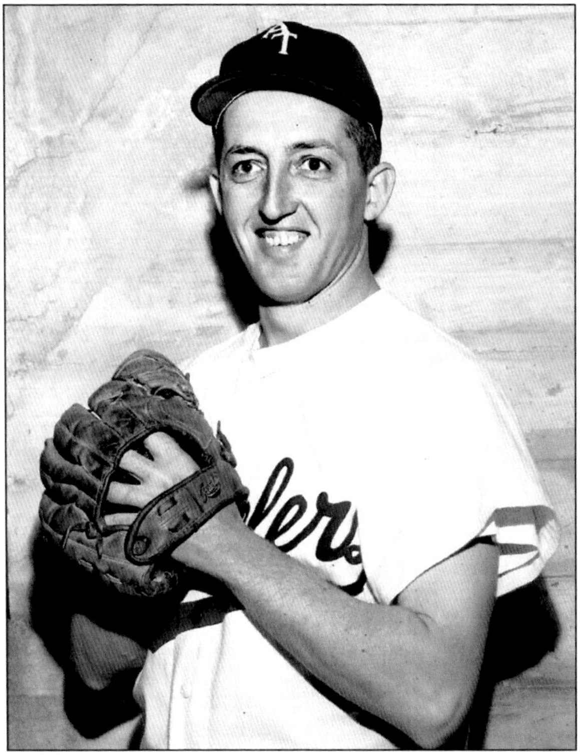

Allen "Dutch" Romberger led the Southern Association with an 18-5 record and a .783 winning percentage in 1958. All of his wins were in relief. He posted a 6-4 record in 1957 was 2-1 in 1959. Romberger was 1-1 in 10 games with the 1954 Philadelphia Athletics. (Courtesy of the Arkansas Travelers.)

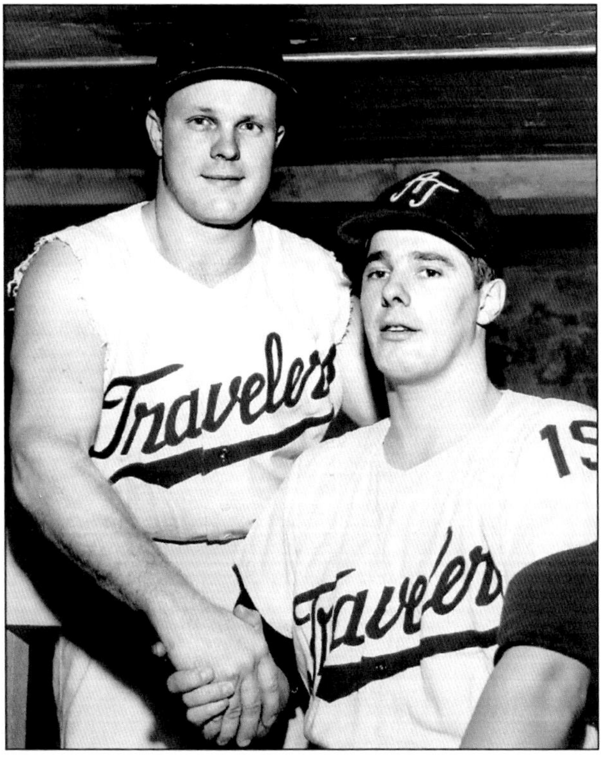

Eric Rodin (left) and George Brunet were road roommates in 1957. Rodin, an outfielder, hit .341 to provide what little offense the Travelers could muster. Brunet led the league with 235 strikeouts, but received little run-support from his team. By June 21, he was 10-3, but for the next five weeks and 52 innings, his team failed to score. Brunet went on to pitch for 32 professional league seasons, striking out 3,175 batters, a feat no other minor league pitcher has matched. (Courtesy of the Arkansas Travelers.)

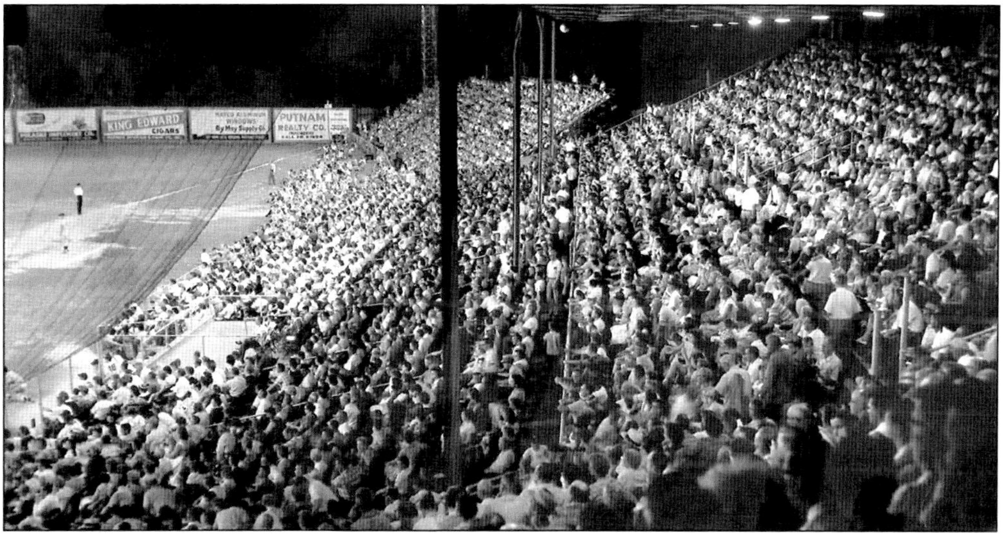

In 1960, Arkansas Travelers baseball returned to Little Rock. The turnstiles clicked for 179,471 fans. A large crowd enjoys a night game on April 20 of that year. Ray Winder assembled a team from all corners of pro baseball and Fred Hatfield managed the castoffs to a third place finish. The team's .543 winning percentage put them three and a half games behind Atlanta and Shreveport. The Travelers attendance was the highest in the Southern Association in 1960 and Arkansas's highest since 1951 when they won the pennant. That figure would not be surpassed until 1980. (Courtesy of the Arkansas Travelers.)

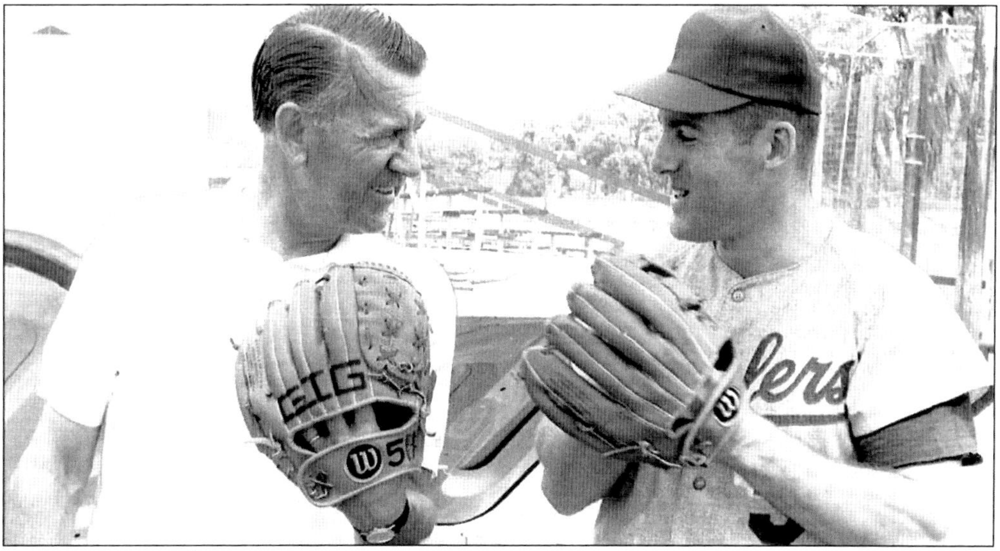

Major league Hall of Famer Vernon "Lefty" Gomez displays the latest fielding glove to Norm Gigon. Gomez served as a representative of the Wilson Sporting Goods Company following his career as a player. During his major league pitching career, Gomez racked up 189 wins and a .649 winning percentage. Gigon, leading off for the Travelers in 1964, hit 30 homers. The Travelers were a Philadelphia Phillie farm team that season and amassed 208 homers. They won the East Division of the Pacific Coast League their first year in the league, but lost to San Diego in a seven-game playoff. Gigon went on to play one year for the Chicago Cubs in 1967. (Courtesy of the Arkansas Travelers.)

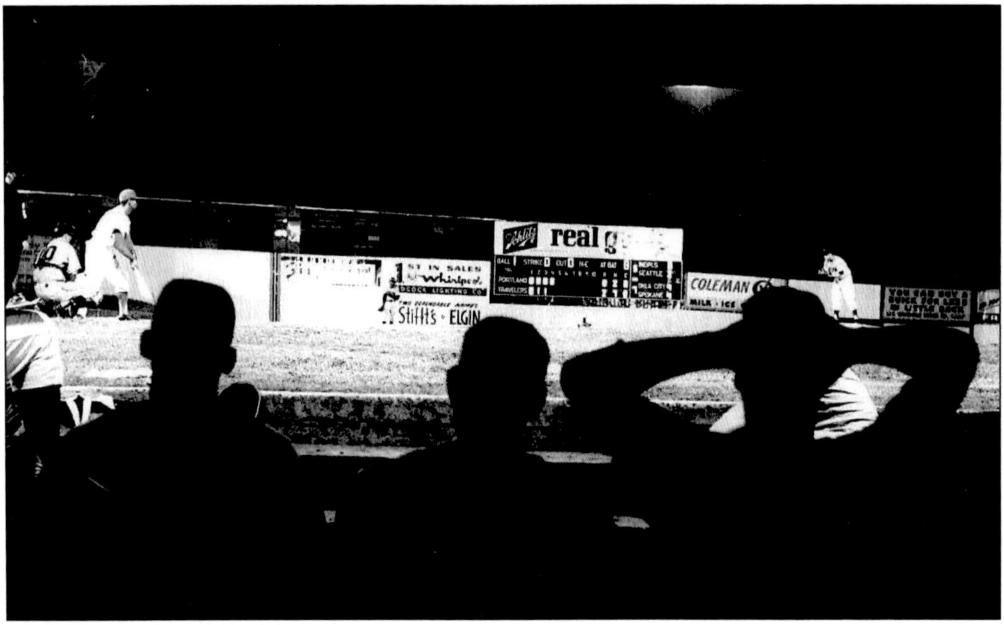

Arkansas players relax in the home half of the fourth in a Pacific Coast League game against Portland. The Travelers played two years in the PCL and took first place in 1964. Arkansas competed against Indianapolis, Oklahoma City, Denver, Salt Lake City, and Dallas in the Eastern Division. San Diego, Portland, Spokane, Seattle, Tacoma and Hawaii made up the Western Division. (Courtesy of the Arkansas Travelers.)

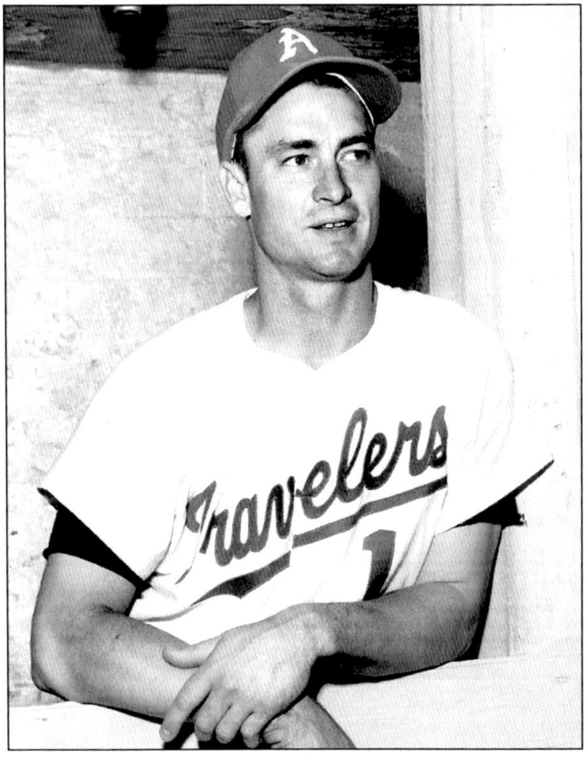

Fred Hatfield managed the Travelers to back-to-back third-place finishes in 1960 and 1961.As a third baseman-manager, he hit .277 with a .315 batting average. The Travelers ceased Southern Association play in 1961. He had a solid nine-year major league career before he came to the 1960 Travelers. Hatfield played for Boston, Detroit, Chicago and Cleveland in the American League and Cincinnati in the National. In 1952, as a Tiger, he led the American League outfielders in fielding percentage. (Courtesy of the Arkansas Travelers.)

Les "Gooch" Peden managed the Travelers one year, 1958, and the team placed sixth with a 74-80 record. As a catcher-manager, Peden hit 26 homers, 88 RBIs, with a .334 average. In 1957, as a player only, Peden hit 15 homers, had 81 RBIs and hit .297. Peden played briefly with the Washington Senators. (Courtesy of the Arkansas Travelers.)

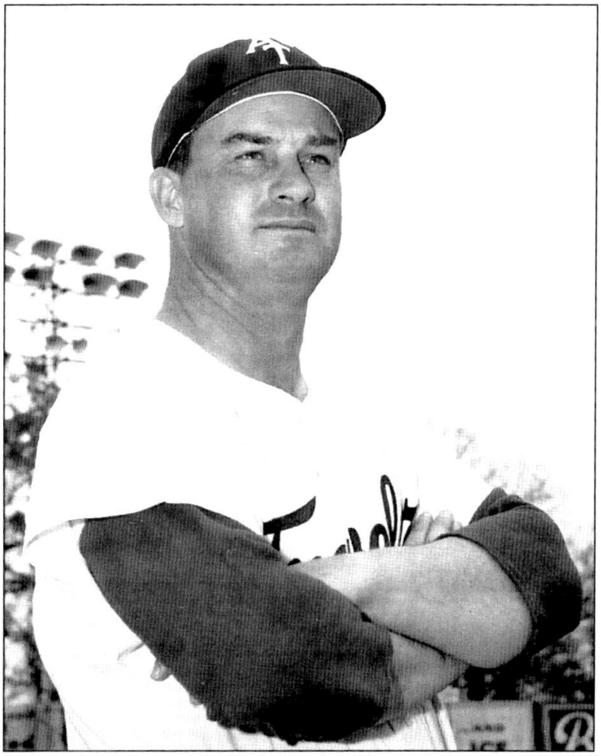

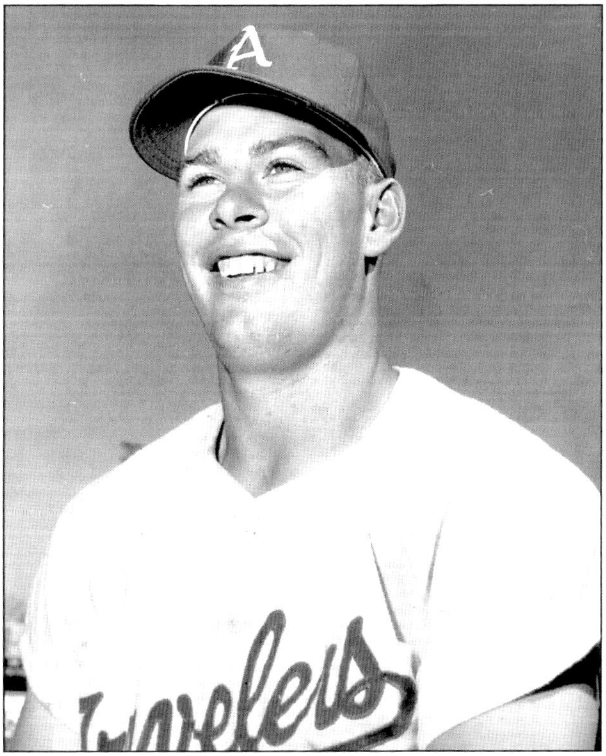

Costen Shockley was a left-handed slugger for the Travelers in 1964. He led the Pacific Coast League with 36 homers and set a Travelers record for lefties that still stands. He also led the PCL in RBIs with 112. Shockley was the big noise in the "Boom-Boom" team of that year. Shockley played two seasons in the majors, one year with Philadelphia and one with California. He hit three homers in 51 games. (Courtesy of the Arkansas Travelers.)

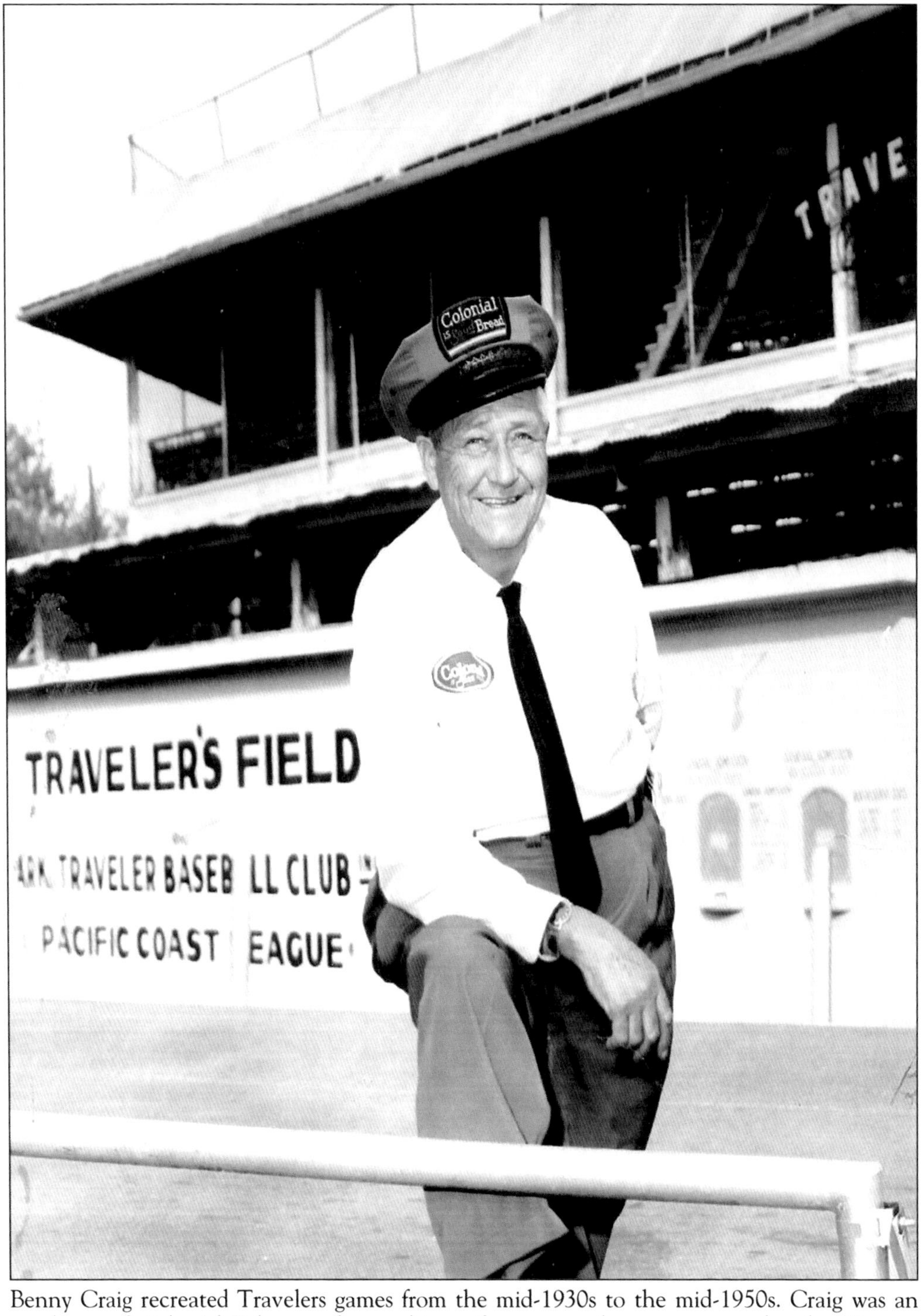

Benny Craig recreated Travelers games from the mid-1930s to the mid-1950s. Craig was an employee of Colonial Bakery and wore his uniform everywhere—even to church. Western Union operator Earle Little gave him the cues and Craig broadcast the games from a special public booth at the bakery. During an inning Craig would say, "put a loaf on the radio and we'll get a rally going." (Courtesy of the Arkansas Travelers.)

Frank Lucchesi managed the most power-packed teams in Arkansas Travelers' history. The San Francisco native managed the 1963 and 1964 teams that set team home run records. The 1963 squad was a Phillies' farm team in the International League. Led by Richie Allen, Cal Emery and John Hernstein, the team hit 148 home runs. The following year, their first in the Pacific Coast League, the Travelers hit 208 homers. They won the title but lost to San Diego in the playoffs. During the 1970s, Lucchesi managed the Philadelphia Phillies and the Texas Rangers for brief periods and piloted the Cubs briefly in 1987. (Courtesy of the Arkansas Travelers.)

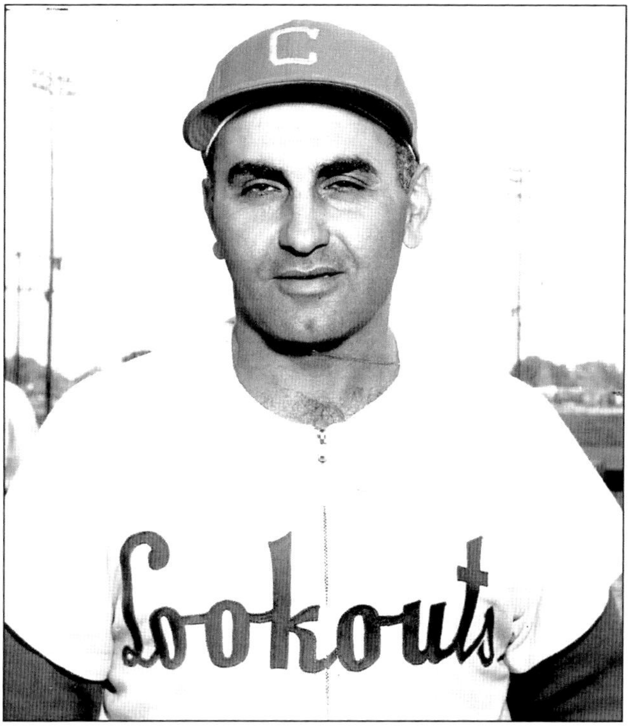

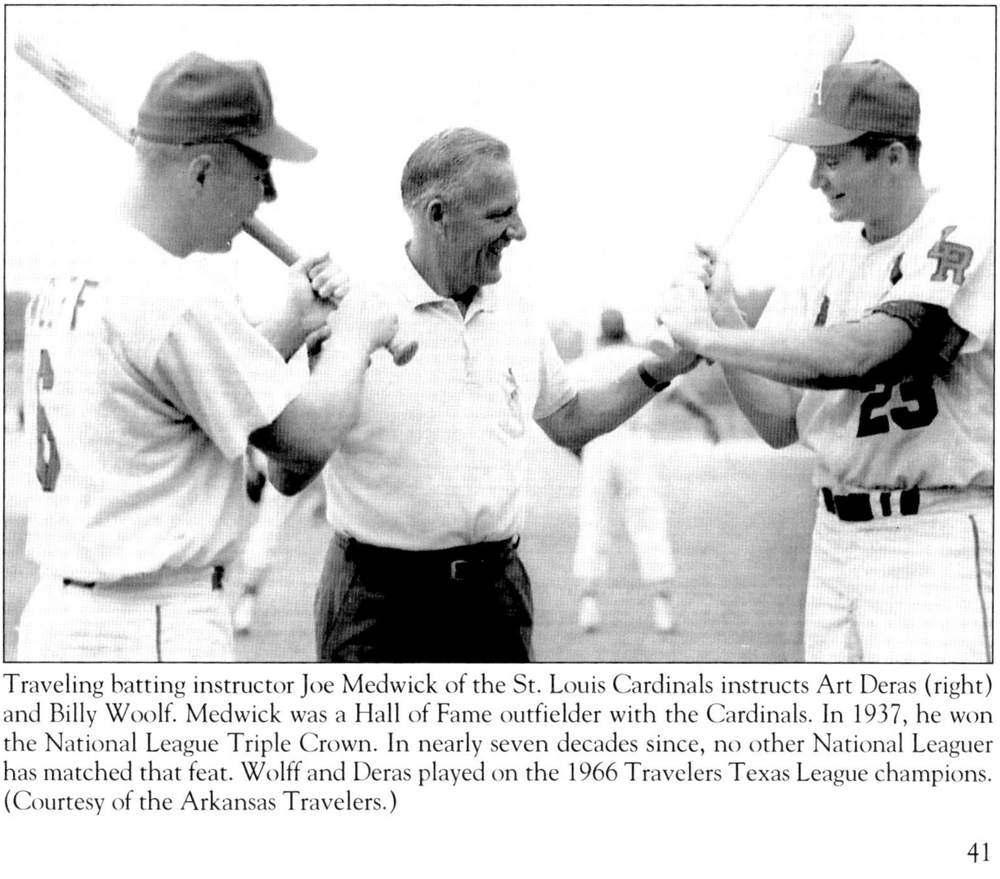

Traveling batting instructor Joe Medwick of the St. Louis Cardinals instructs Art Deras (right) and Billy Woolf. Medwick was a Hall of Fame outfielder with the Cardinals. In 1937, he won the National League Triple Crown. In nearly seven decades since, no other National Leaguer has matched that feat. Wolff and Deras played on the 1966 Travelers Texas League champions. (Courtesy of the Arkansas Travelers.)

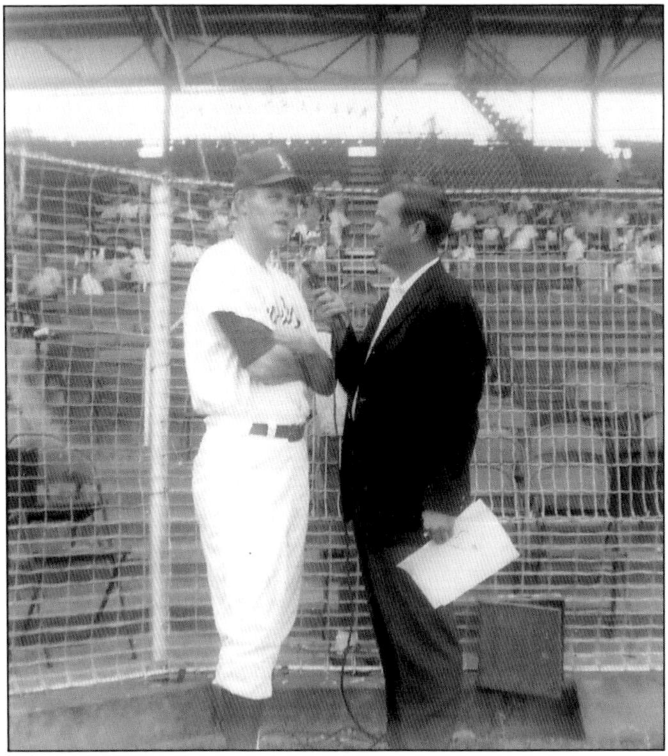

Pitcher Joel Gibson answers a question from Little Rock Travelers play-by-play announcer Bud Campbell. Gibson threw a no-hitter against the Dallas Rangers 3-0 in a 1964 Pacific Coast League contest. (Courtesy of Shirley Rieve.)

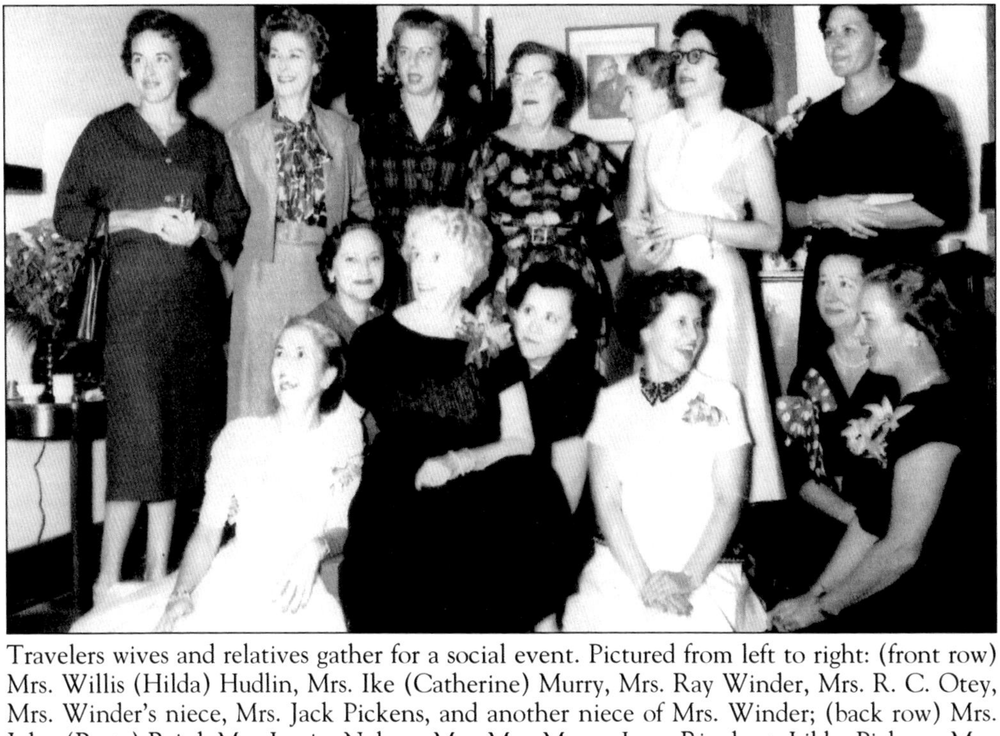

Travelers wives and relatives gather for a social event. Pictured from left to right: (front row) Mrs. Willis (Hilda) Hudlin, Mrs. Ike (Catherine) Murry, Mrs. Ray Winder, Mrs. R. C. Otey, Mrs. Winder's niece, Mrs. Jack Pickens, and another niece of Mrs. Winder; (back row) Mrs. John (Betty) Baird, Mrs. Louise Nelson, Mrs. Max Moses, Lena Rinehart, Libby Pickens, Mrs. Newell and Mrs. Green. (Courtesy of Betty Baird.)

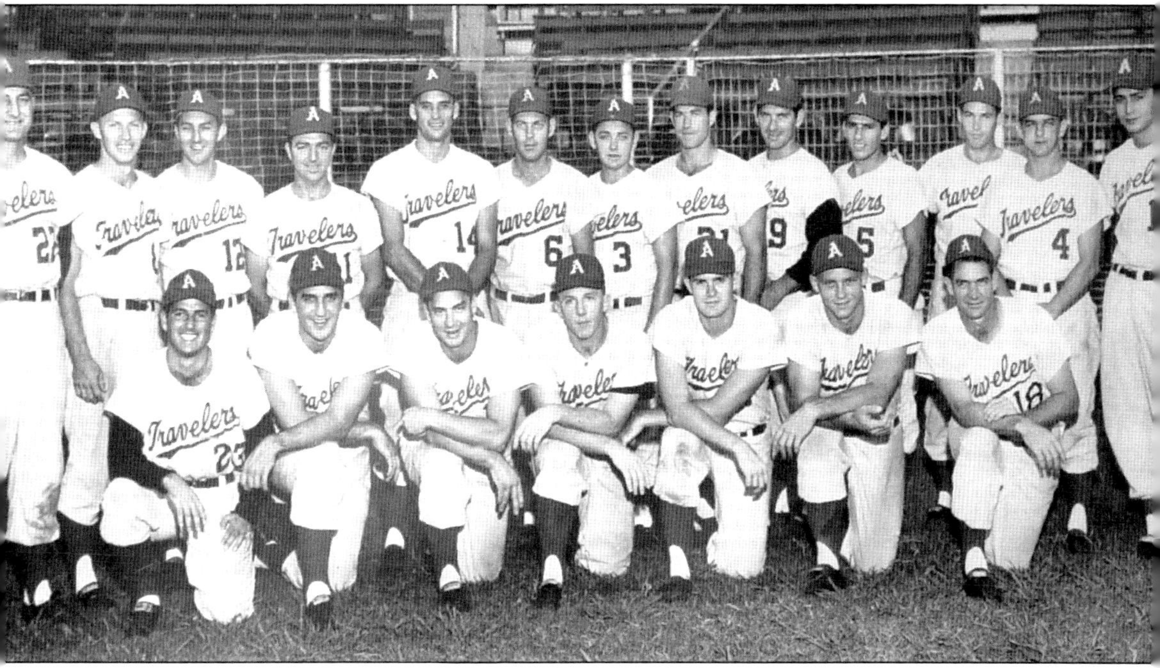

The 1961 edition of the Little Rock Travelers played in the last year of the Southern Association. They finished third and the organization did not field a team in 1962. (Courtesy of the Arkansas Travelers.)

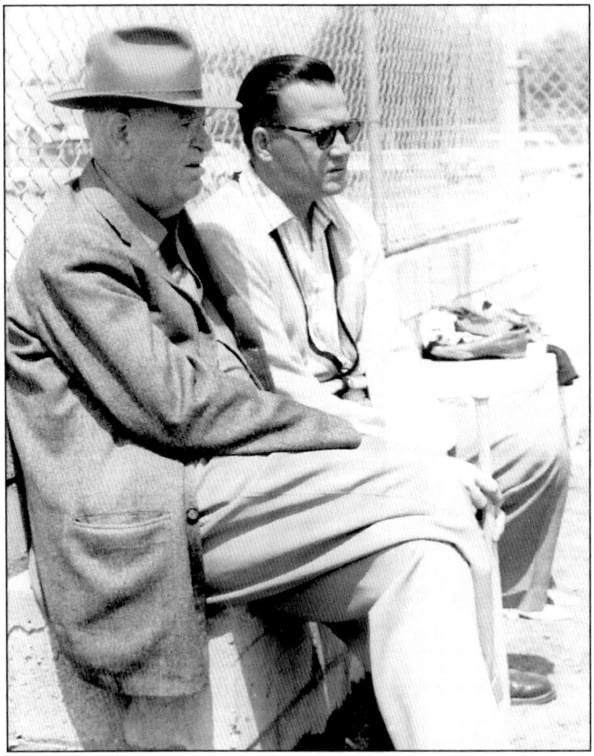

Ray Winder, Travelers general manager, and Hank Peters, Kansas City farm director, watch a team-workout in 1957. The Travelers were a farm team for Kansas City Athletics in 1957 and 1958. (Courtesy of the Arkansas Travelers.)

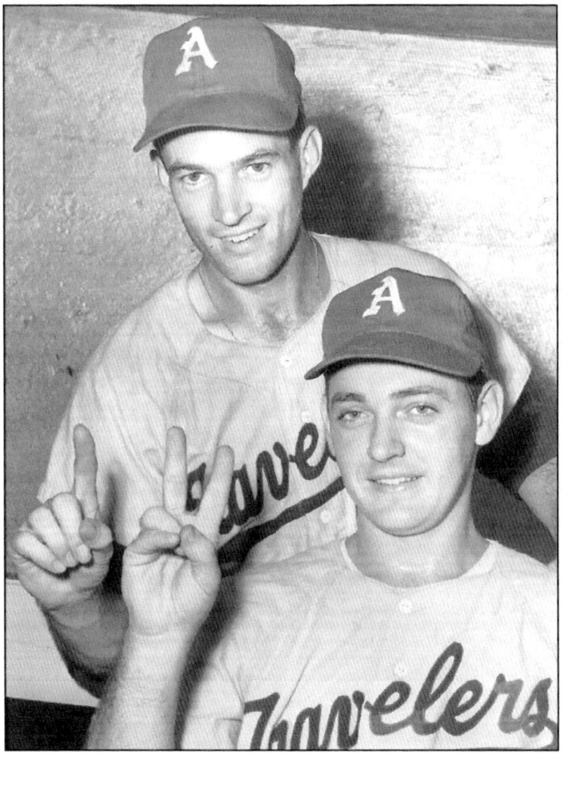

Pitchers Charley Ready and Don Bradey made up the Travelers one-two pitching punch in 1961 for Manager Fred Hatfield. In the last year of the Southern Association, Ready had a 12-7 record and a 3.51 ERA. Bradey was 9-10 and posted an ERA of 4.73. Their production led to a third-place finish and an 80-73 record, placing them 10 1/2 games behind Chattanooga. (Courtesy of the Arkansas Travelers.)

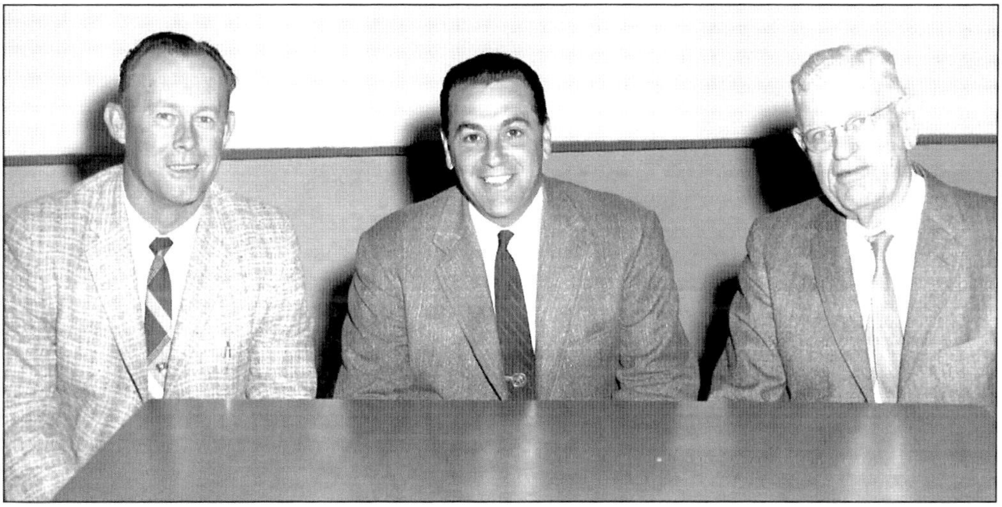

Kansas City manager Lou Boudreau (center) is pictured with Traveler general manager Ray Winder prior to the 1957 season. Boudreau was a Hall of Fame shortstop and a player-manager with the Cleveland Indians. In 1948, he was Most Valuable Player in the American League and managed the Indians to a World Series championship. His last year as manager was in 1960 with the Cubs. He became a Cubs announcer. (Courtesy of the Arkansas Travelers.)

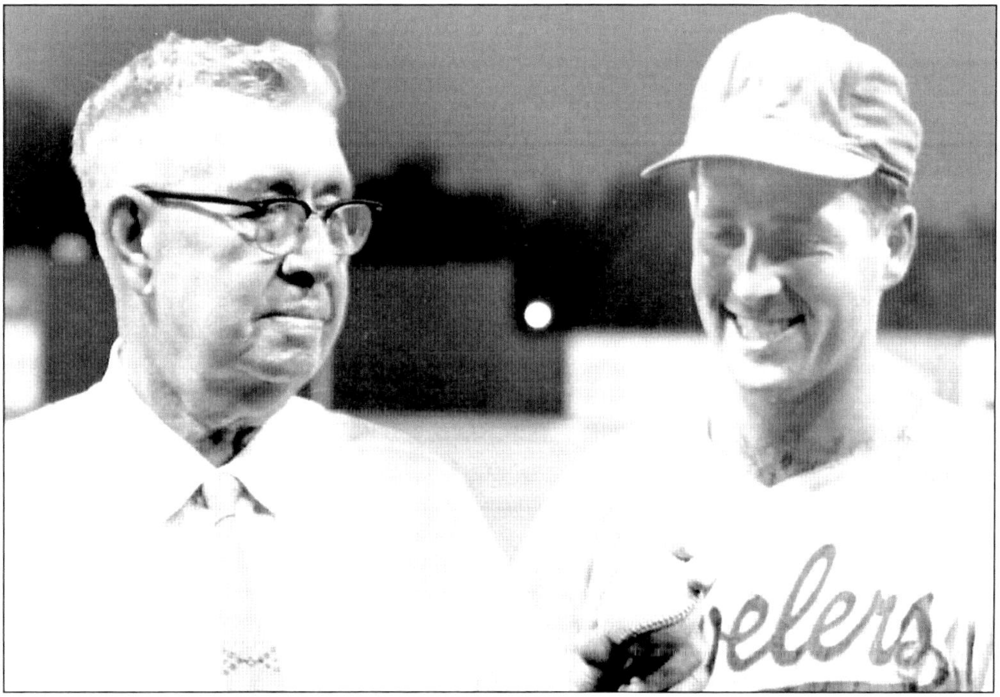

Arkansas Sports Hall of Famer and legendary Southern Association pitcher Rube Robinson shows Travelers pitcher Pat Gillick his grip. Robinson pitched six years in the major leagues and compiled a 42-37 record, playing mainly for the Pittsburgh Pirates early in the 20th century. He also won over 200 games in the Southern Association. Gillick was a key asset for Manager Fred Hatfield's 1961 Travelers, with a record of 10-7, a .588 winning mark and a 4.38 ERA. (Courtesy of the Arkansas Travelers.)

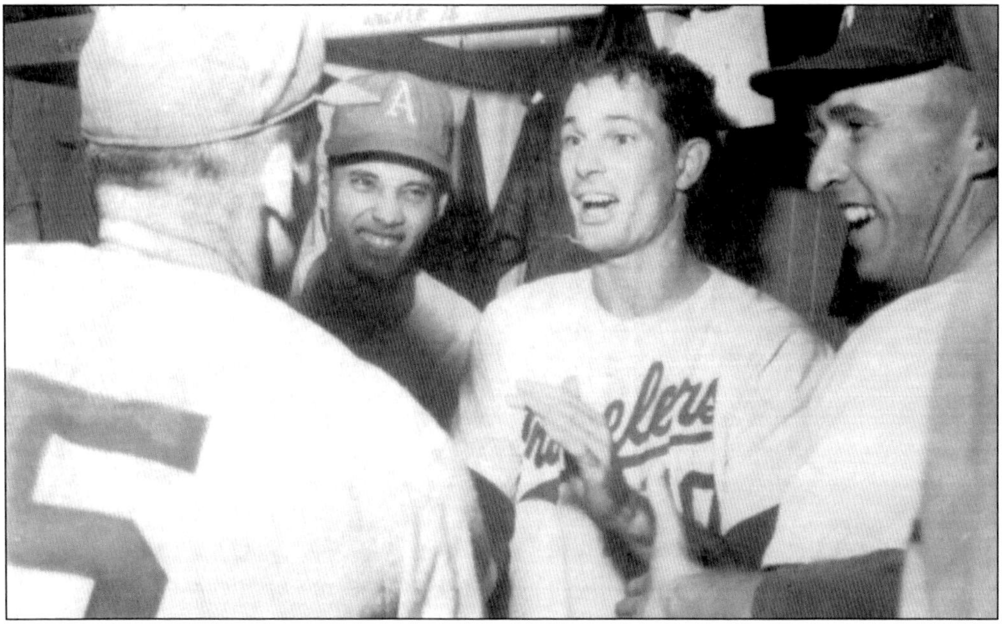

Morrie Steevens pitched a no-hitter on September 9, 1964. He just missed a perfect game, allowing only one batter to reach base. Steevens blanked the Dallas Rangers 3-0 in a Pacific Coast League contest, allowing the Travelers to win the East Division. A crowd of 3,516 was on hand to honor Arkansas General Manager Ray Winder as he celebrated his 50th year in organized baseball. It was Traveler Appreciation Night. Gifts, including $100 checks, were passed out to each Travelers player and fans collected $390 for Steevens after his brilliant performance. (Courtesy of the Arkansas Travelers.)

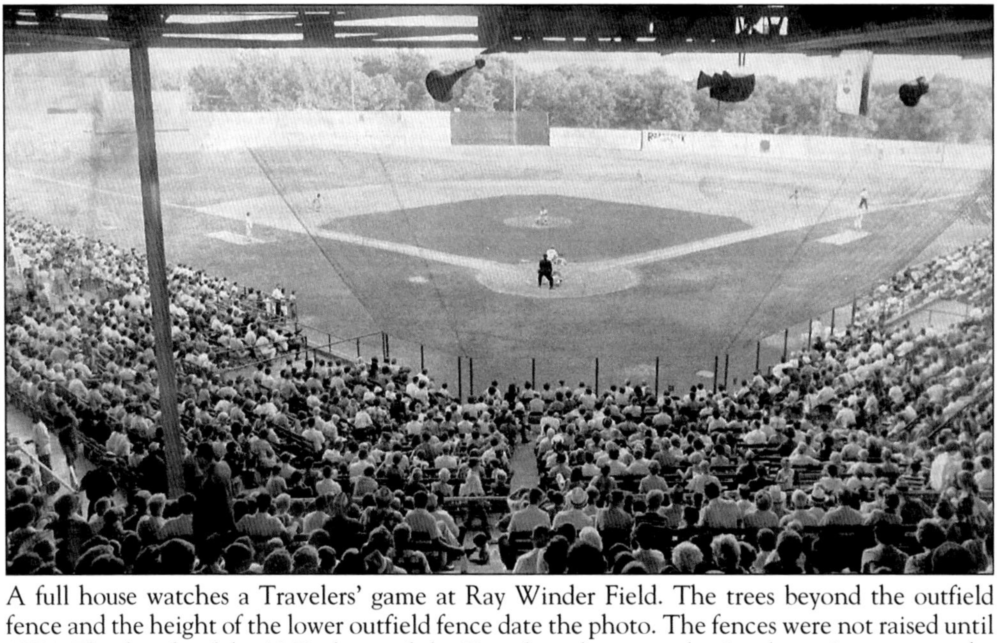

A full house watches a Travelers' game at Ray Winder Field. The trees beyond the outfield fence and the height of the lower outfield fence date the photo. The fences were not raised until 1974. The decade of the 1960s featured the Travelers playing in the Southern Association, the International, the Pacific Coast and the Texas League. (Courtesy of the Arkansas Travelers.)

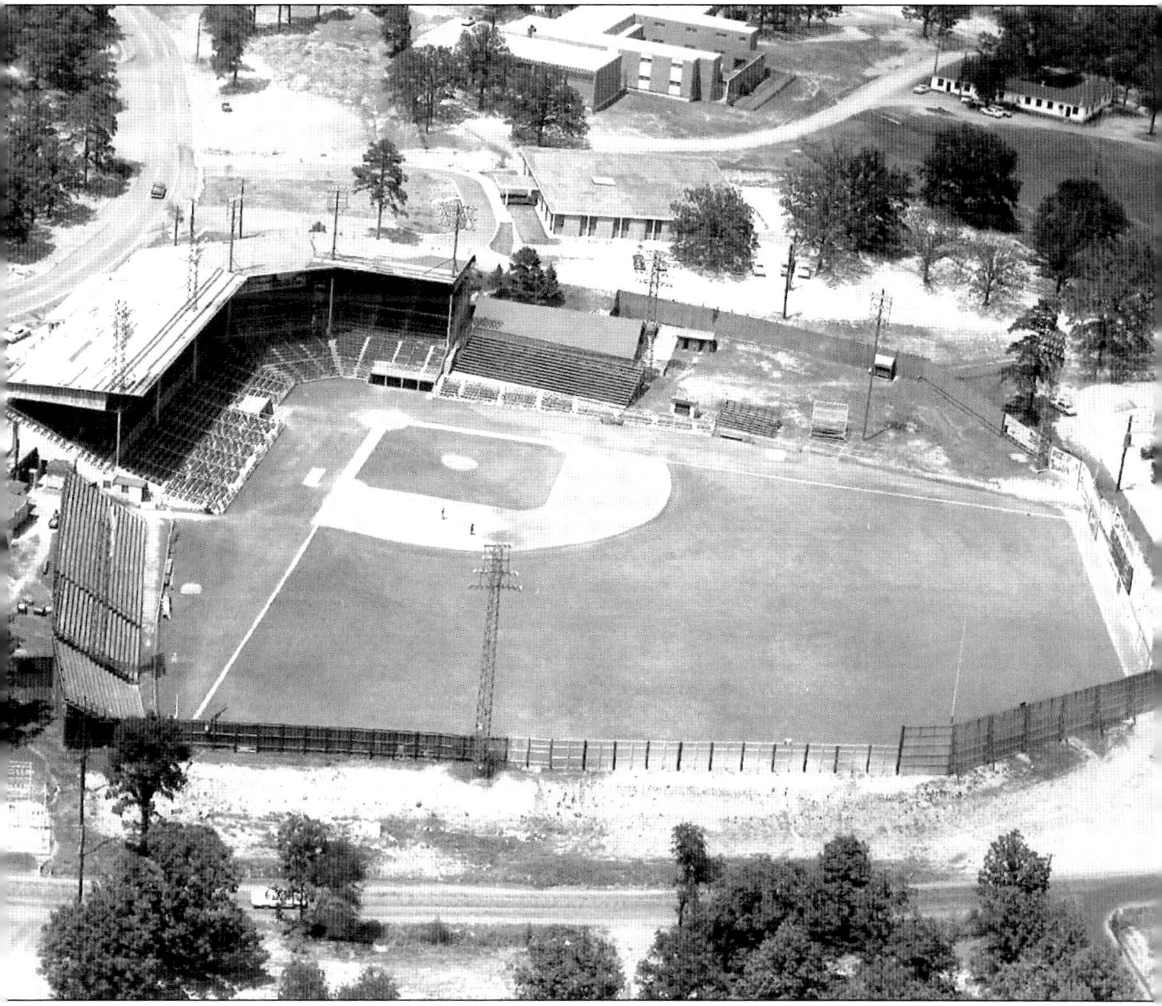

In 1964, Travelers Field underwent a major change in left and centerfield. A dusty trail, visible beyond the rightfield fence, became the path for busy Interstate 630 in the 1970s. (Courtesy of the Arkansas Travelers.)

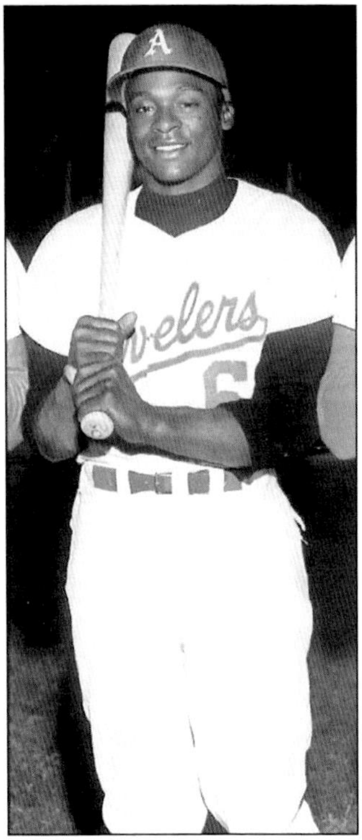

Richie Allen was the first African American to play at Travelers' Field. In 1963, the Phillies assembled the first-ever Triple A team during Arkansas' only year in the International League. Allen led the league that year with 33 home runs, 97 RBIs and 299 total bases. He was part of a powerful team that hit 148 homers. Allen made the Phillies' line-up in 1964 and was named National League Rookie of the Year. In 1972, Allen was the American League Most Valuable Player. (Courtesy of the Arkansas Travelers.)

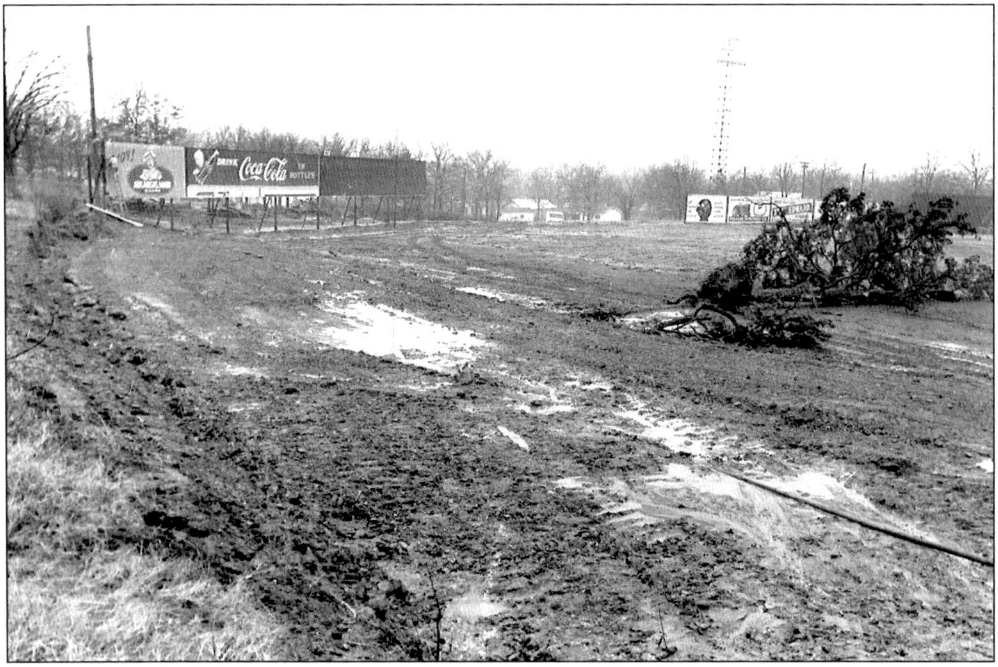

"The dump" is what Little Rock players called the rise in the playing field that ran from left field to centerfield. The Philadelphia Phillies were concerned that key prospects such as Richie Allen might get injured playing on the uneven turf. In the winter of 1965, workers set about to level the outfield. (Courtesy of the Arkansas Travelers.)

THREE

The Texas League Years 1966–Present

After playing in three leagues over four years, the Travelers found stability in the Texas League in 1966. Contrary to their name, the Travelers were weary of traveling. Arkansas was much more at home against El Paso and Albuquerque than playing teams as far away as Syracuse, Portland and Hawaii. Triple-A ball was much more expensive and team officials wanted to return to Double-A ball.

Through Little Rock businessman Jack Pickens' wartime association with St. Louis owner Gussie Busch, the Travelers made the switch to Double-A ball. This new contract brought Arkansas into the Texas League where they were an instant success. They won the Texas League title their first year and two of the first three years.

Attendance at Arkansas games was terrific in the 1980s and 1990s. The Travelers drew over 200,000 fans for 17 consecutive years. The team's association with the St. Louis Cardinals led to much larger crowds. After winning only four pennants in the Southern Association, the Travelers won 17 league titles or half-championships from 1966 through 2001.

The 1989 Travelers drew a franchise record attendance total of 296,428. The exploits of Ray Lankford, Bernard Gilkey, Geronimo Pena, Rod Brewer, Craig Wilson, Ray Stephens and Roy Silver helped the Travelers win the first half of the season. Arkansas almost won the second half. Anxiety was in the air as the Travelers were down 0-3, but pulled off four straight wins to reign as Texas League champs.

In 1998, the Travelers won a half season title featuring four future major leaguers and several outstanding individual performances. Joe McEwing took advantage of a chance to play daily and batted .354 in 60 games. He moved on to Memphis, batted .334 in 78 games and advanced to the Cardinals and a September 1 roster spot. Future 2002 American League playoff MVP Adam Kennedy starred for the Travelers in 1998 and 1999. Kennedy hit .278 in 52 games in 1998 and .327 in 91 games in 1999. J.D. Drew brought headlines and excitement in 1998. The popular Drew broke into the Cardinals' system by hitting .328 in 19 games.

Tyrone Horne was the Texas League Player of the Year for 1998. He became the first professional player to hit for the "Homer Cycle." Horne hit a solo homer, a two-run shot, a three-run homer and a grand slam all in one game. His bat was sent to the Baseball Hall of Fame in Cooperstown, New York. Jose Jimenez threw a no-hitter for the Travelers and won 15 games. He went on to become the Colorado Rockies closer. Stubby Clapp, an exciting hustler who scored 113 runs that season, became a fan favorite. Clapp earned a promotion to the Cardinals' Triple-A farm team in Memphis.

The 2001 Travelers drew 185,905 fans and led the Round Rock Express 2-0 in the Texas League finals on the morning of September 11, 2001. Professional baseball play was suspended and league officials cancelled the playoff games after the atrocities in New York, Washington and Pennsylvania. The Travelers were declared Texas League champs. The

2001 team featured four future World Series stars: John Lackey, Chone Figgins, Francisco Rodriquez, and Brendan Donnelly.

The move to the Texas League has paid off for the Travelers, both on the field and at the turnstiles. The franchise is in contention more often in the Texas League than it ever was in the Southern Association. The team has become more competitive, more profitable and draws more fans.

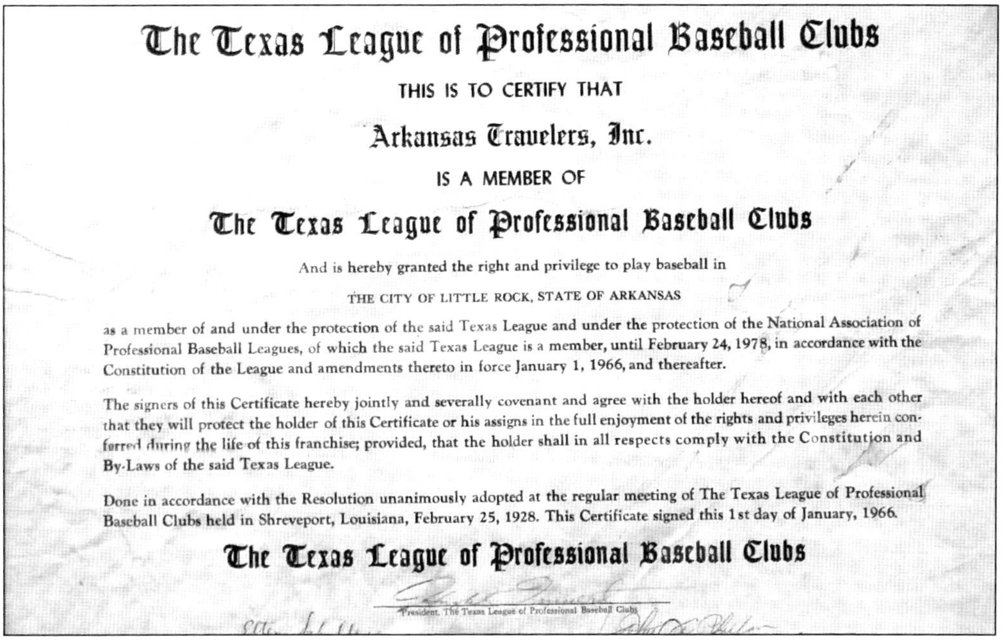

The Texas League of Professional Baseball Clubs

THIS IS TO CERTIFY THAT

Arkansas Travelers, Inc.

IS A MEMBER OF

The Texas League of Professional Baseball Clubs

And is hereby granted the right and privilege to play baseball in

THE CITY OF LITTLE ROCK, STATE OF ARKANSAS

as a member of and under the protection of the said Texas League and under the protection of the National Association of Professional Baseball Leagues, of which the said Texas League is a member, until February 24, 1978, in accordance with the Constitution of the League and amendments thereto in force January 1, 1966, and thereafter.

The signers of this Certificate hereby jointly and severally covenant and agree with the holder hereof and with each other that they will protect the holder of this Certificate or his assigns in the full enjoyment of the rights and privileges herein conferred during the life of this franchise; provided, that the holder shall in all respects comply with the Constitution and By-Laws of the said Texas League.

Done in accordance with the Resolution unanimously adopted at the regular meeting of The Texas League of Professional Baseball Clubs held in Shreveport, Louisiana, February 25, 1928. This Certificate signed this 1st day of January, 1966.

The Texas League of Professional Baseball Clubs

President, The Texas League of Professional Baseball Clubs

After playing in three leagues over four years, the Travelers found stability in the Texas League in 1966. After playing against teams as far away as Syracuse, Portland and Hawaii, the Travelers were much more at home against El Paso and Albuquerque. They were also an instant success. They won the Texas League title their first year and two of the first three years. (Courtesy of the Arkansas Travelers.)

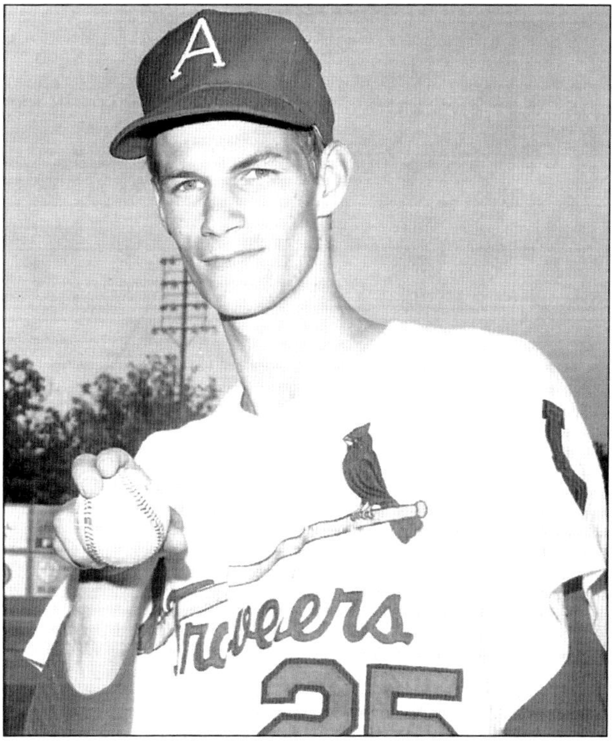

Wayne Granger participated in several Travelers firsts in 1966: first time Arkansas was part of the St. Louis Cardinal farm system, first time the team was in the Texas League, and the first time Arkansas won a Texas League championship, with an 81-59 record under Manager Vern Rapp. They nipped second-place Amarillo by four games thanks to Granger. The slim reliever beat Amarillo eight times and posted an 11-2 record. Granger moved up to the Cardinals for one season in 1968. Twice he led the National League in Games (1969 and 1971) with Cincinnati and in 1970 he topped the National League in saves with 35, appearing that same year in the World Series with the Reds. (Courtesy of the Arkansas Travelers.)

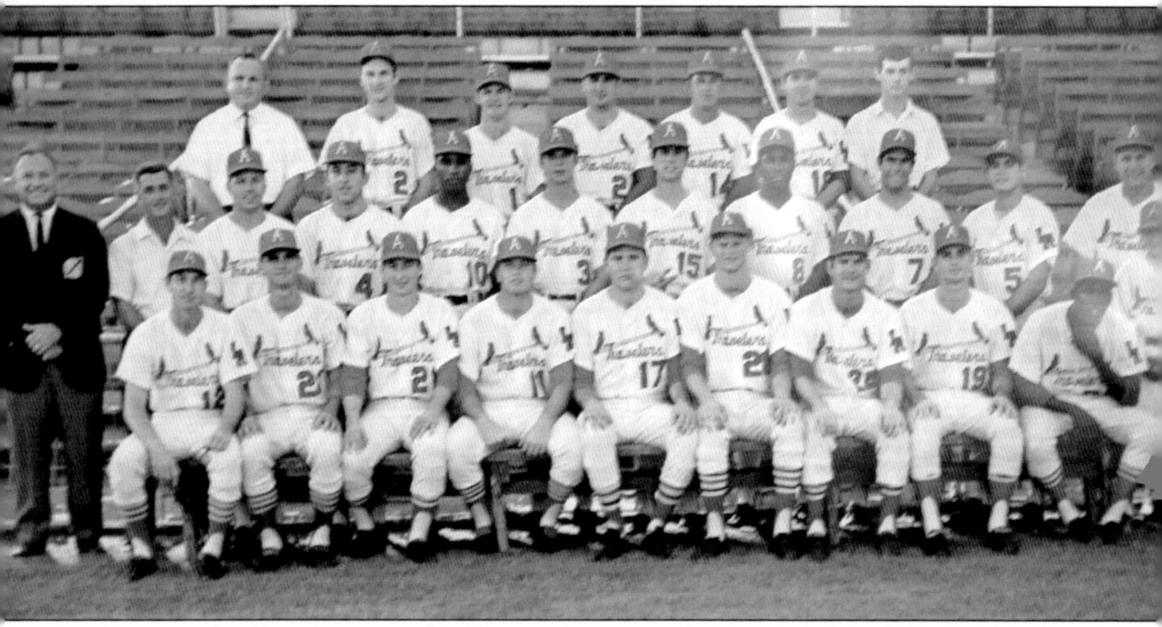

In 1968, the Travelers won the Eastern Division title. Pictured from left to right: (front row) Bobby Dews, Harry Parker, Phil Knuckles, Len Boyer, Jim Cosman, Jerry Reuss, Dave Dowling, Andy Martin, Santiago Guzman, and batboy Jim Rice; (middle row) general manager Carl Sawatski, park superintendent R.C. Otey, Billy Wolff, Gary Stone, Bill Murphy, Mike Christino, John Sipin, Leon Lee, Jerry DaVannon, Quique Rivera, and manager Vern Rapp; (back row) concession manager Tom Moore, Manager Sonny Robertson, Boots Day, Joe De Fabio, Leo Newton, Joe Hamende, and trainer Jim Bell. (Courtesy of the Arkansas Travelers.)

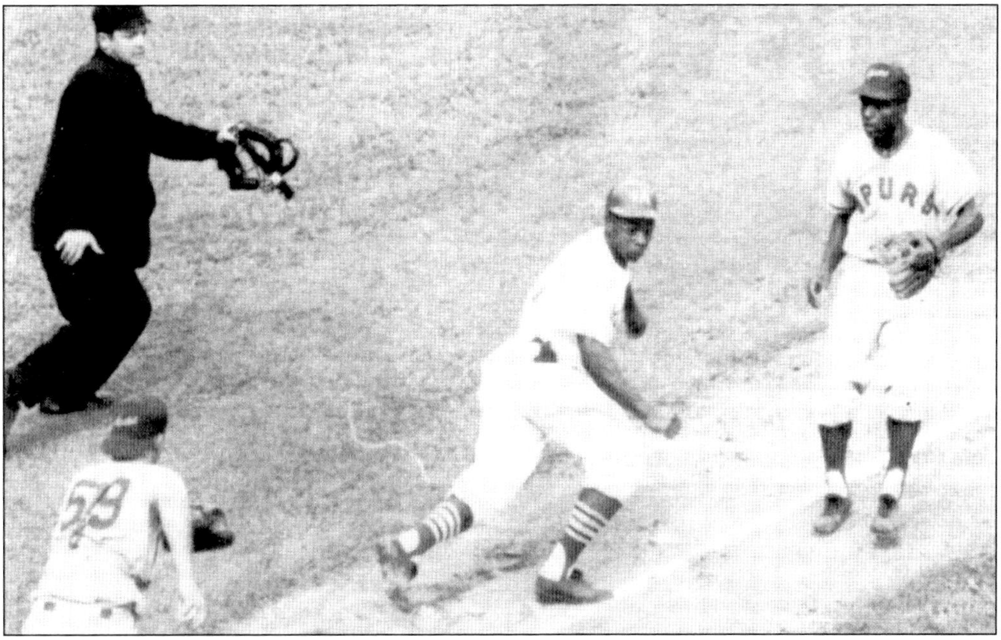

Travelers Joe Patterson avoids a rundown against the Dallas-Ft. Worth Spurs. Patterson, an outfielder for Arkansas in 1966 and 1967, swiped 30 bases in 1966 to finish second in the league. In 1967, he had 12 steals. Patterson kept Traveler fans alert with his base-running antics. (Courtesy of the Arkansas Travelers.)

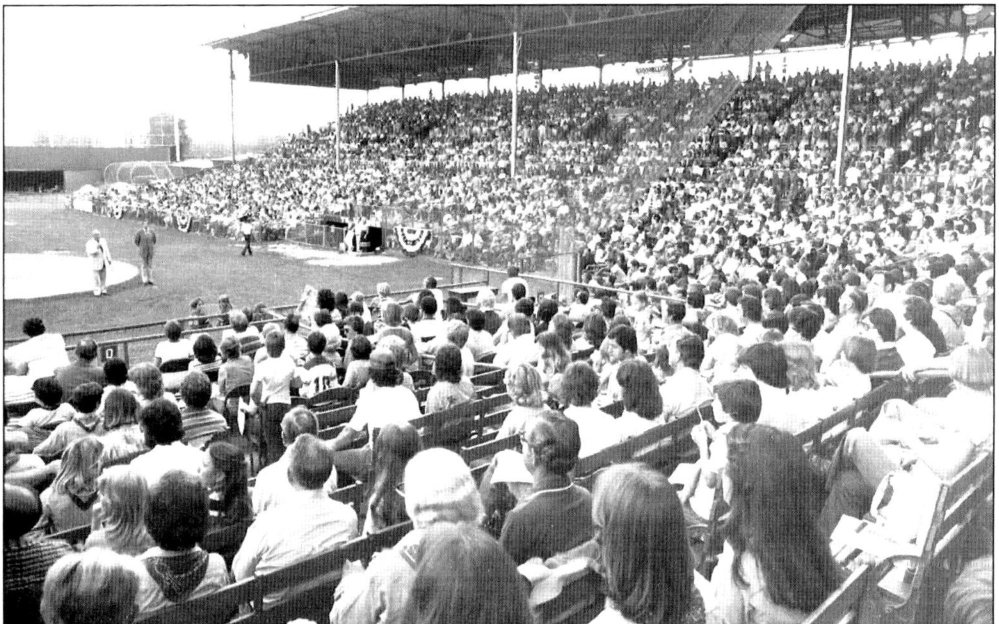

General Manager Carl Sawatski, a former Travelers player, addresses an Opening Day crowd. Sawatski served as Texas League president from 1976 to his death in 1991. He had an 11-year major league career as a catcher for the Cubs, Braves, Phillies and Cardinals. (Courtesy of the Arkansas Travelers.)

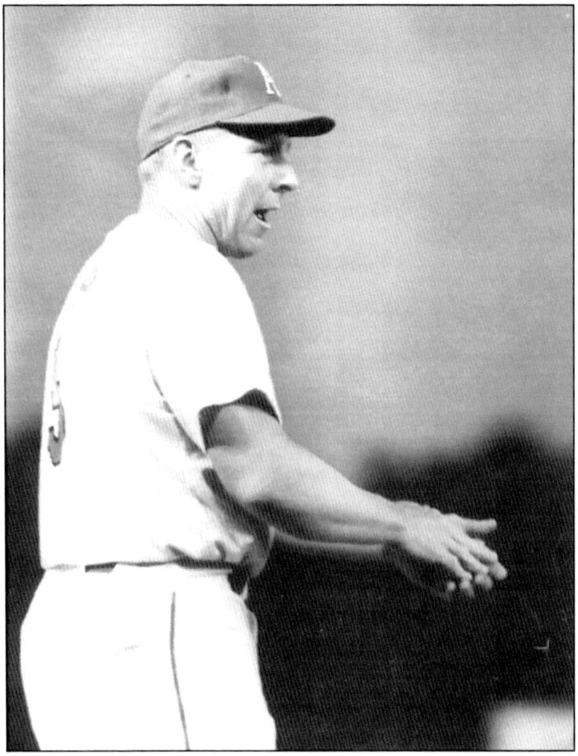

Manager Vern Rapp piloted the Travelers to their first Texas League title in 1966 and again in 1968. Rapp's teams specialized in the speed game, and he drove opponents to distraction with squeeze plays, delayed steals and the hit-and-run. Rapp managed the Cardinals in 1977, part of 1978, and finished his managing career with a 51-70 season in 1984 with Cincinnati. (Courtesy of the Arkansas Travelers.)

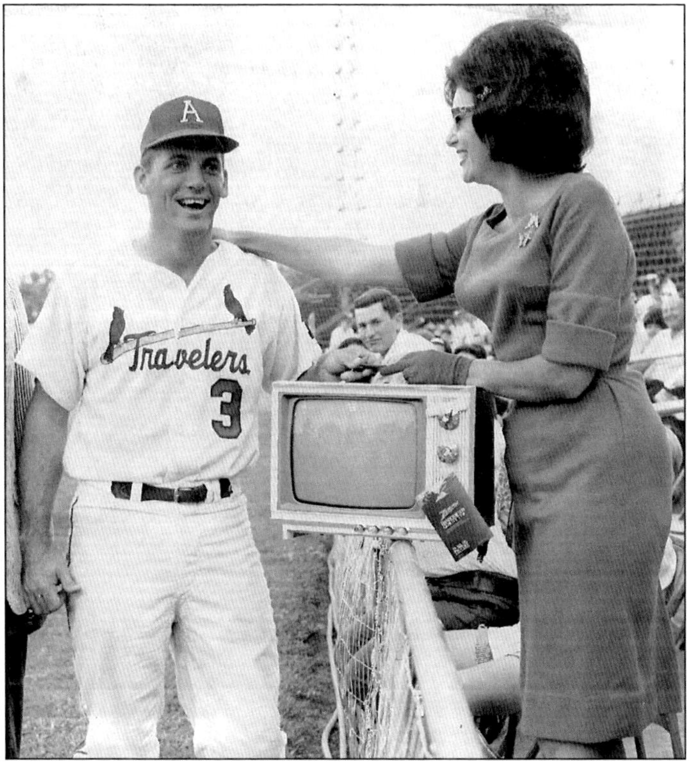

Faithful Travelers fan Beulah Barton presents a gift to slugger Joe Hague. Barton was known for her loud disagreements with the umpires during disputed calls. For over 15 years, she attended all the Travelers' games except on Tuesday nights when she shifted her attention to the wrestling matches. She was just as vocal with wrestling referees as she was with the baseball umpires. (Courtesy of the Arkansas Travelers.)

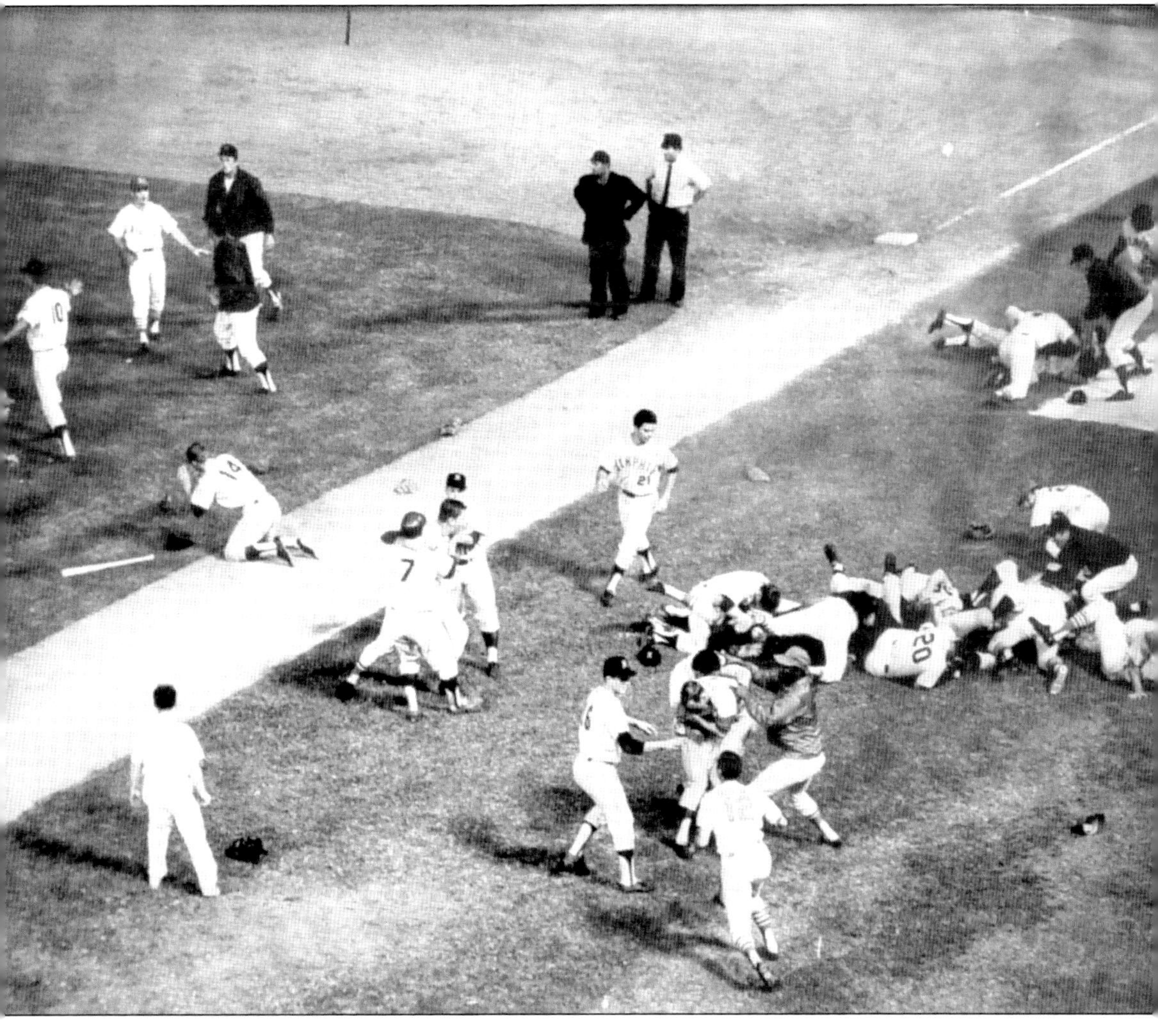

In a year full of discontent nationally, the 1968 Travelers were involved in three huge beanball wars. The one pictured was late in the season and involved Memphis. The only cool heads seem to be the two umpires near first base. The fighting Travelers won the East in 1968, but lost to El Paso in the playoffs, three games to one. (Courtesy of the Arkansas Travelers.)

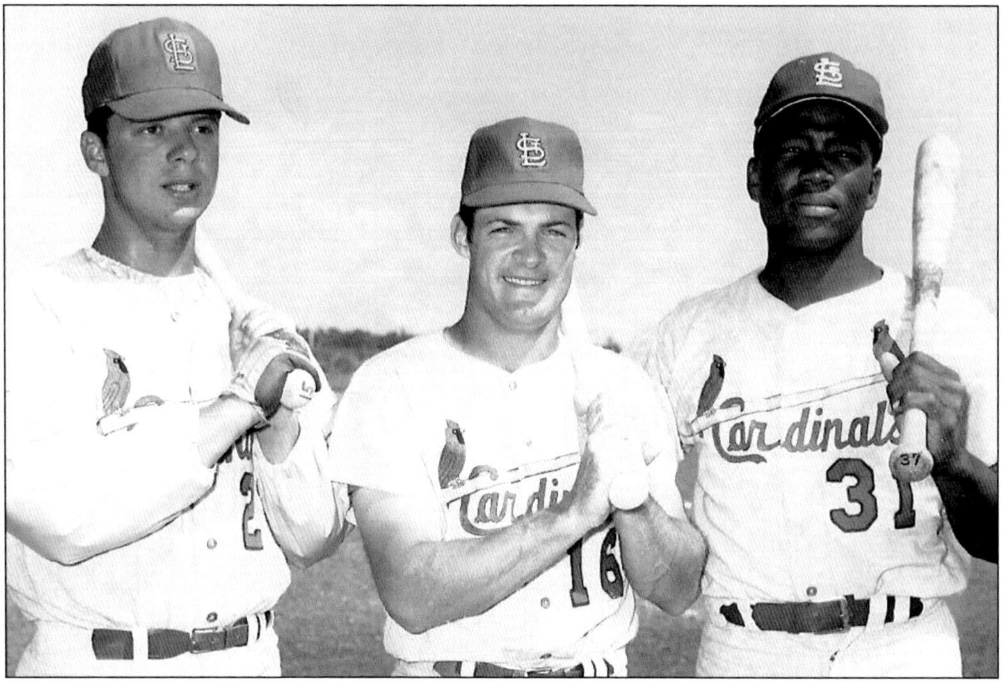

Mike Christino, Boots Day and Leon Lee led the Travelers into the Texas League playoffs in 1968. Arkansas had a record of 82-58 and won the division by four games. Christino had 17 homers and 68 runs batted in. Day had 17 homers, 67 RBIs and batted .295. Lee hit 13 homers and drove in 65 runs. (Courtesy of the Arkansas Travelers.)

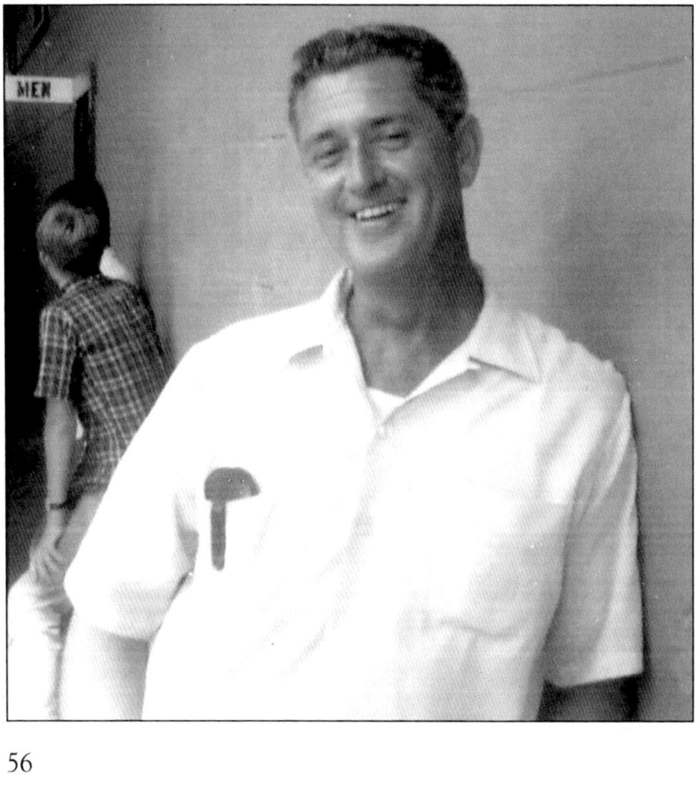

Former Traveler second baseman R.C. Otey is pictured in 1968. After a 10-year career with the Travelers, Otey became groundskeeper and served there from 1963 to the early 1990s. His decade with Little Rock as a player was the longest continuous service in Traveler history. A Levy native, Otey was an important part of the 1951 pennant with a .305 average and 110 runs scored. (Courtesy of Shirley Rieve.)

Danny Napoleon and Jose Cruz were mainstays for the Travelers in 1970. Napoleon hit 12 homeruns for an average of .291 and drove in 64 runs. Cruz finished eighth in the league in hitting with a .300 average. He also led the league with 254 total bases and 29 doubles. (Courtesy of the Arkansas Travelers.)

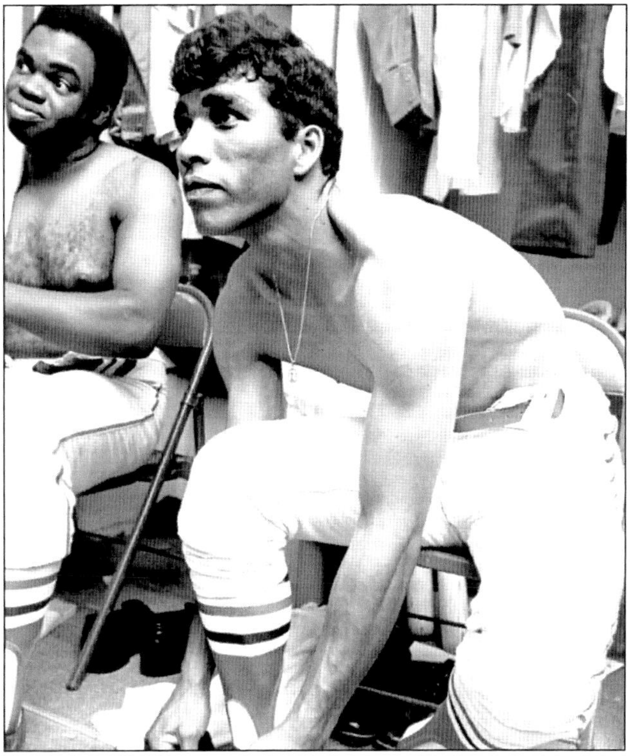

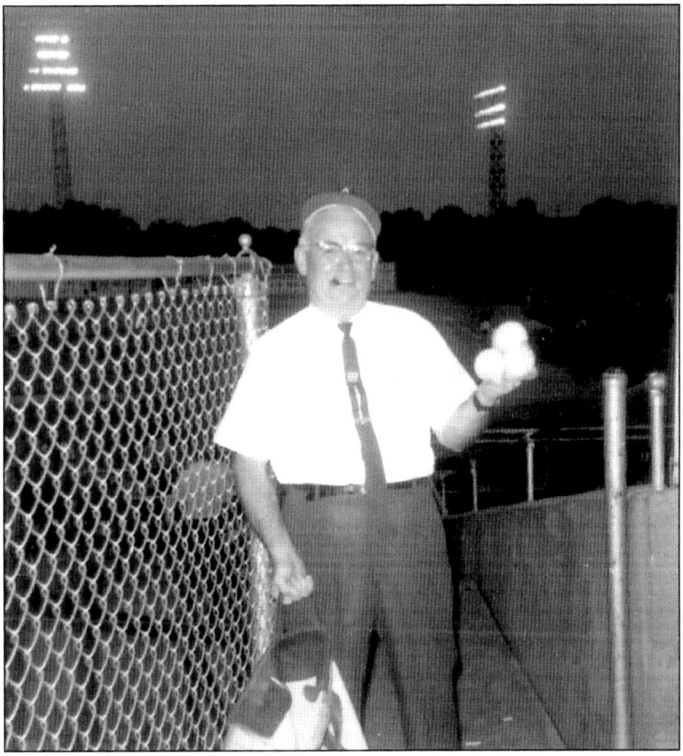

Mr. Reno was the caretaker of the baseballs for each game at Ray Winder Field. It was his job to replenish the balls gathered from the ballboys for the homeplate umpire. (Courtesy of Shirley Rieve.)

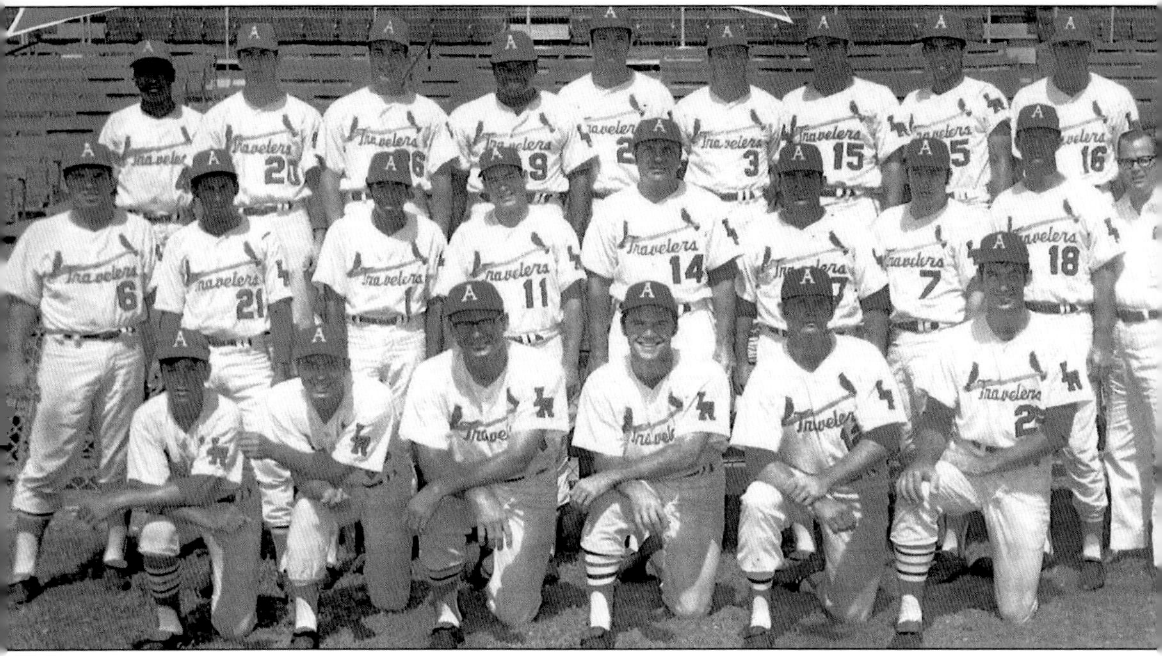

The 1970 Travelers are pictured from left to right: (front row) batboy David Boyer, John Schroeppel, coach Dick Hughes, Mike McDonald, Bruce VonHoff, and Steve Evans; (middle row) Lucky Thompson, Dionicio Gonzalez, Charlie Stewart, Quique Rivera, Ken Boyer, manager, Joe Difabio, Skip Jutze, Ed Gagle, and trainer Lee Landers; (back row) Manuel Abreu, George Winslow, Dick Seminoff, Danny Napoleon, Ray Bare, Bill Stein, Wayne Dees, Jose Cruz, and Tim Thompson. (Courtesy of the Arkansas Travelers.)

Jack Krol managed the Travelers to one-two-three finishes in the 1970s. The team won a Central Division title in the Dixie Association in 1971, but lost the league title to Charlotte in the playoffs. In 1974, Krol's team finished second to Victoria, and third in 1976 after Shreveport and Jackson. Krol managed just three games in the major leagues for the Cardinals in 1978 and 1980. (Courtesy of the Arkansas Travelers.)

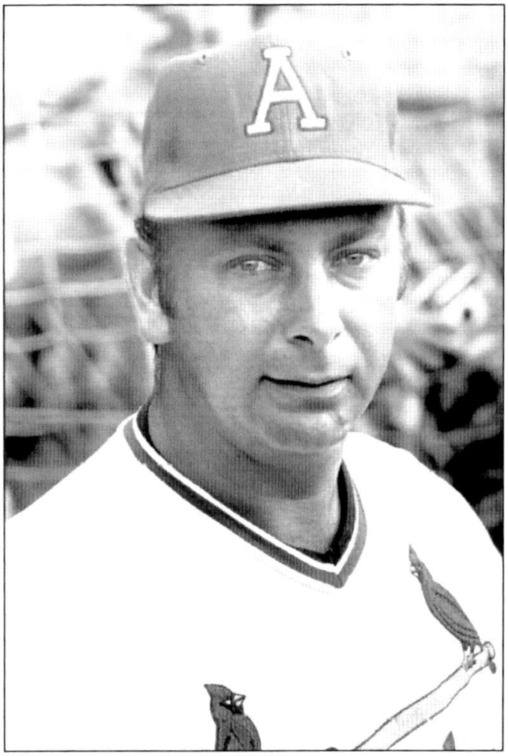

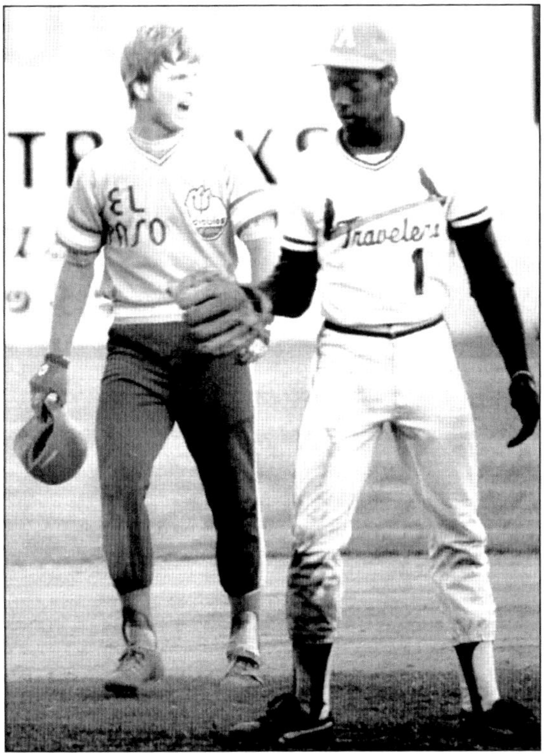

Garry Templeton (No. 1) batted .401 in a six-week stay with the Travelers in 1975. He played part of a season with the Cardinals in 1976 and in 1977, became the St. Louis starter as shortstop. His career got off to a blazing start and he led the National League in triples his first three full years. He also paced the league in hits with 211 in 1979. Templeton had a 16-year career, mostly with San Diego. He was part of the Ozzie Smith trade in 1982 with San Diego. The exchange was the beginning of the Cardinals' turnaround in the mid-80s. It helped lead the Cards to the World Series in 1982, 1985 and 1987. (Courtesy of the Arkansas Travelers.)

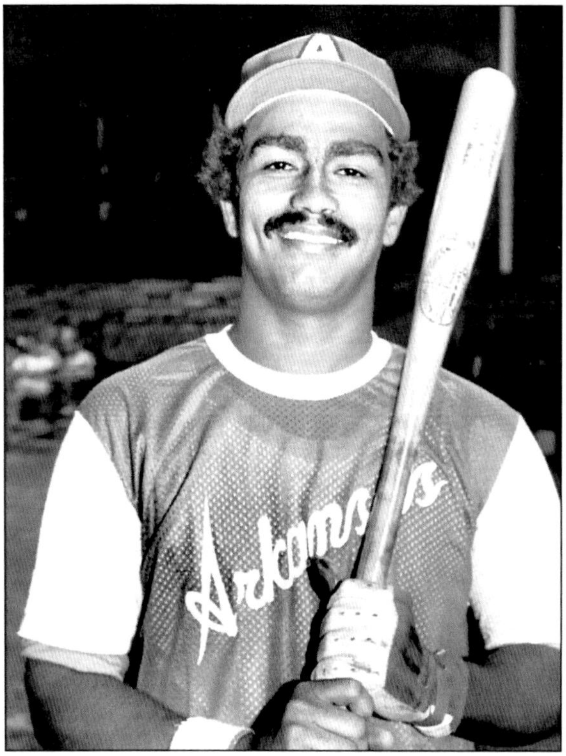

Joey DeSa was a part of the surprising 1979 Travelers managed by Tommy Thompson. The left-handed hitter batted .317 and hit 13 homers. (Courtesy of the Arkansas Travelers.)

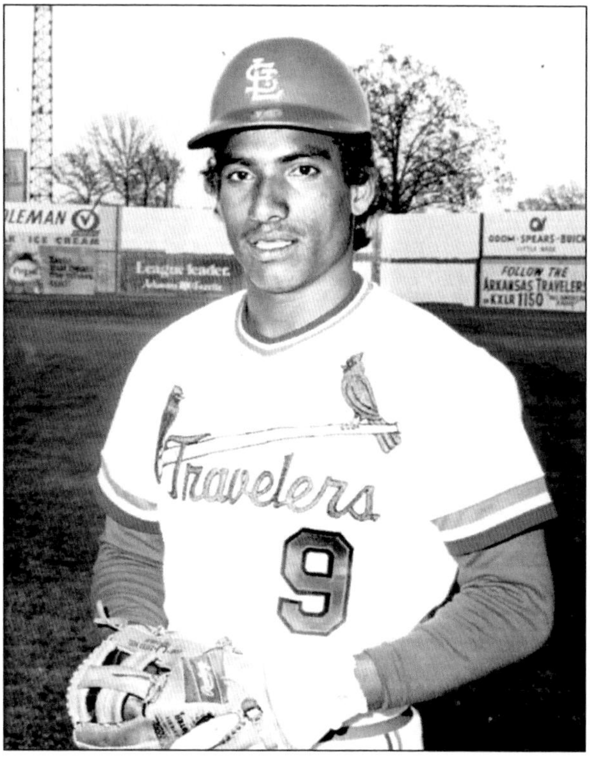

Hector Cruz was the last Travelers hitter to take advantage of the lower fences in right and right centerfield at Ray Winder Field. In 1974, the walls were raised to their present height of 55 feet. In 1973, Cruz led the Texas League with 30 home runs and 105 RBIs and made the All-Star team. Oddly, in a nine-year major league career, he had only 39 homers and batted .225. (Courtesy of the Arkansas Travelers.)

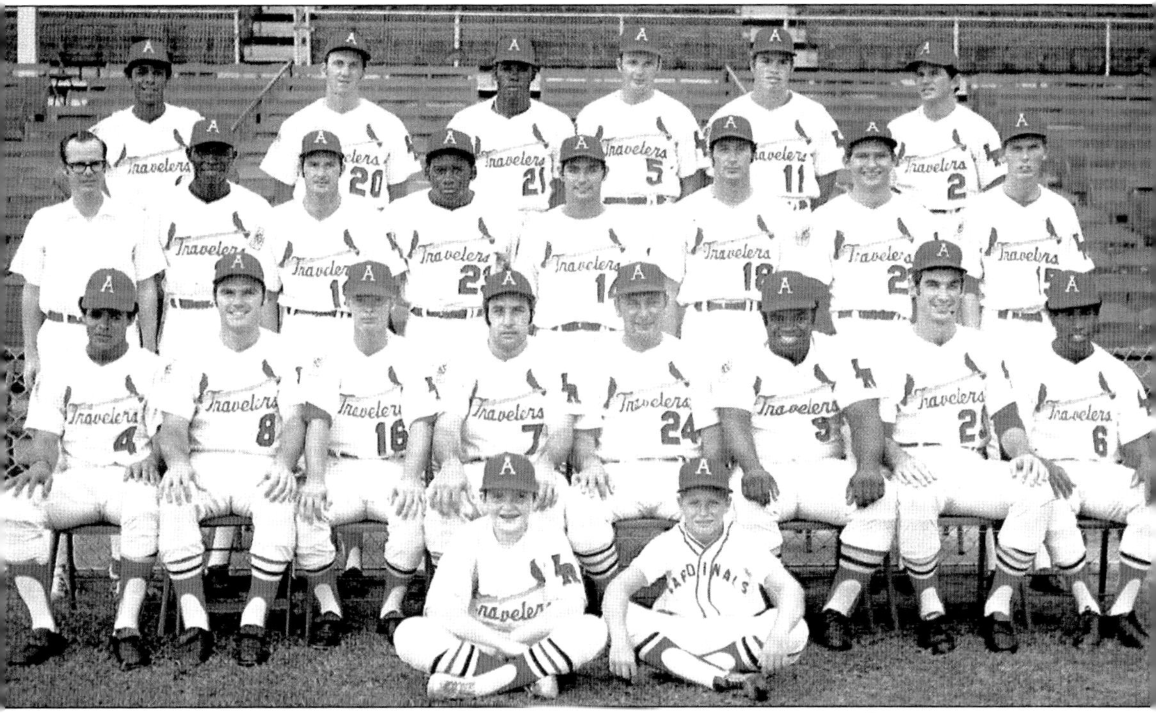

The 1971 Travelers won the Central Division of the Dixie Association with a 75-64 record. Pictured from left to right: (first row) batboys Kevin Alexander and John Krol; (second row) Jorge Roque, Mike McDonald, Gary Marion, Skip Jutze, manager Jack Krol, Danny Napoleon, Steve Evans, and Bill Brooks; (third row) trainer Lee Landers, Jesse Huggins, Aubrey Gatewood, Jackie Stripling, Wayne Dees, Tim Plodinec, Greg Terlecky, and Ike Brookens; (fourth row) Milt Ramirez, Danny Ford, Santiago Guzman, George Greer, Tom Heintzelman, and Kenny Reitiz. (Courtesy of the Arkansas Travelers.)

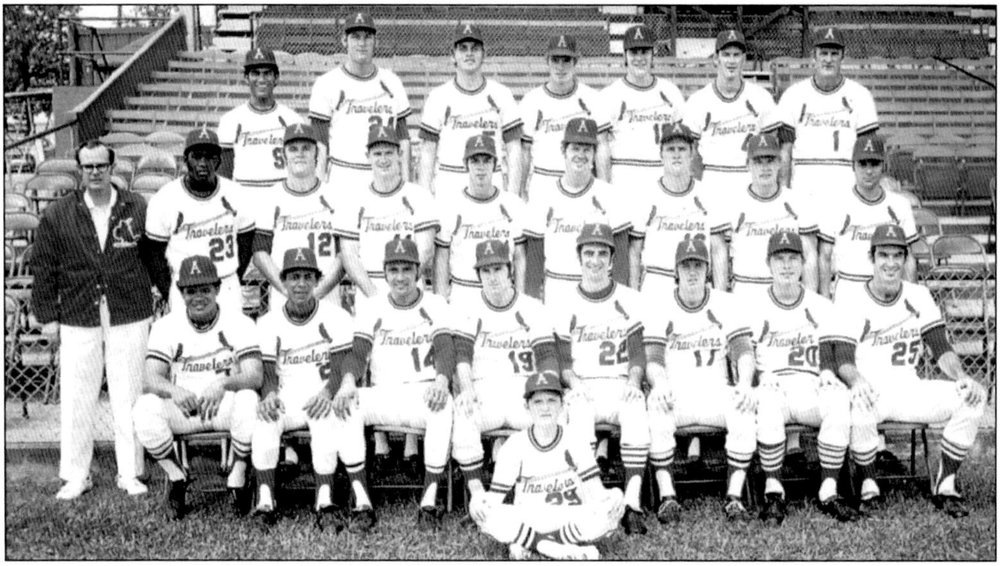

The 1972 Travelers are pictured from left to right: (first row) batboy Kevin Alexander, (second row) Jorge Roque, Milt Ramirez, Rudy Arroyo, Al Hrabosky, Rich Stonum, Brian Bach, Bob Forsch, and Steve Evans; (third row) trainer Lee Landers, Jack Stripling, Greg Millikan, Buzz Nitschke, Bill Bright, Stan Kmet, Dennis Parks, Alan Putz, and Tony Auferio; (fourth row) Tommy Cruz, Rick Pope, Dave Kent, Tom Heintzelman, Phil Trombino, Tommy Thompson, and manager Fred Koenig. (Courtesy of the Arkansas Travelers.)

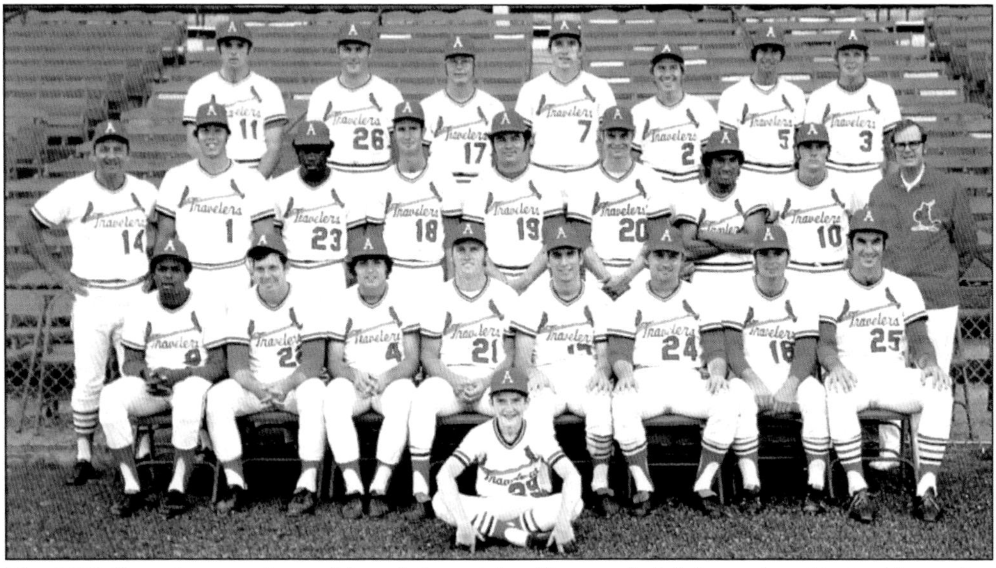

The 1973 Travelers are pictured from left to right: (first row) club house boy Kevin Alexander; (second row) Joe Lindsey, Steve Broege, Gary Barakat, Dennis Parks, Keith Hernandez, Hal Jeffcoat, John Andrews, and Steve Evans; (hird row) manager Tom Burgess, Ed Kurpiel, Jackie Stripling, Larry Volkening, Doug Clark, John Denny, Hector Cruz, Chuck Loseth, and trainer Lee Landers (fourth row) Marc Hill, Garry Hill, Bruce Thompson, Mike Swenton, Dan Loomer, Rudy Kinard, and Gary Breshears. (Courtesy of the Arkansas Travelers.)

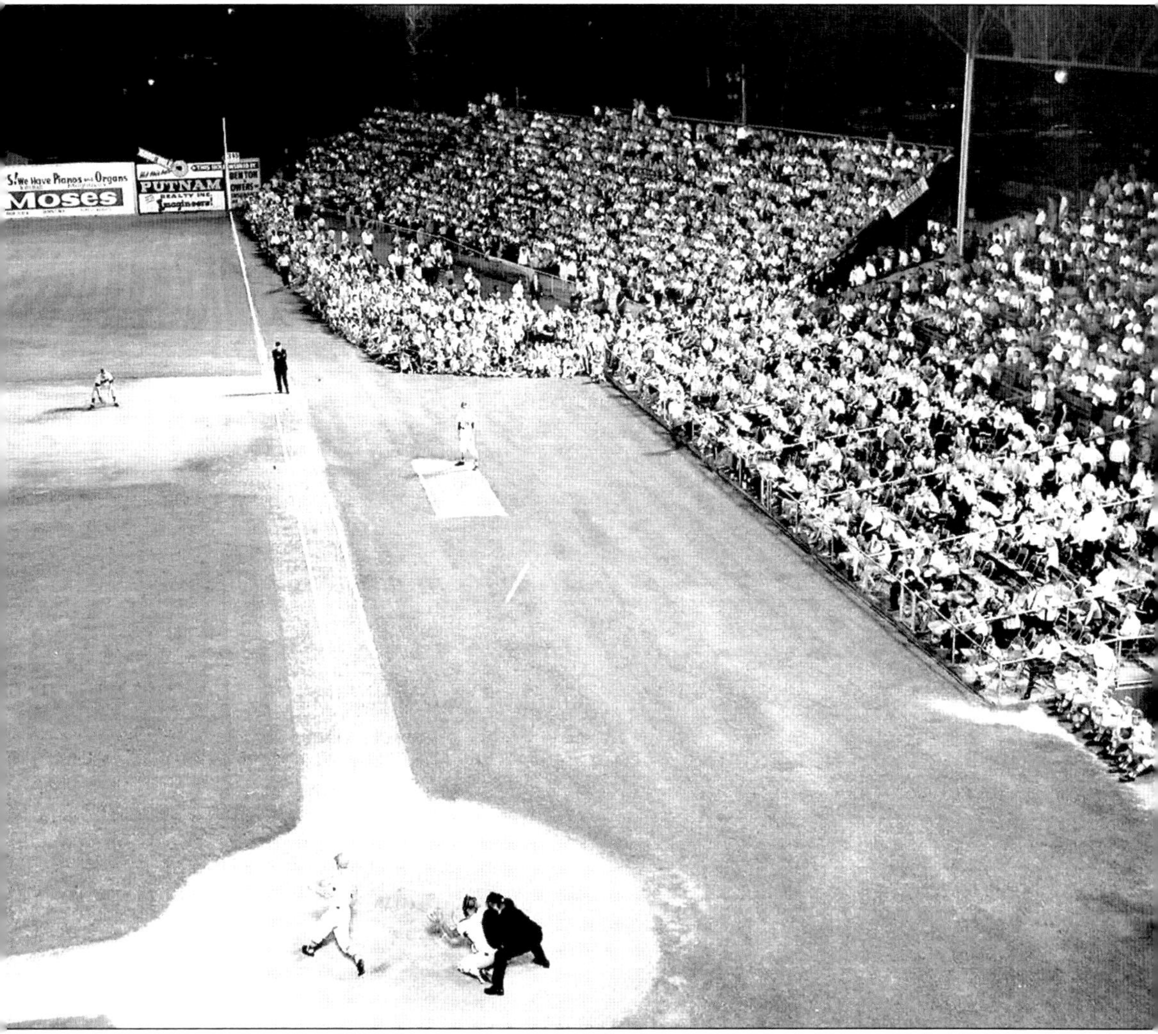

Exhibition games often attracted huge crowds to Ray Winder Field. Large numbers turned out in Little Rock for a special game called the "Eighth" Game of the 1985 World Series between the St. Louis Cardinals and Kansas City Royals. A record crowd of over 12,000 turned out when Fernando Valenzuela pitched during a rehabilitation outing. (Courtesy of the Arkansas Travelers.)

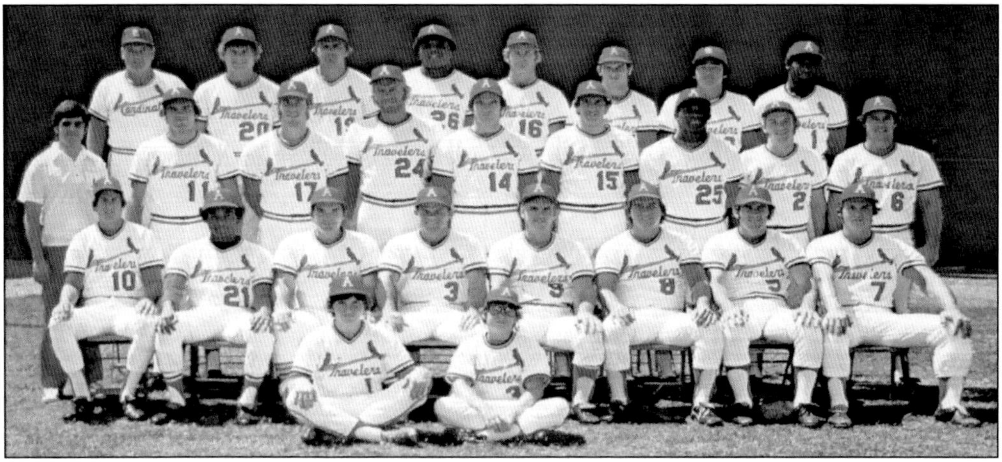

The 1975 Travelers are pictured from left to right: (front row) club house boy Kevin Alexander and batboy Mark Ramer; (second row) Gary Raco, Angel Torres, Tom Harmon, Tom Zimmer, manager Roy Majtyka, Dave Bialis, Doug Clarey, and Ed Daves; (third row) trainer Tony Garofalo, Monte Bolinger, Mark Covert, Kris Sorensen, Bob Stewart, Randy Benson, Cardell Camper, Ed Bowman, and Mike Potter; (fourth row) pitching coach Bob Milliken, Jay Schlueter, Stan Butkus, John Young, Randy Wiles, Bob Hrapmann, Ryan Kurosaki, and Garry Templeton. (Courtesy of the Arkansas Travelers.)

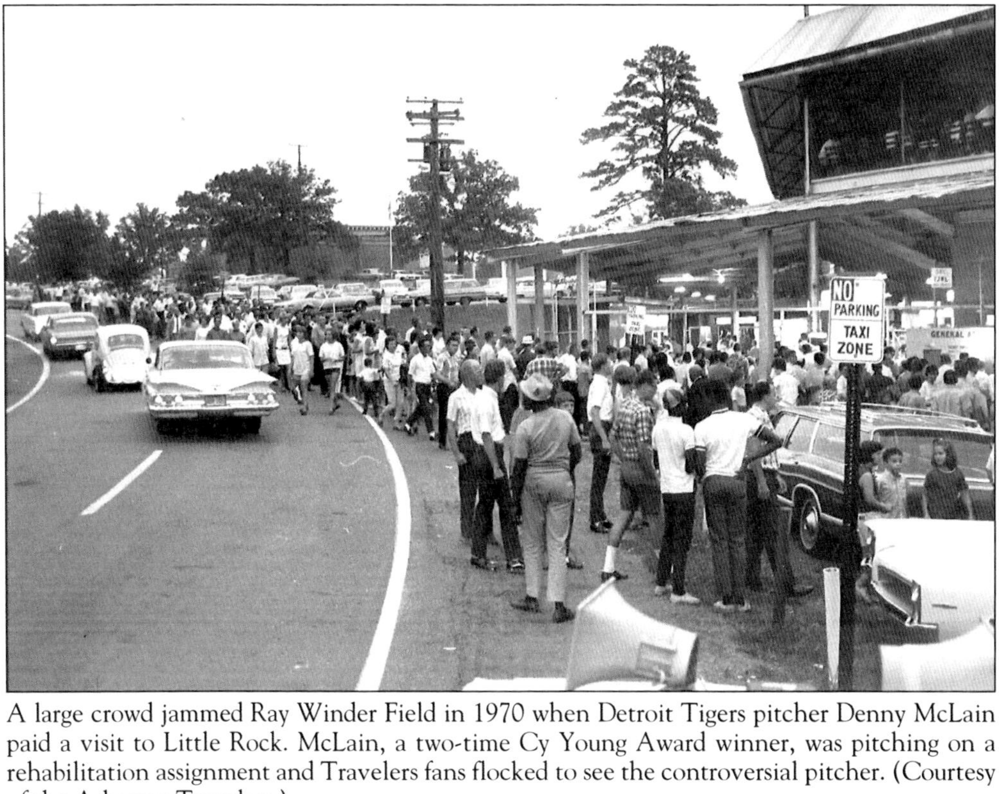

A large crowd jammed Ray Winder Field in 1970 when Detroit Tigers pitcher Denny McLain paid a visit to Little Rock. McLain, a two-time Cy Young Award winner, was pitching on a rehabilitation assignment and Travelers fans flocked to see the controversial pitcher. (Courtesy of the Arkansas Travelers.)

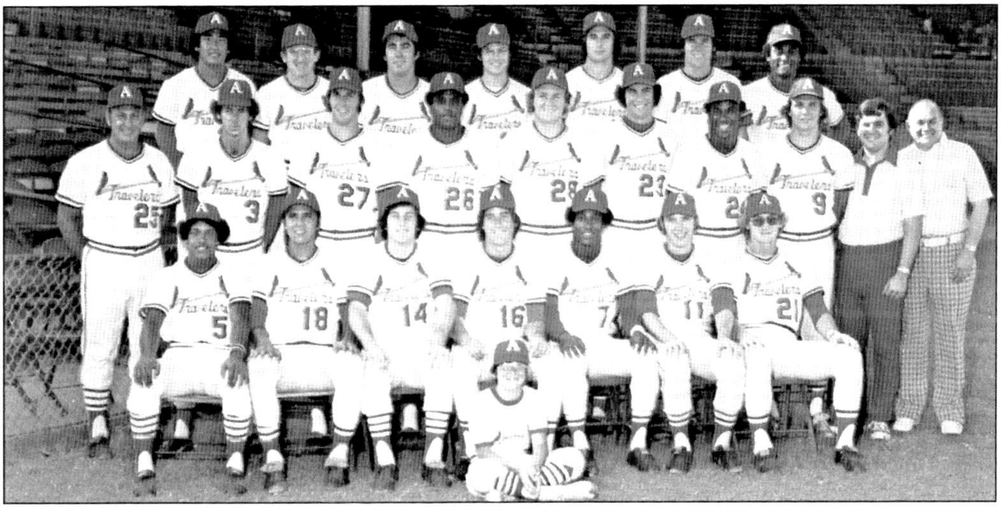

The 1976 Travelers are pictured from left to right: (up front) batboy Dan Troilett; (front row) Manny Castillo, John Urrea, Bill Caudill, Dave Bialas, Tito Landrum, Ken Oberkfell, Bob Detherage; (middle row) manager Jack Krol, Mike Ramsey, Mark Covert, John Young, Steve Staniland, Andy Replogle, Ramon DeLos Santos, Eddy Daves, trainer Tony Garofalo, general manager Bill Valentine; (back row) Ryan Kurosaki, Ernie Rosseau, Nick Leyva, Mike Murphy, Gary Blackwell, Rocky Jordan, and Angel Torres. (Courtesy of the Arkansas Travelers.)

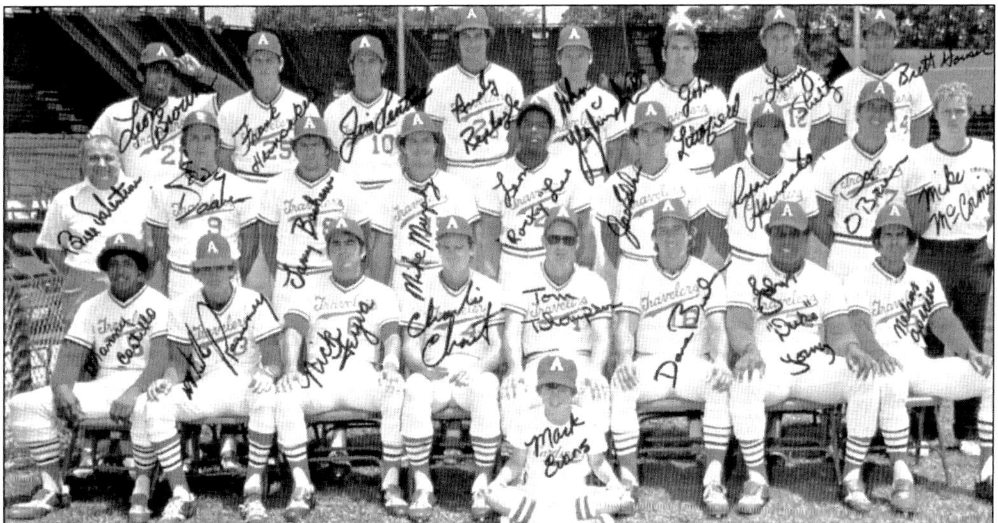

The Travelers of 1977 are pictured from left to right: (up front) batboy Mark Evans; (front row) Manny Castillo, Mike Ramsey, Nick Leyva, Charlie Chant, Tom Thompson, Dave Bialas, John Young, and Nelson Garcia; (middle row) general manager Bill Valentine, Eddy Daves, Larry Bashaw, Mike Murphy, Leon Lee, Joe Edelen, Ryan Kurosaki, Dan O'Brien, and Mike McCormick; (back row) Leon Brown, Frank Hunsaker, Jim Lentine, Andy Replogle, John Yeglinski, John Littlefield, Lenny Strelitz, and Brett Houser. (Courtesy of the Arkansas Travelers.)

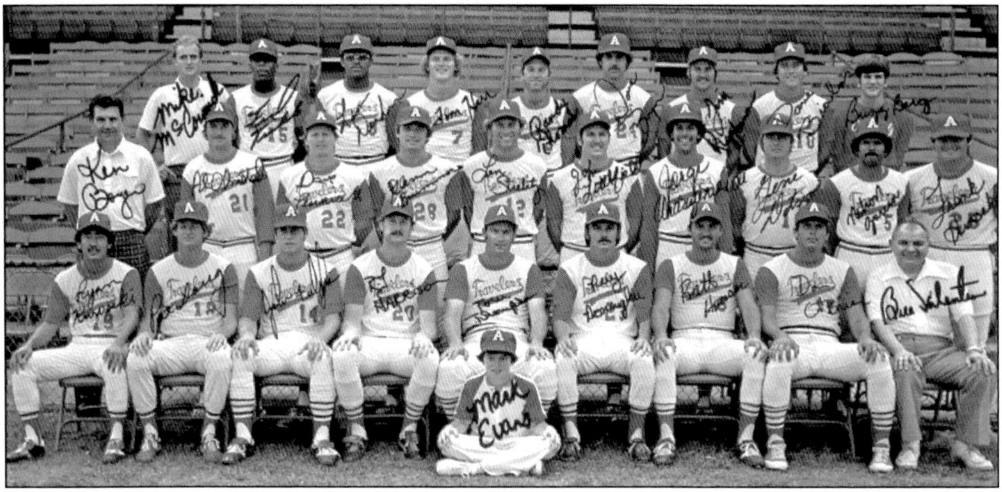

The 1978 Travelers won the Eastern Division Championship. Pictured from left to right: (up front) batboy Mark Evans; (front row) Ryan Kurosaki, Pat Darcy, John Fulgham, R.L. Harrison, Tom Thompson, Ray Douglas, Brett Houser, Dan O'Brien, and general manager Bill Valentine; (middle row) manager Ken Boyer, Al Olmstead, Dave Penniall, Glenn Brummer, Len Strilitz, John Littlefield, Jorge Aranzamendi, Gene Dotson, Nelson Garcia, and Frank Hunsaker; (back row) trainer Mike McCormick, Fred Tisdale, Leon Durham, Tom Herr, Randy Thomas, Dave Boyer, Jim Riggleman, Dave Bialas, and Buzz Berg. (Courtesy of the Arkansas Travelers.)

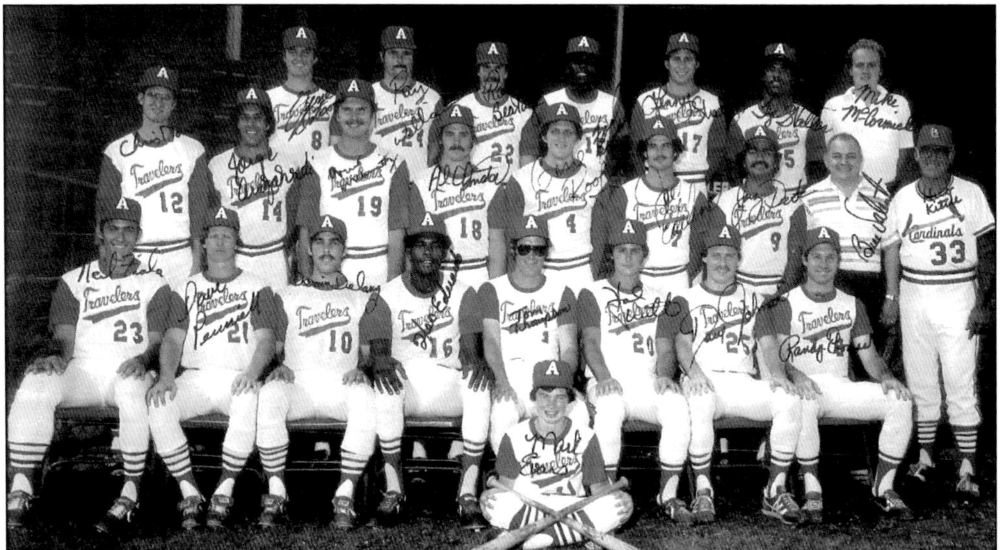

The 1979 Texas League Champion Travelers swept through the playoffs with a perfect 5-0 record. Pictured from left to right: (up front) batboy Mark Evans; (front row) Neil Fiala, Dave Penniall, Dennis Delany, Hector Eduardo, Tom Thompson, Hal Witt, Dave Johnson, and Randy Thomas; middle row) Davis, Jorge Aranzamendi, Arno Kirchenwitz, Al Olmstead, Gene Roof, Joe Edelen, Joey DeSa, general manager Bill Valentine, and Hub Kittle; (back row) Gene Dotson, Ray Williams, Ray Searage, Fred Tisdale, Lenny Strelitz, Ty Waller, and trainer Mike McCormick. (Courtesy of the Arkansas Travelers.)

Teammates celebrate John Young and one of the most historic Traveler home runs. On September 9, 1977, Young blasted a majestic homer over the 55-foot rightfield fence and over Interstate 630. The three-run homer followed Leon Lee's "beaning" and helped the Travelers to a Texas League championship. They beat El Paso two games to none. Young was considered a "franchise man" by the team. (Courtesy of the Arkansas Travelers.)

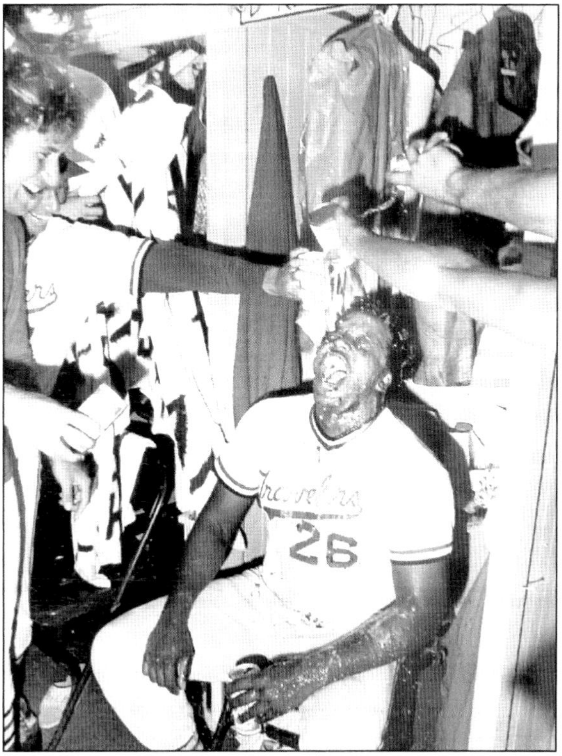

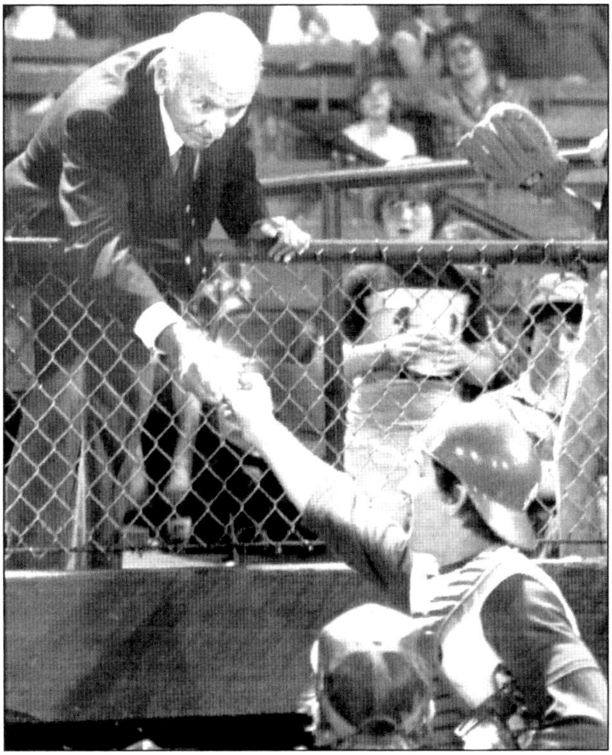

Travelers President Max Moses receives the opening game ball from Catcher George Bjorkman on April 22, 1980. (Courtesy of the Arkansas Travelers.)

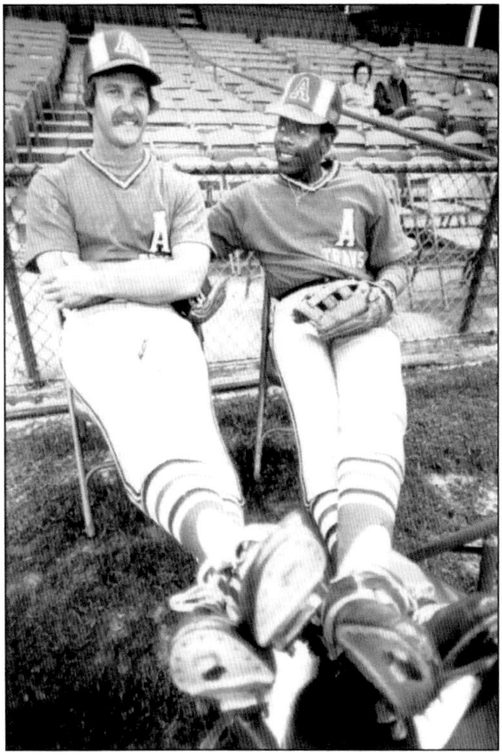

Teammates and friends Jim Riggleman (left) and "Sweet" Fred Tisdale relax before a game in 1980. That year the pair helped lead the Travelers to the Texas League championship. Third baseman Riggelman hit 21 homers, had 90 RBIs and batted .245. Tisdale, a first baseman, homered 17 times, batted in 85 and hit .268. (Courtesy of the Arkansas Travelers.)

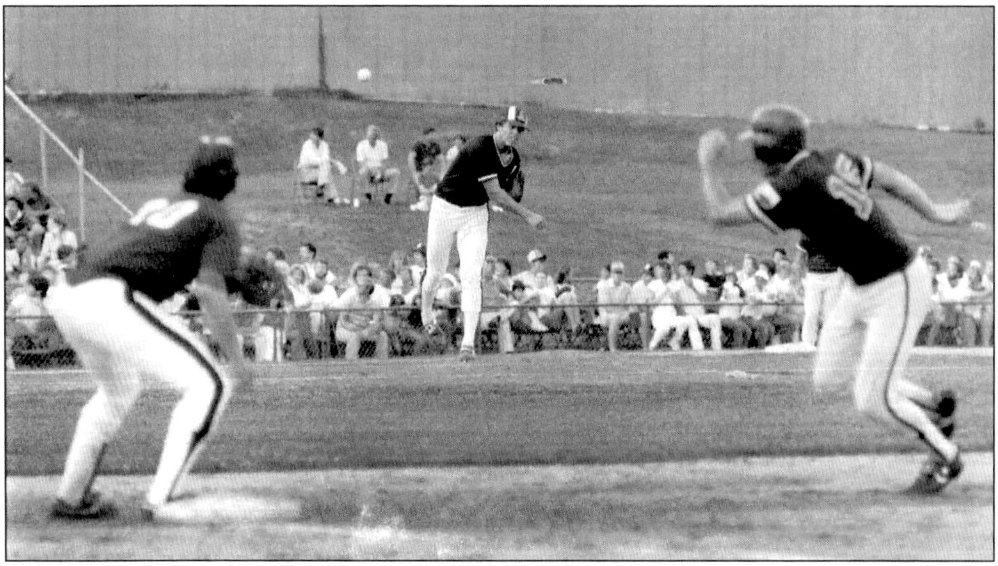

Arkansas pitcher Danny Cox fires the ball to Travelers first baseman Alan Hunsinger. Shreveport's Don Mazzilli hurries back to the bag. The action took place in the second inning of a June 27, 1983 game at Ray Winder Field. (Courtesy of the Arkansas Travelers.)

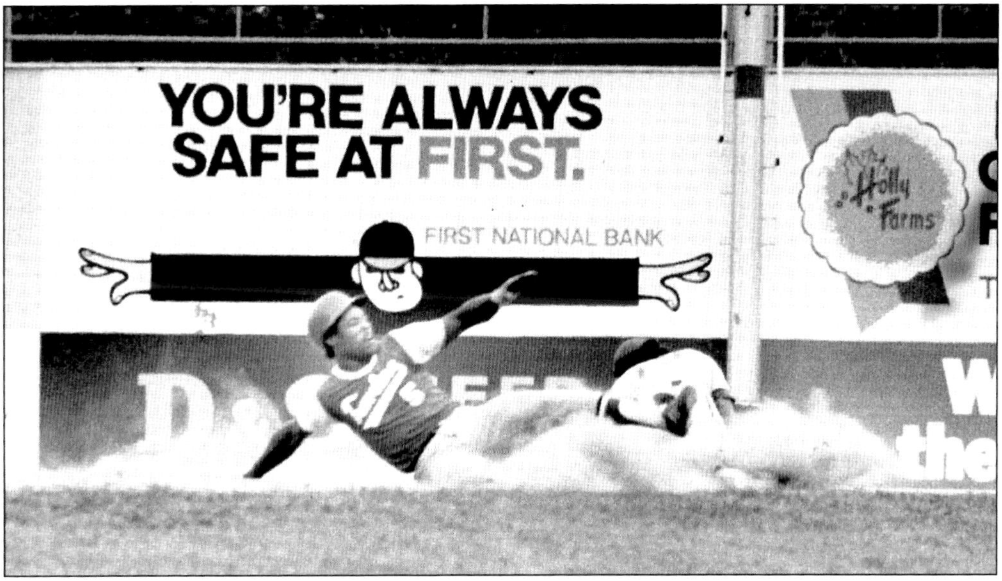

Despite what the sign says, Traveler Ty Waller is tagged out on a return to first base. This action took place early in the 1979 season. (Courtesy of the Arkansas Travelers.)

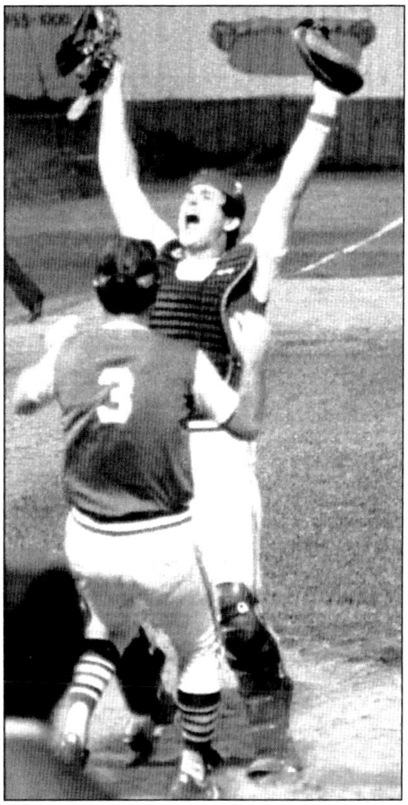

Travelers catcher Frank Hunsaker and manager Sonny Ruberto celebrate a Texas League championship win in 1980. Arkansas went undefeated in the playoffs sweeping Jackson and San Antonio. The title was the second straight for the Travelers who also had a clean sweep in 1979. Hunsaker batted a solid .325, led the league in fielding and handled the second best pitching staff in the Texas League. Ruberto managed the Travelers to an 81-55 record and won the East by six games. (Courtesy of the Arkansas Travelers.)

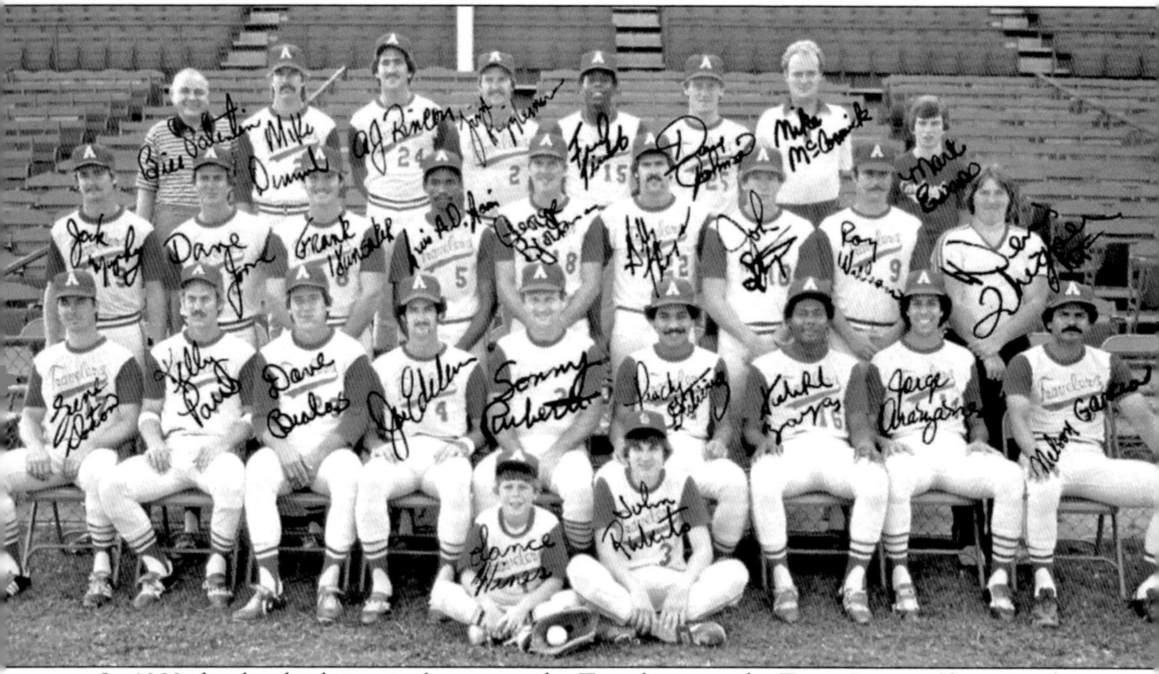

In 1980, for the third time in four years, the Travelers won the Texas League Championship. Pictured from left to right: (up front) batboys Lance Hines and John Roberts; (front row) Gene Dotson, Kelly Paris, Dave Bialas, Joe Edelen, Sonny Ruberto, Julian Gutierrez, Felipe Zayas, Jorge Aranzamendi , and Nelson Garcia; (middle row) Jack Murphy, David Jorn, Frank Hunsaker, Luis DeLeon, George Bjorkman, Billy Thomas, John Stuper, Roy Williams, and trainer Dennis Thigpen; (back row) general manager Bill Valentine, Mike Dimmel, Andy Rincon, Jim Riggleman, Fred Tisdale, Dave Johnson, trainer Mike McCormick, and clubhouse manager Mark Evans. (Courtesy of the Arkansas Travelers.)

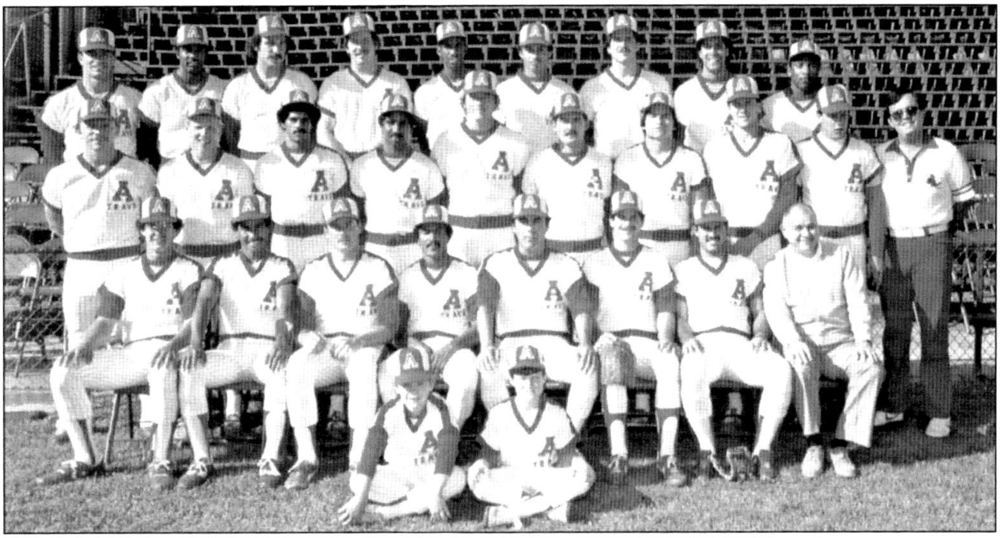

The 1983 Travelers are pictured from left to right: (up front) batboys Chad Avants and B.J. Mack; (front row) Randy Hunt, Frank Batista, John Adams, Gotay Mills, manager Nick Leyva, Mike Rhodes, Luis Ojeda, and general manager Bill Valentine; (middle row) Greg Guin, Doug Wabeke, Rafael Rimentel, Ruben Gotay, Steve Winfield, Alan Hunsinger, Mark Salas, Jerry Johnson, Kurt Kepshire, and trainer Dave England; (back row) Mike Barba, Larry Reynolds, Terry Clark, Jack Ayer, Mike Harris, Rod Booker, Walt Pierce, Coach Jorge Aranzamendi, and Terry Pendleton. (Courtesy of the Arkansas Travelers.)

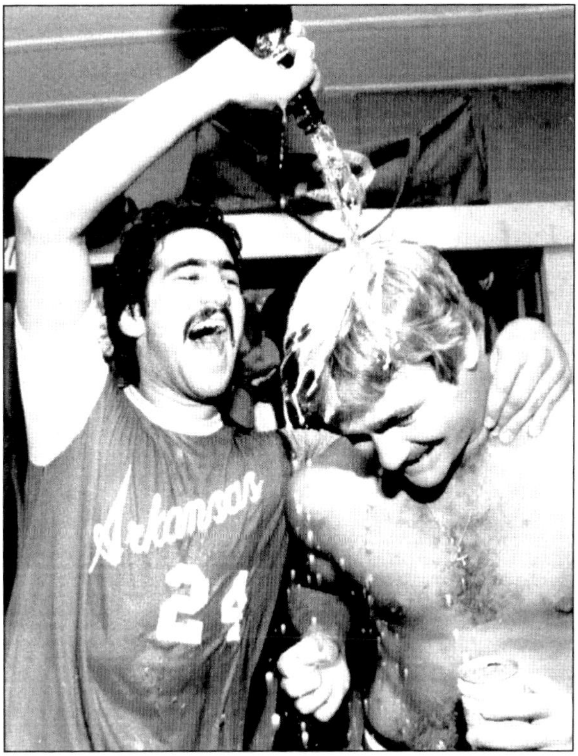

Pitchers Andy Rincon and Jack Murphy celebrate the 1980 Texas League Championship. Arkansas stormed through the playoffs with a 5-0 record, downing Jackson in two games and San Antonio in three. (Courtesy of the Arkansas Travelers.)

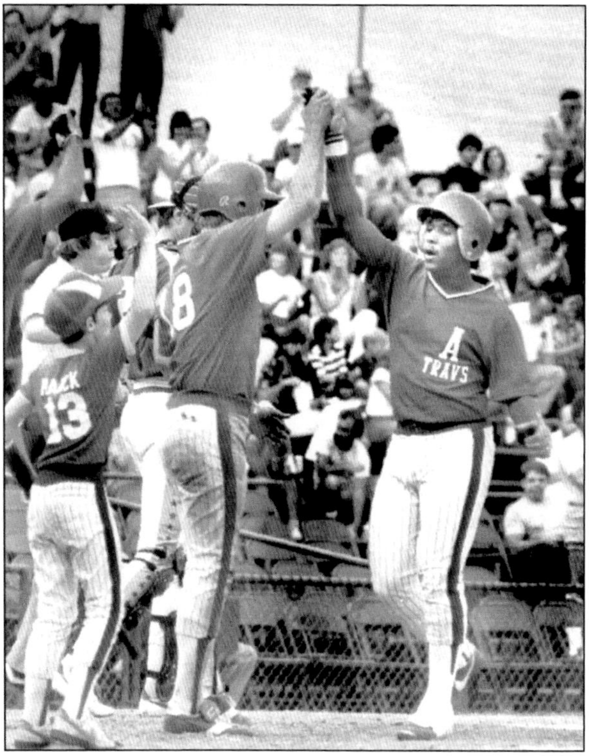

Terry Pendleton crosses homeplate and receives a happy greeting from Traveler teammates. Because of injuries, Pendleton only played in 48 games in 1980. He hit .275 and was a member of the second half champions. Pendleton won an MVP award for the Atlanta Braves. (Courtesy of the Arkansas Travelers.)

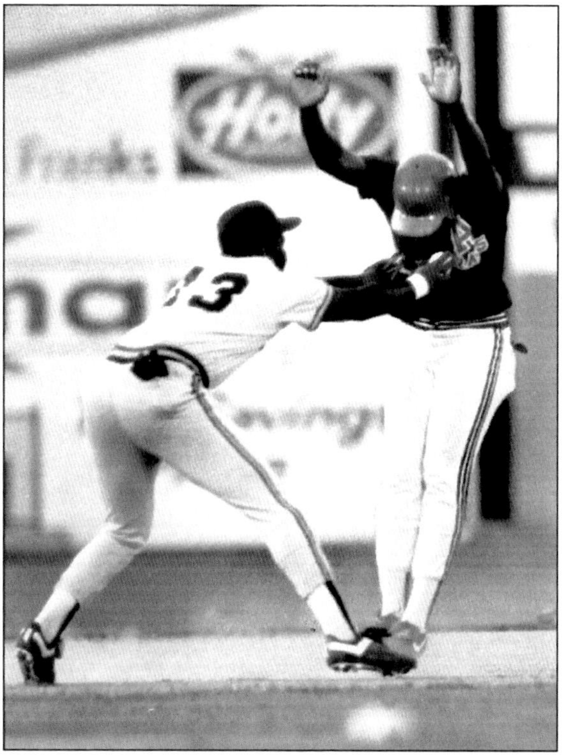

Charlie Hayes tags Traveler Craig Wilson out in a rundown in this 1987 game at Ray Winder Field. Wilson batted .290 in 66 games for the Travelers and then went on to a five-year career with St. Louis. Used mostly in part-time work in the National League, he batted .311 in 1992. (Courtesy of the Arkansas Travelers.)

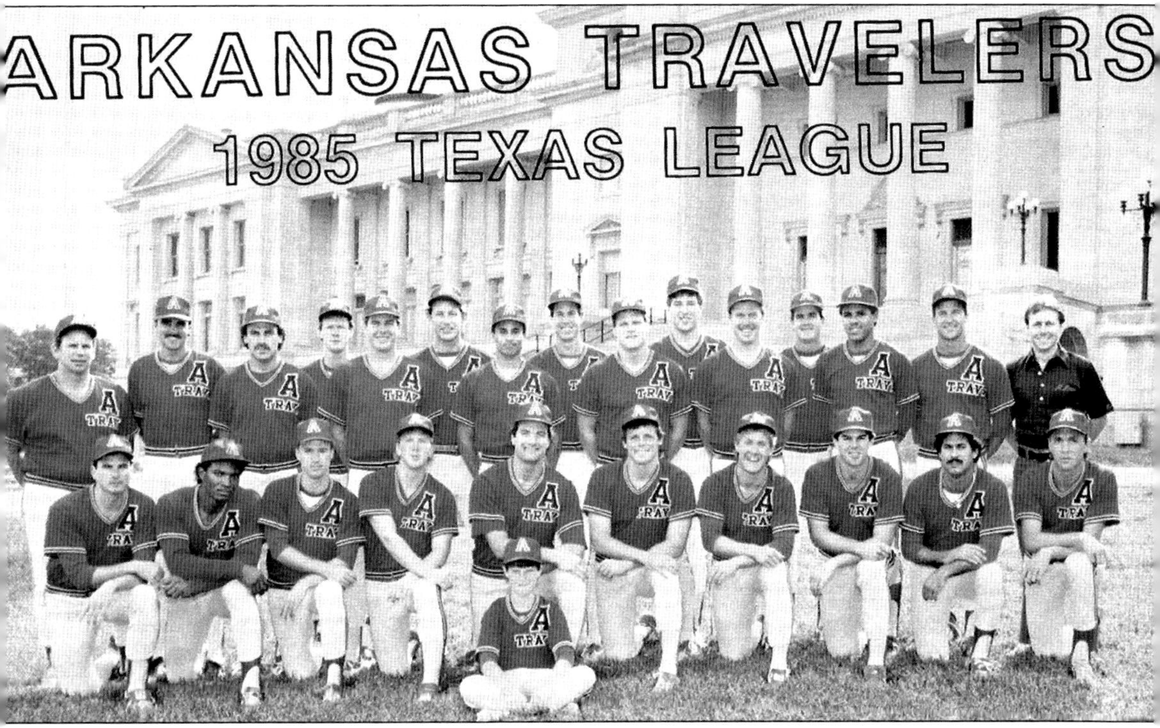

The State Capitol provides the backdrop for the 1985 Arkansas Travelers. Pictured from left to right: (up front) batboy B. J. Mack; (front row) John Adams, Rubin Robles, Marty Mason, Ed Tanner, Bob Geren, Dan Stryffeler, Mark Schulte, Tom Pagnozzi, Luis Roman, and Paul Wilmet; (back row) Dyar Miller, Gary Gill, Terry Clark, Kurt Kavil, John Martin, Rich Buonantony, Rod Booker, Allen Morlock, Jim Lindeman, Mike Dunne, Joe Boever, Mark Dougherty, Jose Rodriguez, manager Jim Riggleman, and Hap Hudson. (Courtesy of the Arkansas Travelers.)

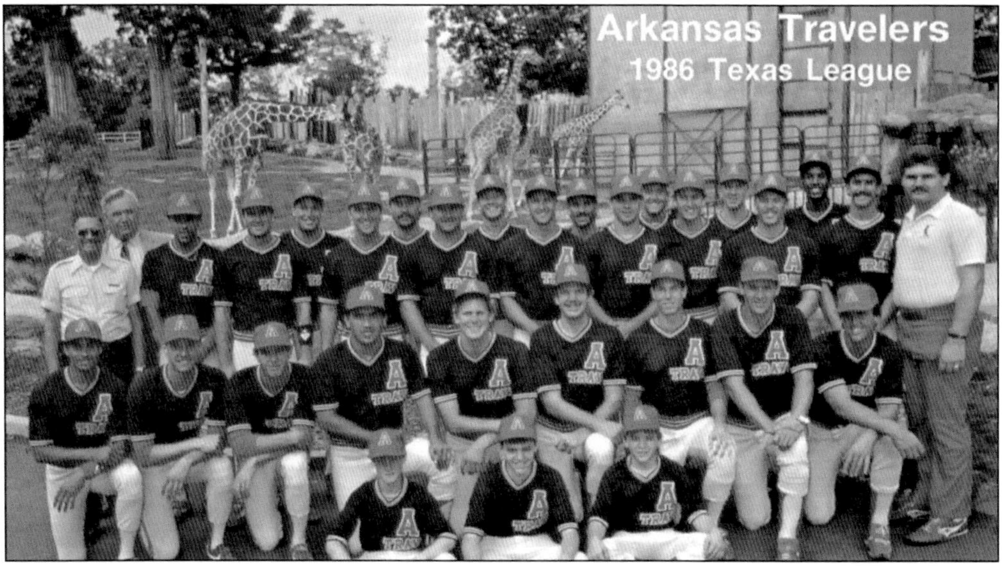

The 1986 Travelers pose at the Little Rock Zoo. Pictured from left to right: (up front) batboys B.J. Mack, Matt Liker, and Chad Avants; (front row) Rod Booker, Rich Embser, John Martin, Ernie Carrasco, Joe Magrane, Scott Young, Allen Morlock, Dave Kable, and Jeff Ledbetter; (back row) driver Buster Hoggard, president Bert Parke, Jose Rodriguez, Mark Dougherty, Harry McCulla, Paul Cherry, Ray Soff, coach Mark Riggins, Mike Robinson, manager Jim Riggleman, Tom Amante, Mike Rhodes, Mark Schulte, Dave Clements, Eddie Tanner, Tim Wallace, Lance Johnson, Jeff Keener, and trainer Curt Metzger. (Courtesy of the Arkansas Travelers.)

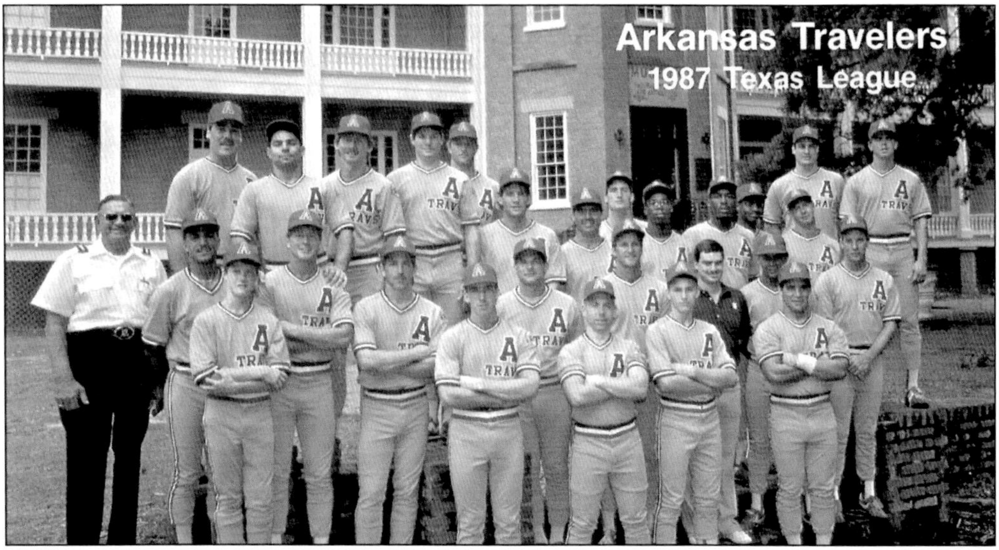

Pictured for the 1987 Travelers from left to right: (front row) Tim Jones, batboys Craig and Jerry Laird, and Roy Silver; (second row) driver Buster Hoggard, Luis Alicea, clubhouse manager B.J. Mack, Mike Robinson, Steve Peters, coach Keith Champion, manager Jim Riggleman, trainer Bra Henderson, Ken Infante, and John Costello; (third row) Matt Kinzer, Sal Agostinelli, Jeff Oyster, Jim Fregosi, Jr., Mike Fitzgerald, Craig Weissmann, Ray Stephens, Charles McGrath, Alex Cole, Dennis Carter, Ken Hill, Jeff Fassero, Scott Arnold, and Marty Pevey. (Courtesy of the Arkansas Travelers.)

Traveler pitcher Jeff Fassero prepares to fire a pitch. Fassero had a no-hitter in 1989 against the Jackson Mets on June 12. Arkansas won 2-0. Fassero's pitching contributions helped lead the Travelers to the 1989 Texas League Championship. (Courtesy of the Arkansas Travelers.)

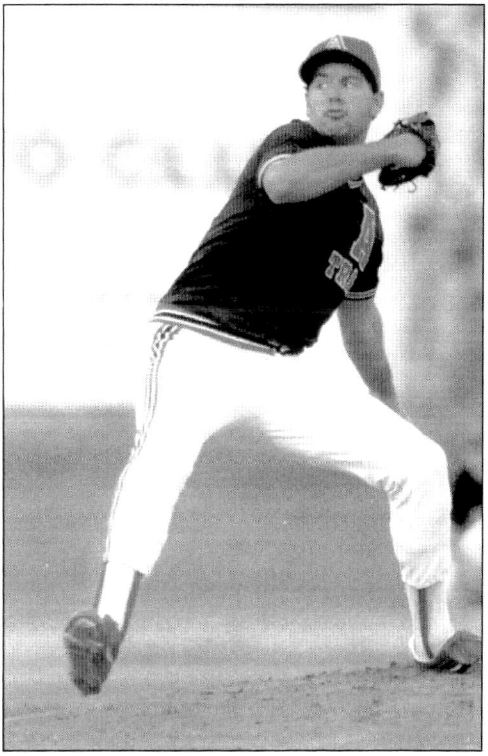

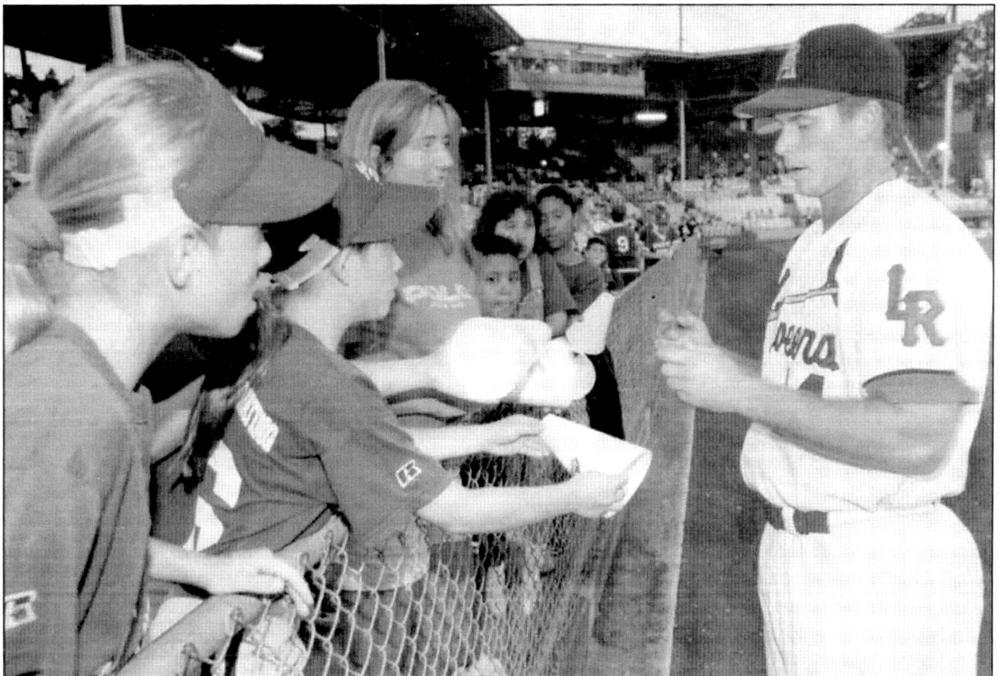

Bill Bright was a fan favorite for the Travelers in 1972. He was a power hitter with 20 home runs and 69 runs batted in. Bright played the next three years for Midland. (Courtesy of the Arkansas Travelers.)

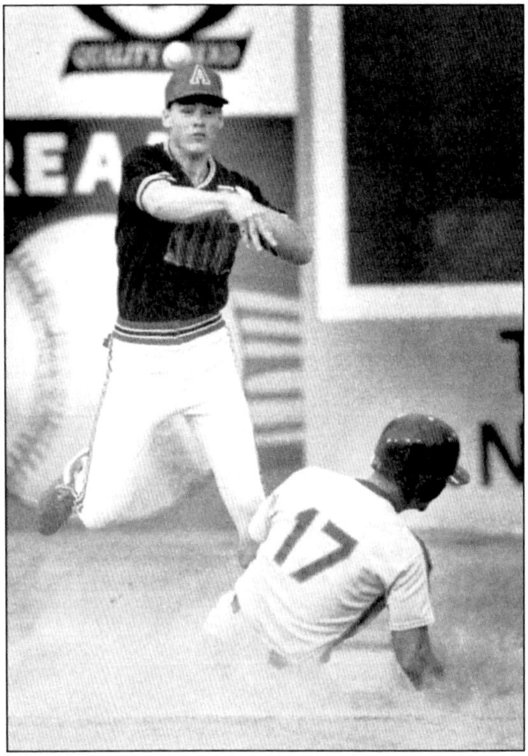

Traveler Brett Harrison turns a double play on Jackson's Kurt DeLuca during first inning action of a June 16, 1988 game. (Courtesy of the Arkansas Travelers.)

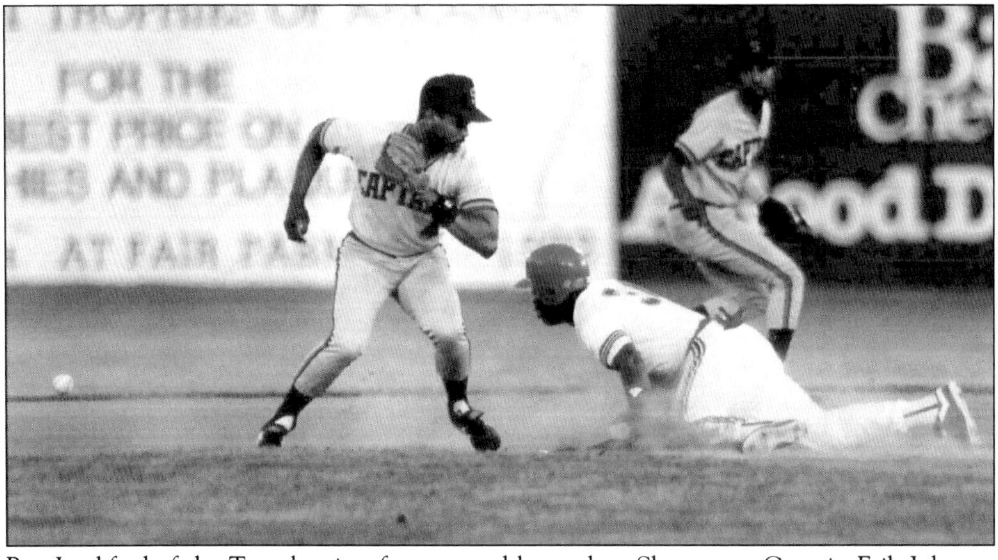

Ray Lankford of the Travelers is safe at second base when Shreveport Captain Erik Johnson misses the ball. The play occurred April 17, 1989, during the Travelers championship season. (Courtesy of the Arkansas Travelers.)

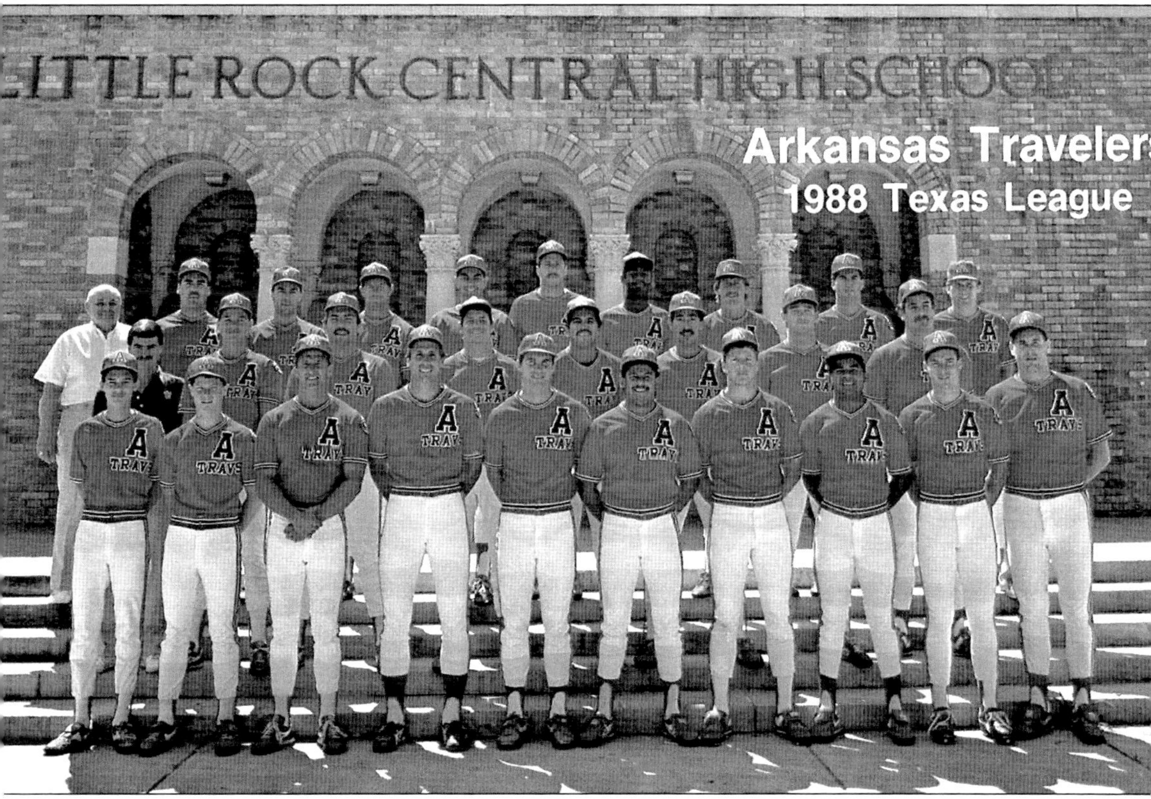

The Travelers of 1988 are shown at Little Rock's historic Central High School. Pictured from left to right: (front row) clubhouse managers Jim Gardner and B. J. Mack, manager Jim Riggleman, coach Rick Colbert, Tom Baine, Jesus Mendez, Mike Robinson, Bien Figueroa, Rick Lockwood, and Howard Hilton; (middle row) trainer Brad Henderson, Brett Harrison, Mike Sassone, Jim Fregosi, Benito Malave, Mauricio Nunez, Mike Robertson, and Scott Arnol; (back row) general manager Bill Valentine, Matt Kinzer, Todd Zeile, Jeff Fassero, Jim Puzey, Al Sontag, Ken Hill, Jeff Oyster, Dave Osteen, and Mike Hocutt. (Courtesy of the Arkansas Travelers.)

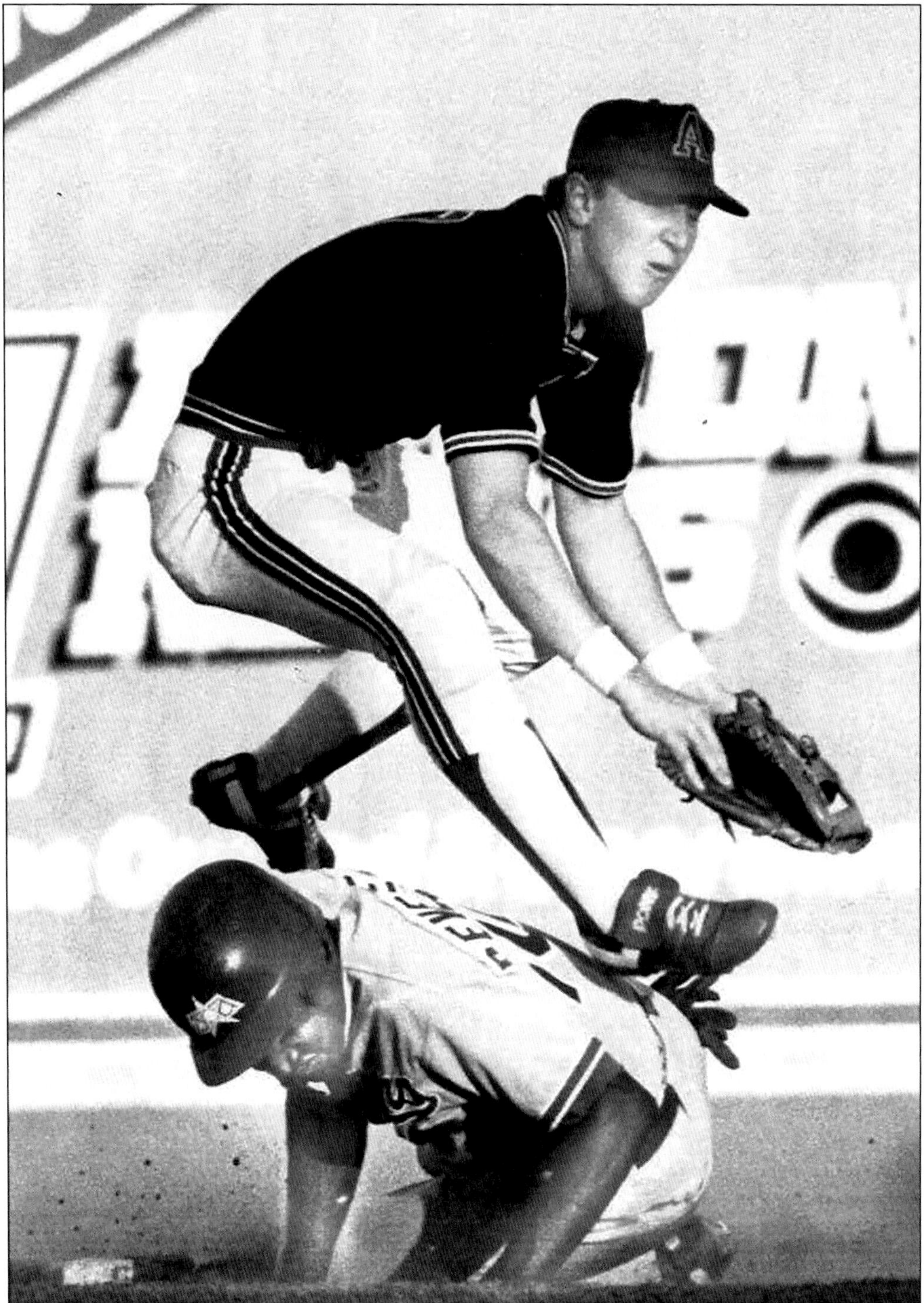

Arkansas' Eddie Tanner dives over Mike Devereaux of San Antonio as Devereaux is forced out on the play. Tanner played from 1984 through 1986 as an outfielder-infielder. He batted .311 in 1986 and was in the .280s the previous two seasons. (Courtesy of the Arkansas Travelers.)

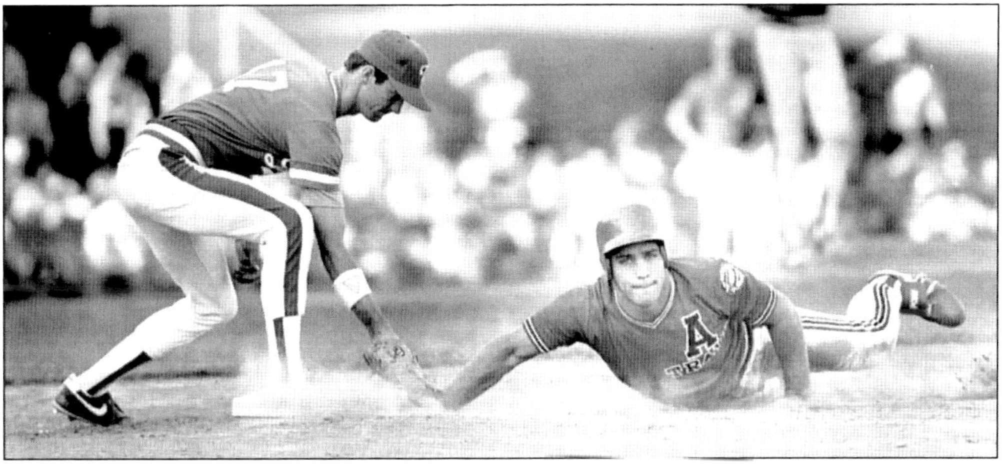

The Travelers Roy Silver beats a pickoff throw to first base. Tulsa's Jeff Melrose applies the late tag. The play occurred in a June 6, 1987 game. (Courtesy of the Arkansas Travelers.)

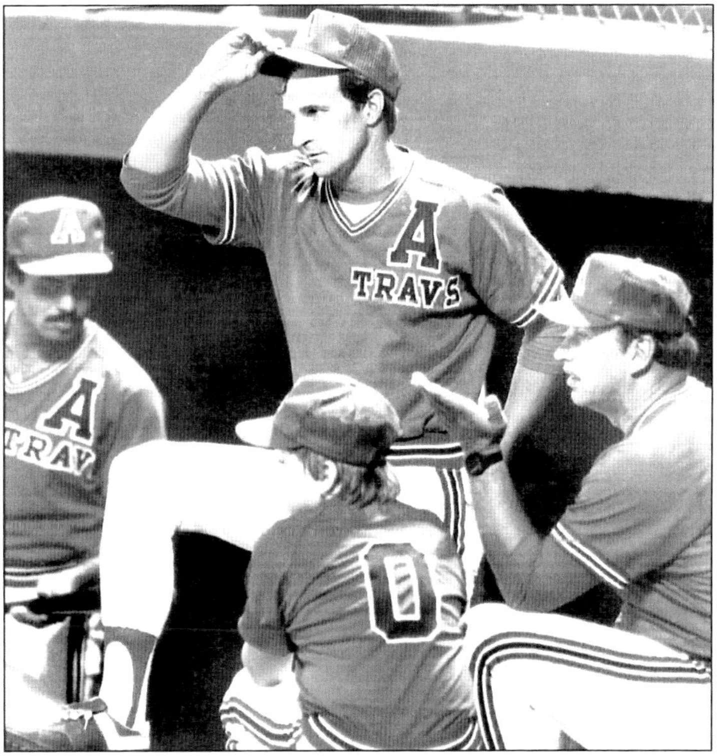

Jim Riggleman listens to Dyar Miller during a game. Riggelman managed the Arkansas Travelers from 1985 through 1988. He took them to a first-place finish in the first half of 1985. Riggleman also managed the San Diego Padres and the Chicago Cubs. Dyar Miller played seven years in the major leagues and had a record of 23-17 as a relief pitcher. (Courtesy of the Arkansas Travelers.)

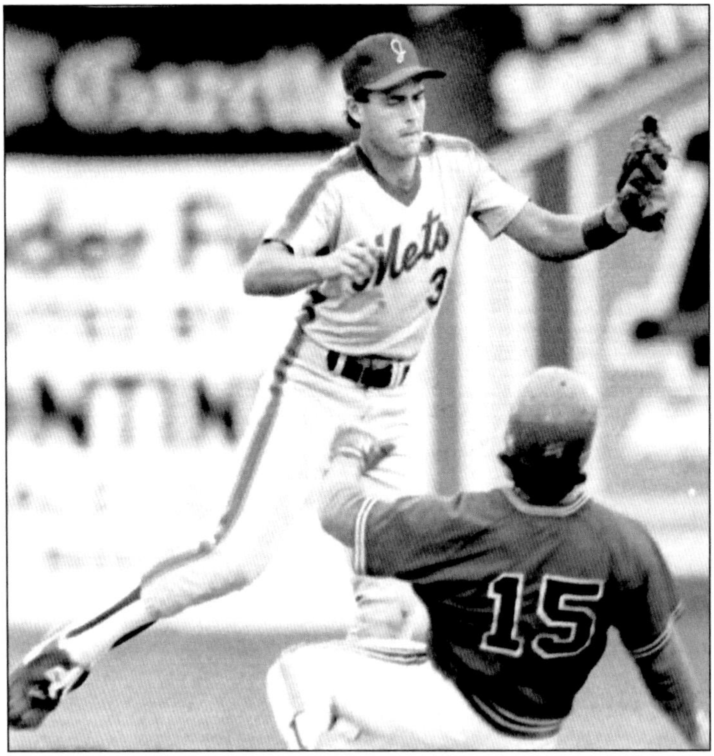

Arkansas' Tom Amante avoids Kevin Elster's tag at second base. Elster played shortshop for the Jackson Mets in a 1985 game. (Courtesy of the Arkansas Travelers.)

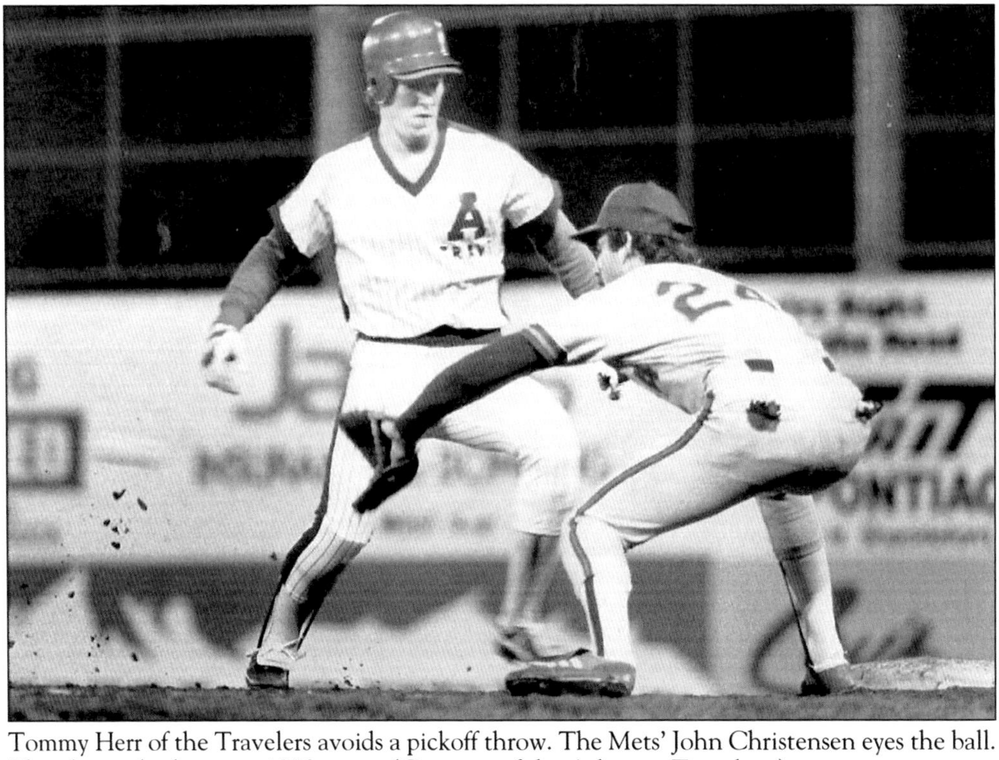

Tommy Herr of the Travelers avoids a pickoff throw. The Mets' John Christensen eyes the ball. The play took place in a 1983 game. (Courtesy of the Arkansas Travelers.)

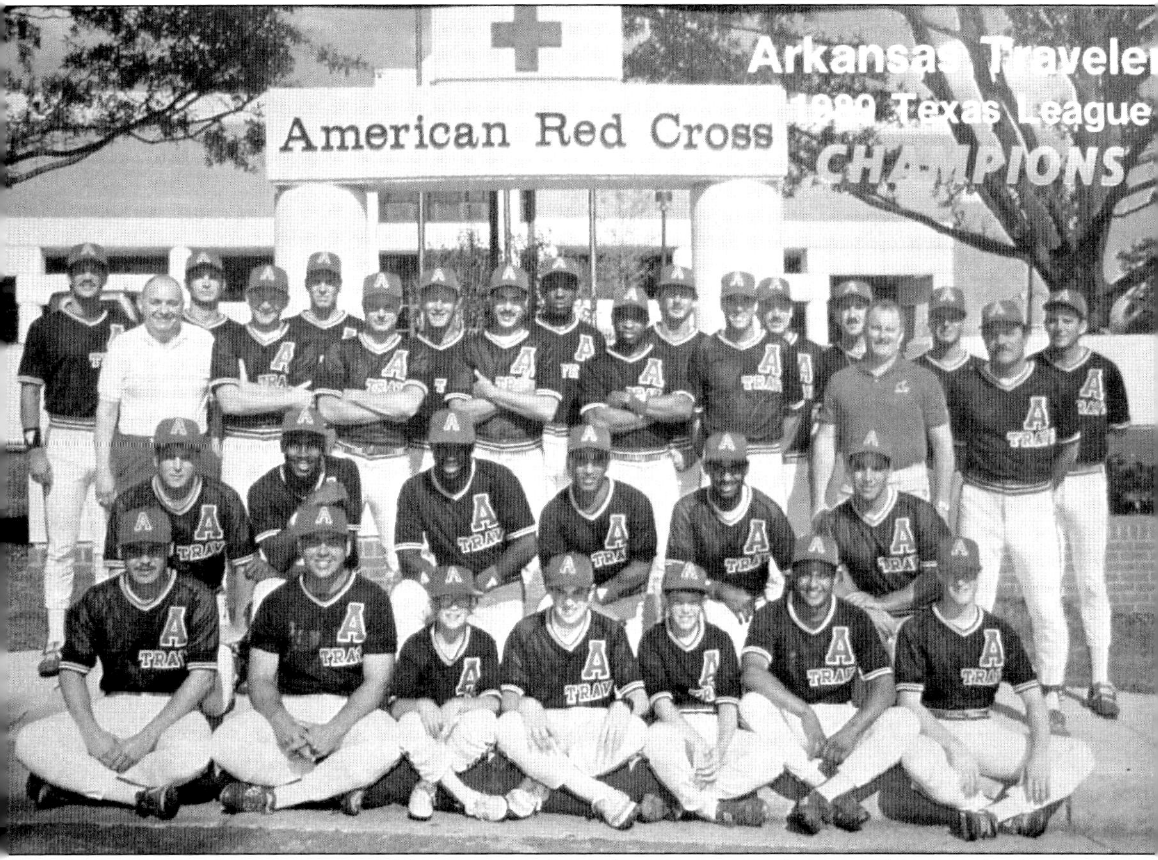

The 1989 Travelers were one of the most popular Arkansas teams in history. They won the first half title by four-and-a-half games. In the playoffs, they dispatched Shreveport 2-0 and scored a dramatic win over Wichita four games to three for the Texas League championship. Pictured from left to right: Back row: (ront row) Mike Perez, Ray Stephens, Brian Hughes, batboys Brian Sternberg and Jeff Markus, Jesus Mendez, and clubhouse manager B. J. Mack; (middle row) Steve Hill, Bernard Gilkey, Craig Wilson, Opie Moran, Julian Martinez, and Roy Silver; (back row) Mike Fox, general manager Bill Valentine, Mike Robertson, Steve Mumaw, Red Brewer, Mike Hinkle, coach Chris Maloney, Len Picota, Dennis Carter, Ray Lankford, Jeff Oyster, John Lepley, Frank Potestio, Andy Rincon, Trainer Pete Fagan, Dave Osteen, manager Gaylen Pitts, and Craig Weissman. (Courtesy of the Arkansas Travelers.)

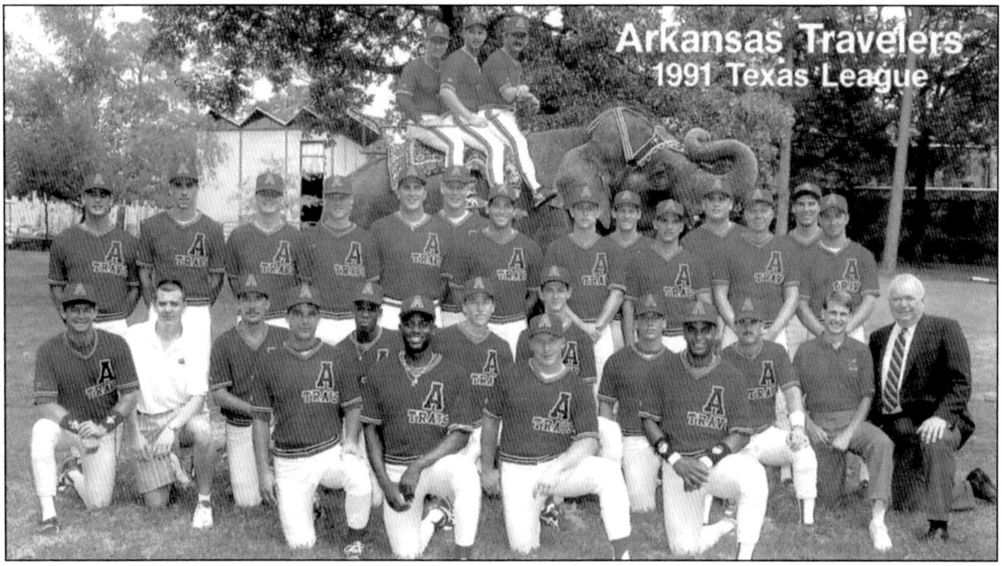

The 1991 Travelers pose at the Little Rock Zoo, across the street from the ballpark. Pictured from left to right: (front row) Luis Martinez, Bob Beumer, David Richardson, Don Pryblinski, Rico Christian, Charlie White, Lee Plemel, Mike Fiore, Tripp Cromer, Tim Redman, Frank Abreu, Jeff Shireman, trainer Mark O'Neal, president Bert Parke; (back row) Donovan Osborne, Cliff Brannon, Dennis Wiseman, Steve Fanning, Mark Clark, John Ericks, John Sellick, Dale Kisten, Steffen Majer, Joe Federico, Luis Faccio, Troy Salvior, Jose Fernandez, and Dean Weese. On the elephant, from left to right, are coaches Marty Mason and Scott Melvin, and manager Joe Pettini. (Courtesy of the Arkansas Travelers.)

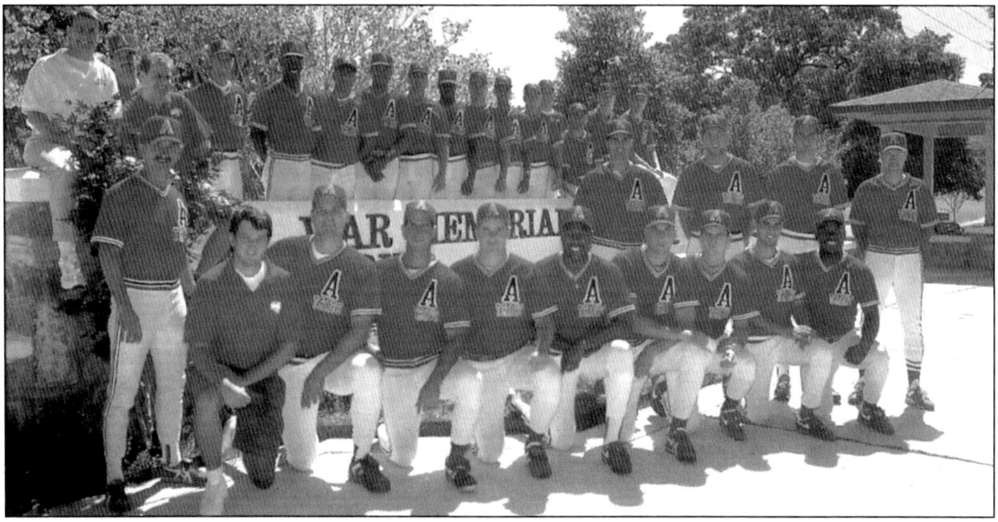

The 1993 Travelers are pictured from left to right: (front row) manager Joe Pettini, John Evans, Craig Faulkner, Kevin Tahan, Bryan Eversgerd, Paul Anderson, John Mabry, Marc Ronan, Frank Cimorelli, and Anthony Lewis; (middle row) Kerry Knox, John Kelly, Duff Brumley, and coach Marty Mason; (back row) trainer Mark O'Neal, Jeff Shireman, Michael Schiff, Joe Aversa, Allen Battle, Rigo Beltran, Odalis Savinon, Darrel Deak, Paul Coleman, Doug Creek, Wander Pimentel, Gerald Santos, Brian Barber, Howard Prager, Steve Fanning, and Rick Shackle. (Courtesy of the Arkansas Travelers.)

Tyrone Horne had a night to remember on July 27, 1998, when the Arkansas slugger achieved the "homer cycle." He hit a solo homer, a two-run homer, a three-run homer and a grand slam all in one game! It is the first known occurrence in professional baseball history of such a feat. Horne was named the Texas League Player of the Year after leading the league with 37 homers and 139 RBIs, both Travelers' single season records. (Courtesy of Jim Vasaldua.)

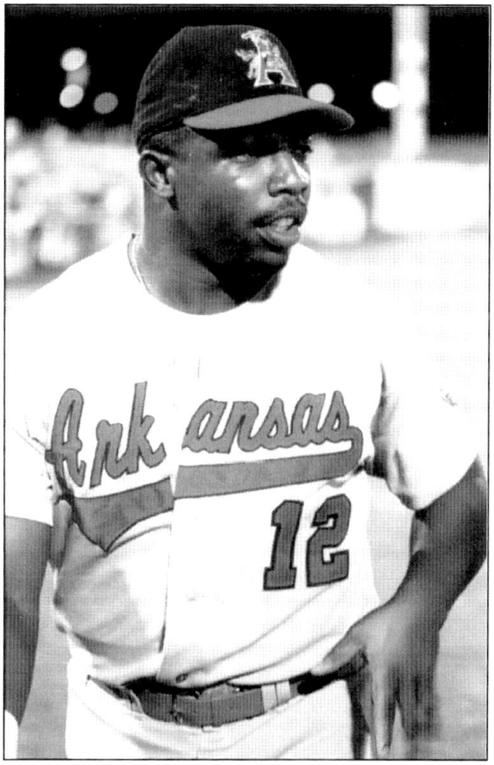

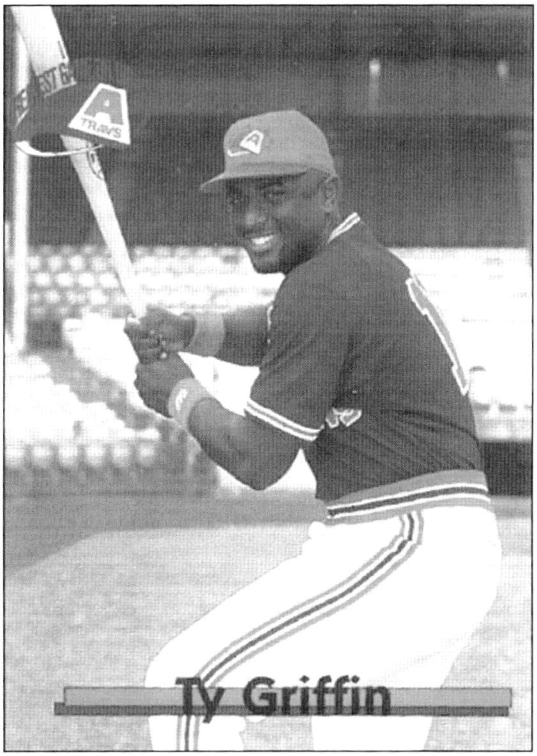

Travelers' second baseman Ty Griffin pulled off a baseball rarity from August 11–14, 1995. In a four-game series in Jackson, Mississippi, Griffin hit leadoff homers to start four consecutive games. His first homer came as Griffin batted right. The next three games he homered as a lefty leading off. Griffin was on a hot streak at the time and hit safely in 18 of 19 games. (Courtesy of the Texas League Archives.)

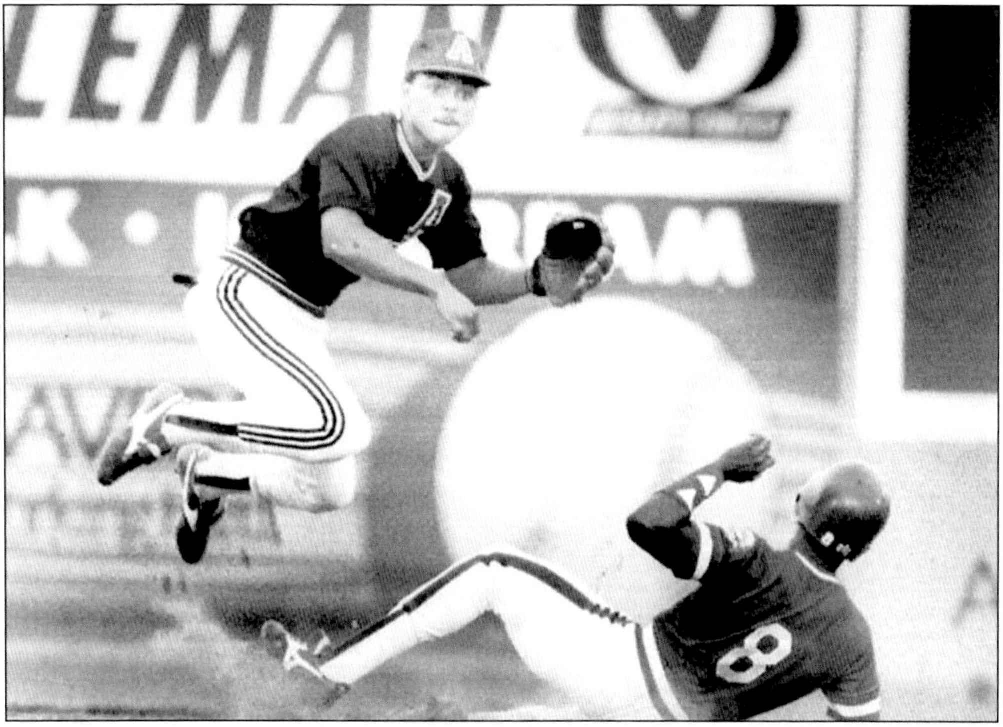

Traveler Luis Alicea avoids George Threadgill of Tulsa for the first out of a double play. The action happened at Ray Winder Field on June 8, 1987. (Courtesy of the Arkansas Travelers.)

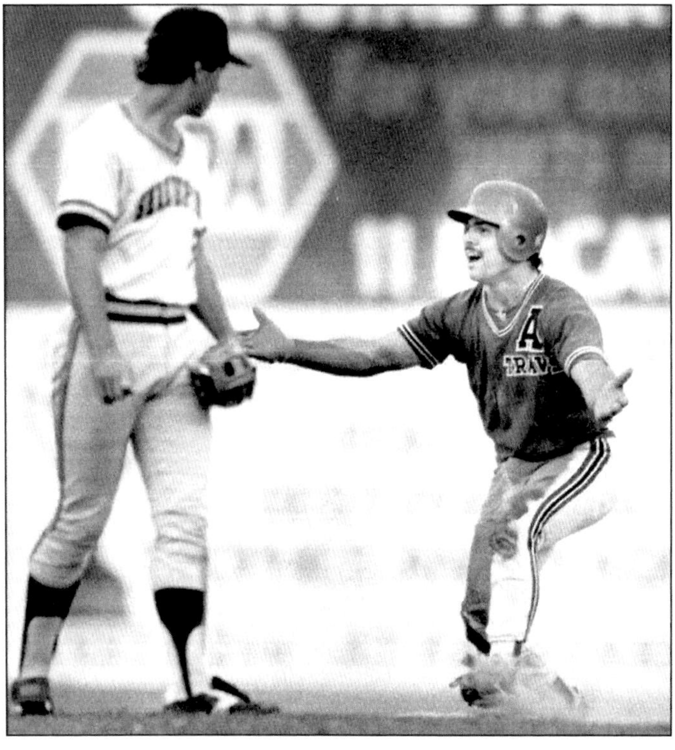

Traveler catcher Sal Agostinelli pleads his case to the second base umpire. He was called out at second base in a 1986 game after a headfirst slide. Agostinelli shared catching duties with Henry McCulla, Marty Pevey, and Tim Wallace. (Courtesy of the Arkansas Travelers.)

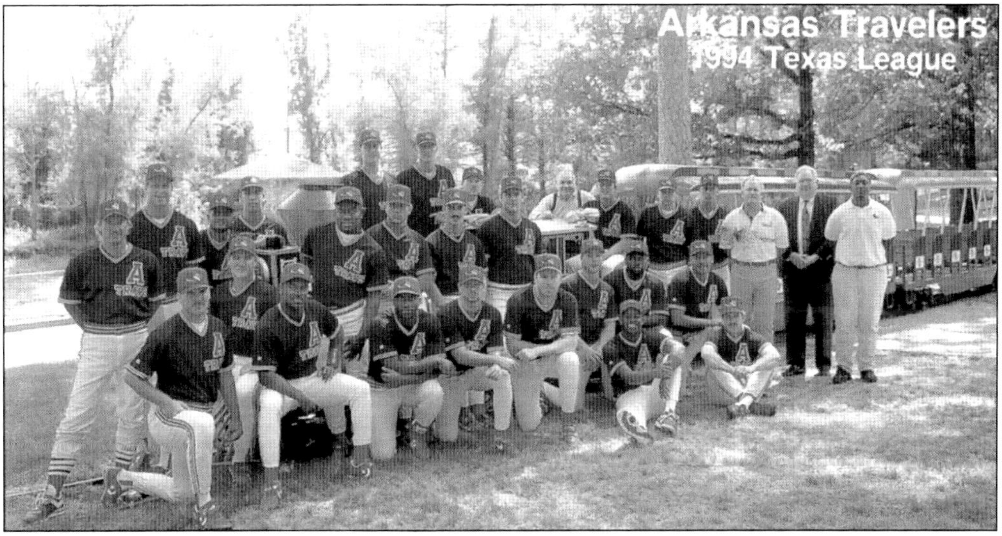

The 1994 Travelers are pictured from left to right: (first row) Aaron Holbert and Jeff Shireman; (second row) Scott Simmons, Doug Radziewicz, Tony Diggs, Terry Bradshaw, Gerry Santos, Jeff Alkire, Dan Cholowsky, Dmitri Young, and John Corona; (third row) coach Marty Mason, Mike Badorek, Gabriel Ozuna, Frankie Martinez, Anthony Lewis, John Frascatore, Joe Biasucci, and Paul Ellis; (fourth row) Steve Montgomery, Ron Warner, John Kelly, general manager Bill Valentine, manager Chris Maloney, Mike Difelice, Andy Bruce, Trainer Pete Fagan, president Bert Parke, and clubhouse manager Clarence Finley. (Courtesy of the Arkansas Travelers.)

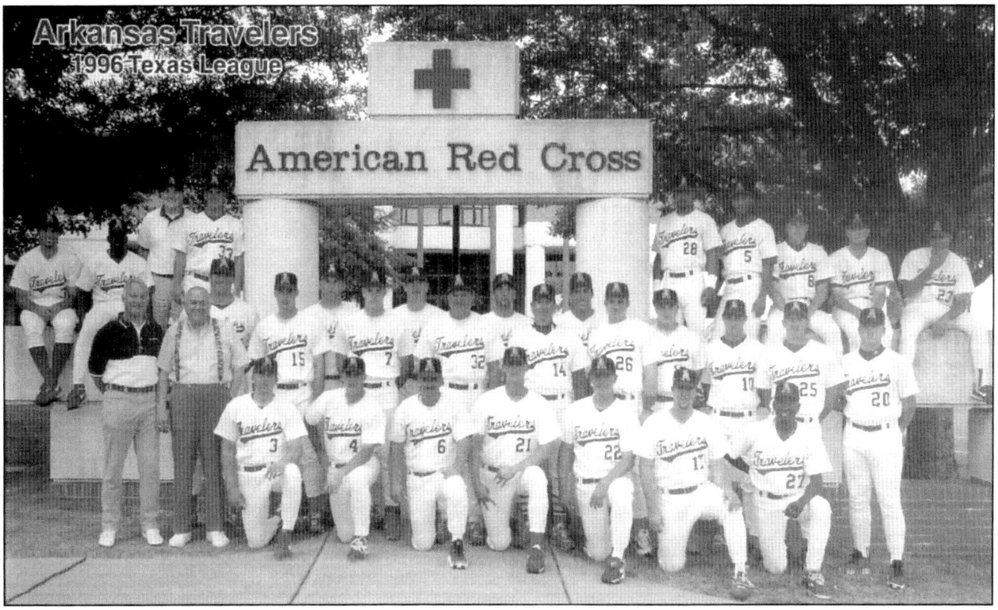

The 1996 Arkansas Travelers are pictured from left to right: (front row) Dee Dalton, Joe McEwing, coach Jeff Shireman, Ron Warner, Sean Lowe, Kevin Lovingier, and Manuel Aybar; (back row) trainer Pete Fagan, general manager Bill Valentine, Brady Raggio, Matt Golden, Kris Detmers, Chris Fick, Rich Croushore , manager Rick Mahler, Jeff Matranga, coach Marty Mason, Paul Torres, Joel Wolfe, Jeff Matulevich, Jeff Berblinger, Brian Carpenter, and Jeff Murphy. (Courtesy of the Arkansas Travelers.)

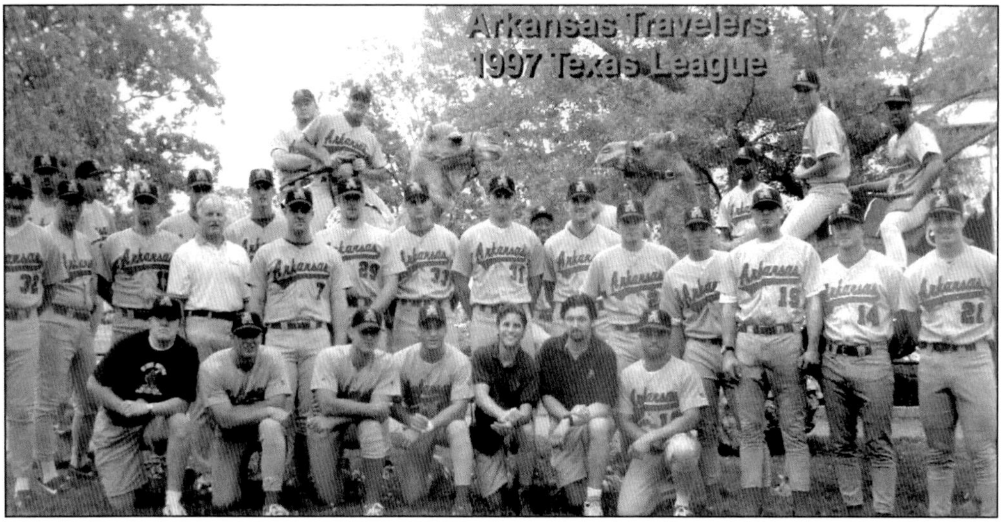

The 1997 Travelers are pictured from left to right: (front row) Ernie Moore, Jason LaRivere, Travis McClendon, Luis Ordaz, Hap Seliga, John Evans, and Placido Polanco; (middle row) Rick Mahler, Marcus Logan, Rich Folkers, Luis Melendez, Kevin Lovingler, David Chavarria, Pete Fagan, Blake Stein, Keith McDonald, Rick Croushore, Curtis King, Kris Detmer, Scarborough Green, Braden Looper, Greg Almond, Mike Matvey, Kerry Robinson, Matt Jarvis, Mike Windham, and Chris Richard; (back row) Rick Heiserman, Joe McEwing, Keith Glauber, and Yudith Ozorio. (Courtesy of the Arkansas Travelers.)

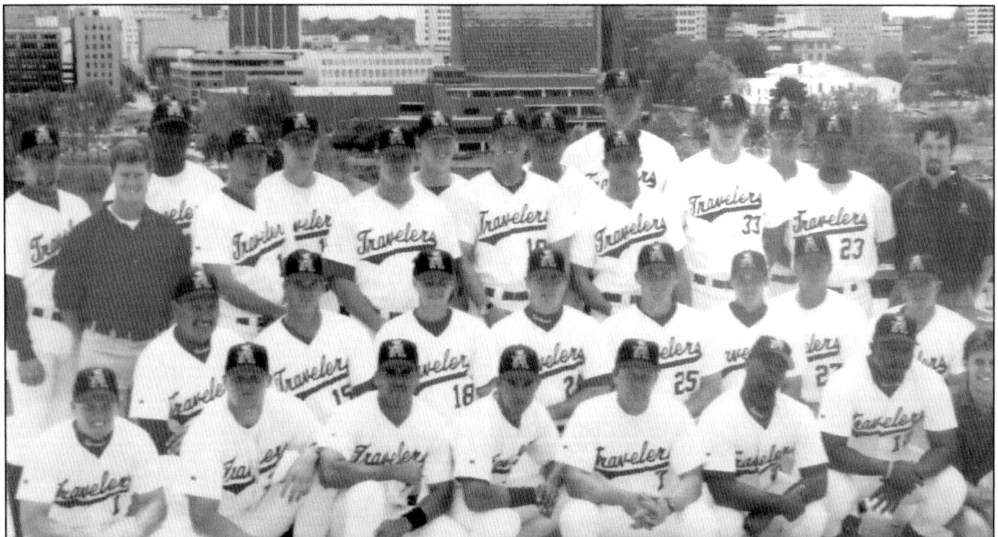

With the skyline of Little Rock behind them, the 1998 Travelers are pictured from left to right: (front row) Stubby Clapp, Nate Dishington, Miguel Rivera, Juan Munoz, manager Chris Maloney, Mike Harage, Tyrone Horne, and Hap Seliga; (middle row) coach Luis Melendez, Mike Windham, Stacy Kleiner, Dave Schmidt, Chris Haas, Joe McEwing, Greg Almond, and Jason LaRivere; (back row) Ossie Garcia, trainer B. J. Mack, Jose Jimenez, Kevin Lovingier, Kevin Cratton, Steve Reed, Clint Weibl, Matt Jarvis, Armando Almanza, Rick Heiserman, Jason Woolf, Kris Detmers, pitching coach Rich Folkers, Marcus Logan, and John Evans. (Courtesy of the Arkansas Travelers.)

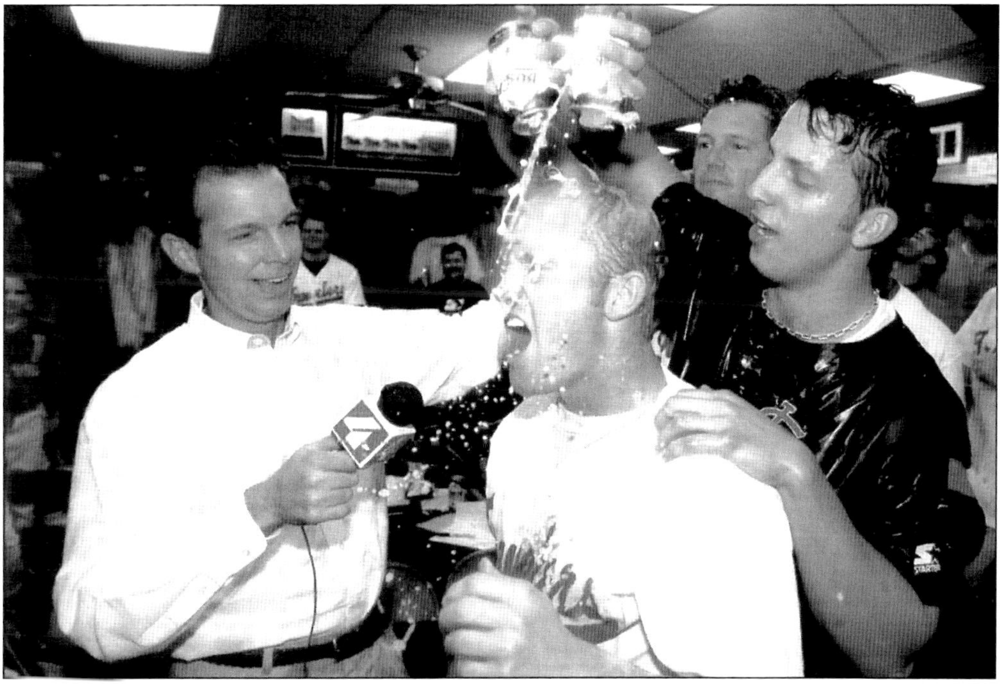

Popular Travelers player Stubby Clapp is "showered" with attention from teammate Jason Woolf during an interview with Channel 4 sportscaster Taylor Carr. Carr was the Travelers announcer during the 1996 and 1997 seasons. (Courtesy of the Arkansas Travelers.)

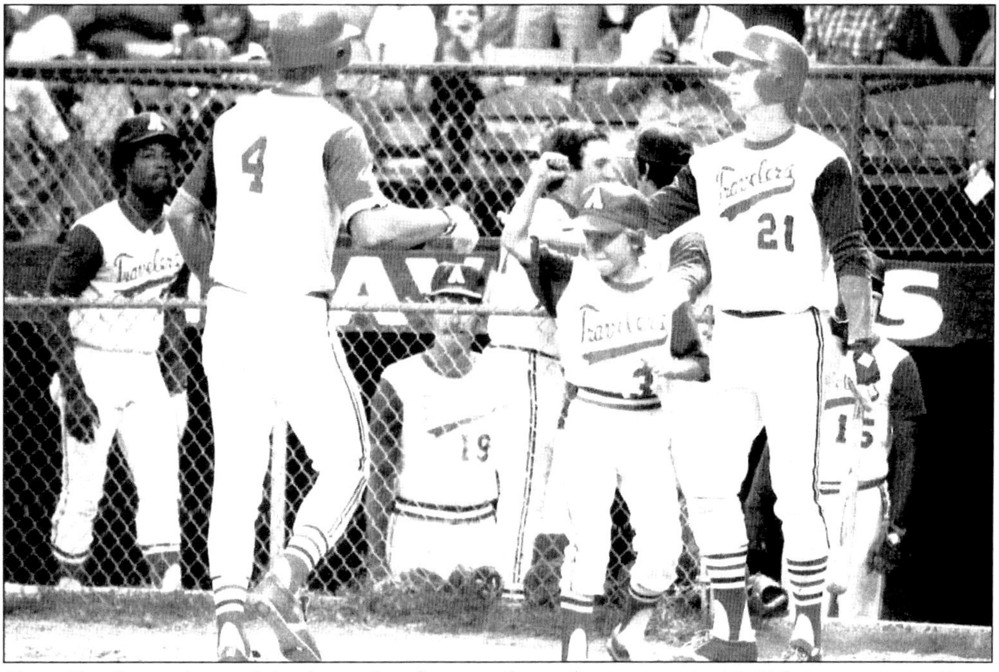

Gene Roof is welcomed back to the dugout after a home run in 1977 by teammates Dave Penniall (No. 21) and, left to right, Ty Waller, Arno Kirkenwitz, and batboy Lance Hines. (Courtesy of the Arkansas Travelers.)

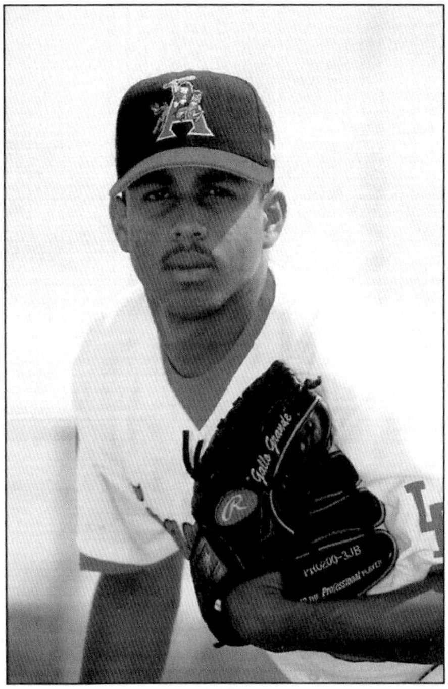

Francisco Rodriquez played for the Travelers in 2002 just before he went up to the Anaheim Angels. In Little Rock, he had a 3-3 record and a sparkling 1.96 ERA. He was a key contributor for the Angels in the World Series that year where he earned the nickname "K-Rod" for his clutch strikeouts. (Courtesy of the Arkansas Travelers.)

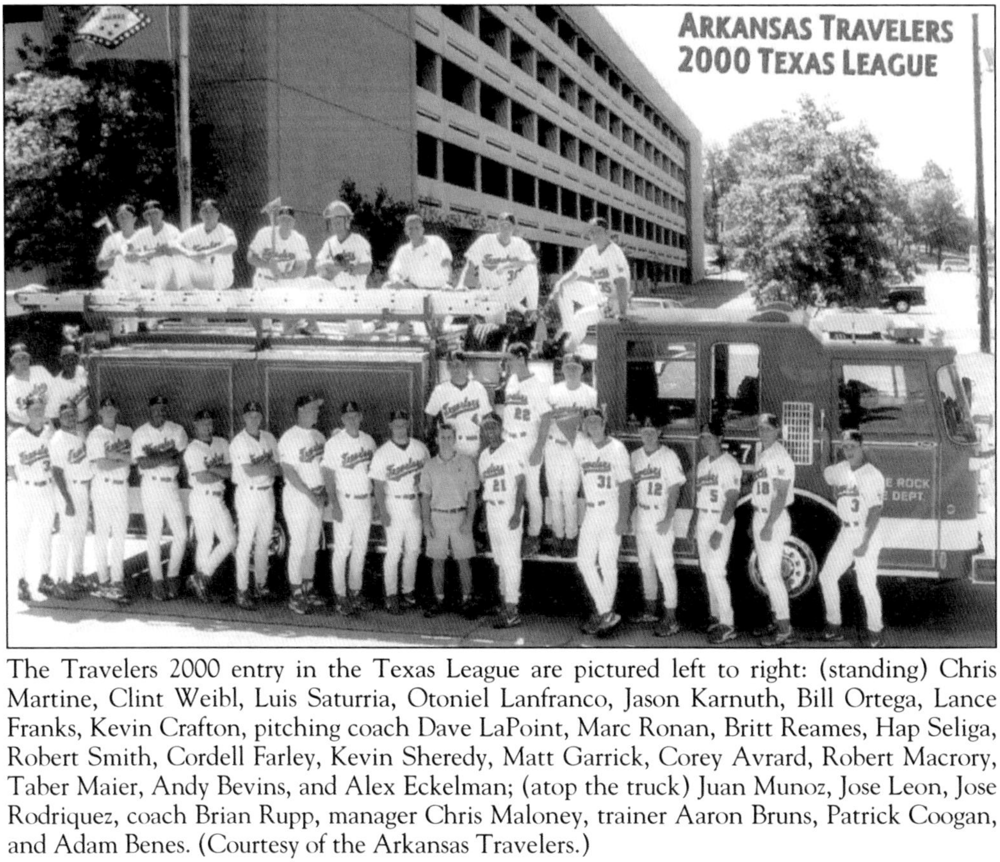

The Travelers 2000 entry in the Texas League are pictured left to right: (standing) Chris Martine, Clint Weibl, Luis Saturria, Otoniel Lanfranco, Jason Karnuth, Bill Ortega, Lance Franks, Kevin Crafton, pitching coach Dave LaPoint, Marc Ronan, Britt Reames, Hap Seliga, Robert Smith, Cordell Farley, Kevin Sheredy, Matt Garrick, Corey Avrard, Robert Macrory, Taber Maier, Andy Bevins, and Alex Eckelman; (atop the truck) Juan Munoz, Jose Leon, Jose Rodriquez, coach Brian Rupp, manager Chris Maloney, trainer Aaron Bruns, Patrick Coogan, and Adam Benes. (Courtesy of the Arkansas Travelers.)

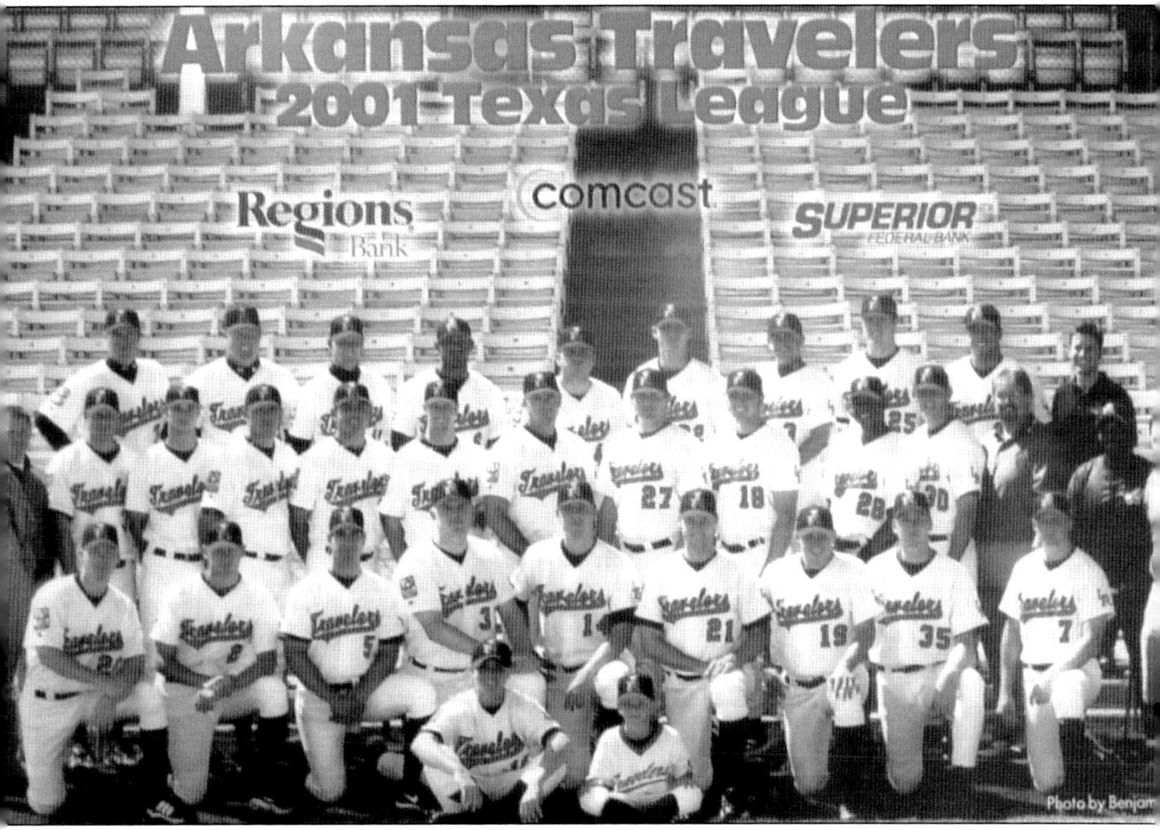

The 2001 Arkansas Travelers brought the Texas League Championship back to Little Rock after a 12-year drought. Arkansas won Texas League titles in 1977, 1979, 1980, and 1989. Playing as an Anaheim Angel farm team for the first time, the Travelers won the first half with a 38-32 record. They downed Wichita and Round Rock to win the post-season. Pictured from left to right: (front row) Mike Christensen, Chris Clark, Tom Gregorio, Daron Kirkreit, John Lackey, Gary Johnson, Robb Quinlan, Dusty Bergman, Jason Huisman, and batboys Jason Belk and Logan Brumley; (middle row) general manager Bill Valentine, trainer Geoff Hostetter, Chris Demouy, E.J. Thoen, Felipe Suarez, Radhames Dyhkoff, Jason Hill, Brendan Donnelly, Ryan Cummings, Mark Harriger, Elpidio Guzman, Derrick Turnbow, clubhouse manager Tony Aragon, strength coach Kevin Burns, director of broadcasting Phil Elson; (back row) coach Mark Budaska, coach Mike Butcher, manager Mike Brumley, Nathan Haynes, Norberto Lopez, Sean Brummett, Alfredo Amezaga, Bill Mott, Jeremy Callier, and assistant general manager Hap Seliga. (Courtesy of the Arkansas Travelers.)

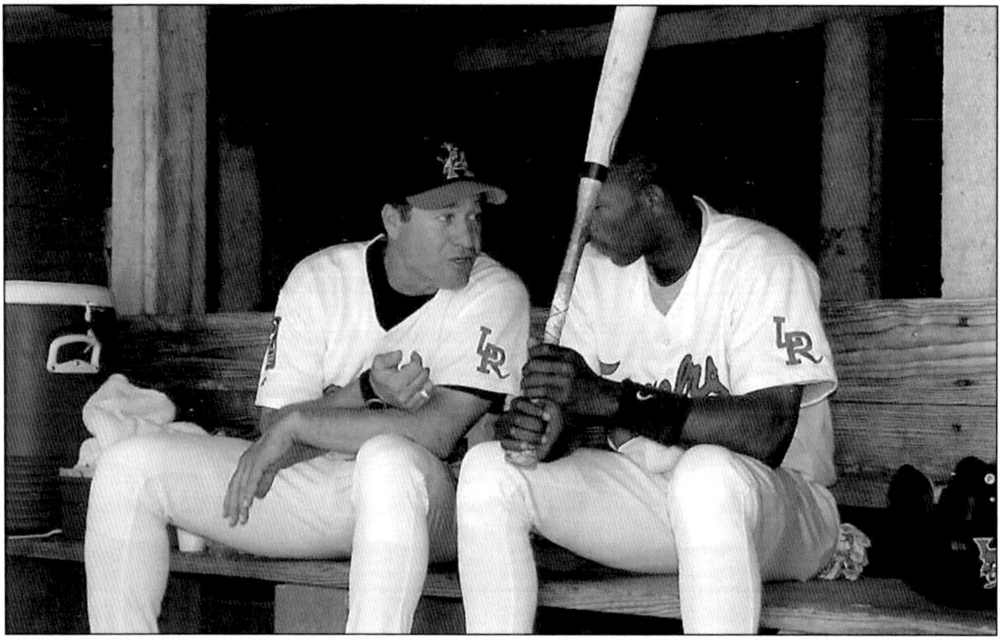

Arkansas hitting coach Mark Budaska advises outfielder Elpidio Guzman. Guzman, a speedy centerfielder, starred for the Travelers during the 2001 championship year. (Courtesy of the Arkansas Travelers.)

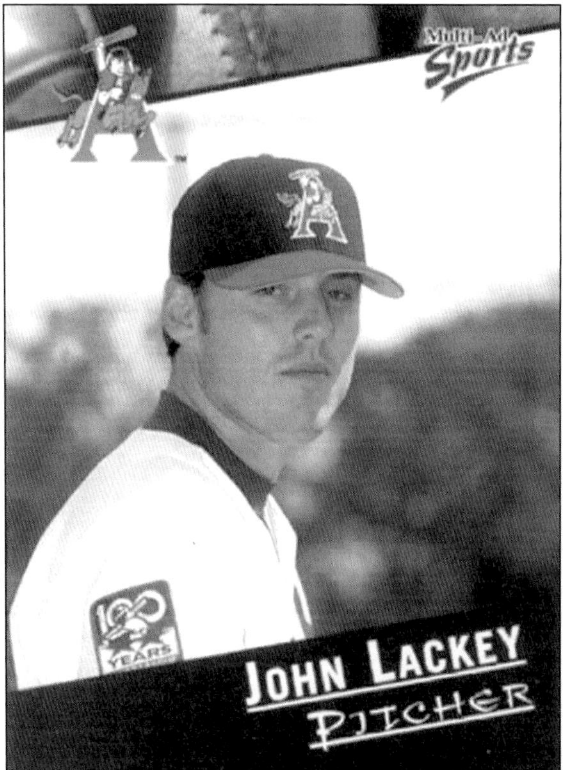

John Lackey had a 9-7 record for the 2001 Travelers. The 6-foot-6, 230-pound right-hander helped lead Arkansas to the first half Eastern Division title. Lackey was promoted to Salt Lake City of the Pacific Coast League on July 6, but still had the Travelers in a position to win the Texas League Championship. One year later, Lackey was on the World Champion Anaheim Angels. He pitched and won the seventh game against San Francisco, becoming only the second rookie to win the seventh game of a World Series. (courtesy of the Texas League Archives.)

Brian Specht was a switch-hitting shortstop for the 2001 Texas League Champions. Specht joined the Travelers in mid-season and helped prepare them for the Texas League playoffs. A popular player, Specht served as shortstop and designated hitter in 2002 and 2003. (Courtesy of Pete Lavan.)

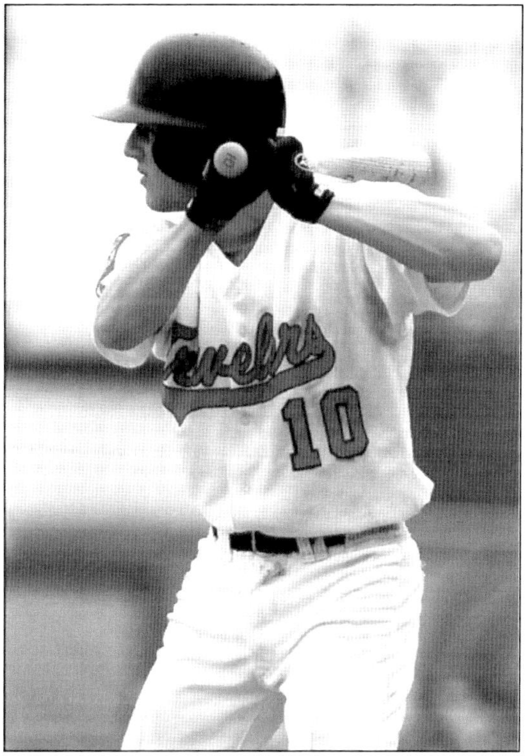

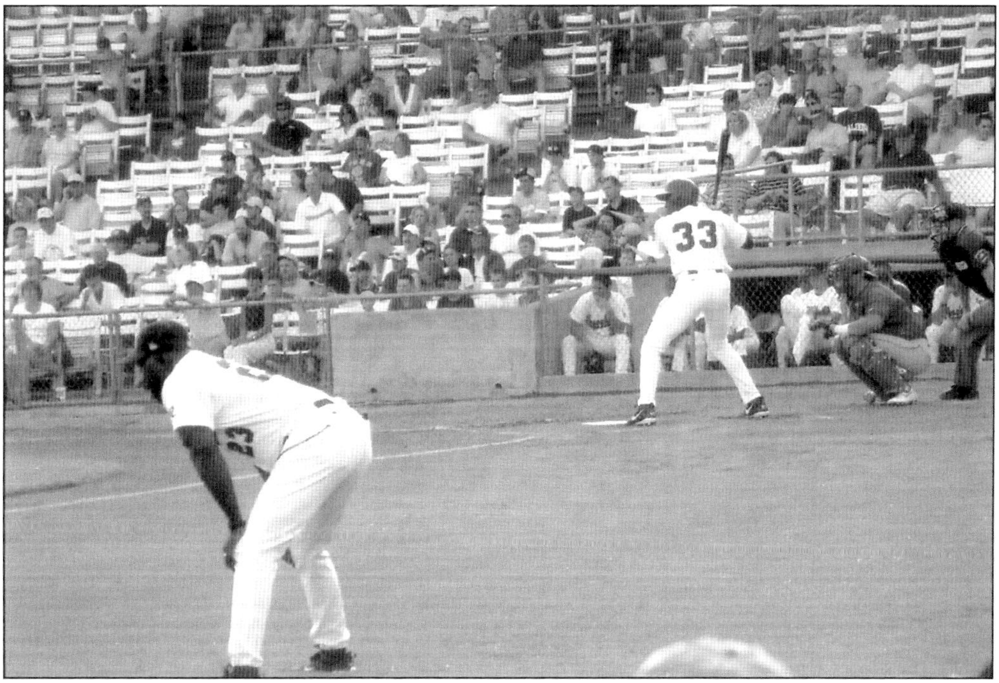

Manager Tyrone Boykin watches a runner on second while Junior Zamora prepares to bat. Boykin's Travelers rallied in early August of 2003, but were derailed by a poor road trip and finished out of the playoffs. (Courtesy of Don Curdie.)

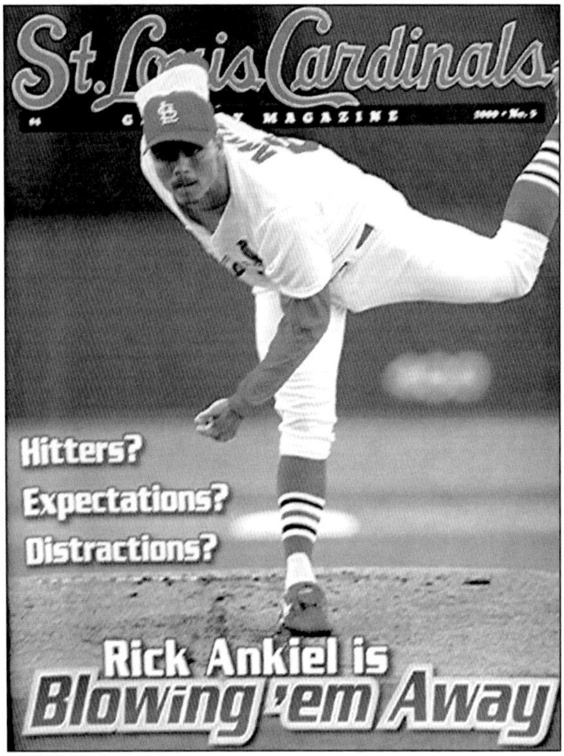

Rick Ankiel wowed Travelers fans in 1999. The powerful lefthander went 6-0 on the mound with an excellent 0.91 ERA. The 1997 second-round draft choice of the St. Louis Cardinals was 7-3 with AAA Memphis and sported a 3.16 ERA. Ankiel was named the 1999 Minor League Pitcher of the Year and advanced to the Cardinals pitching staff. (Courtesy of the St. Louis Cardinals.)

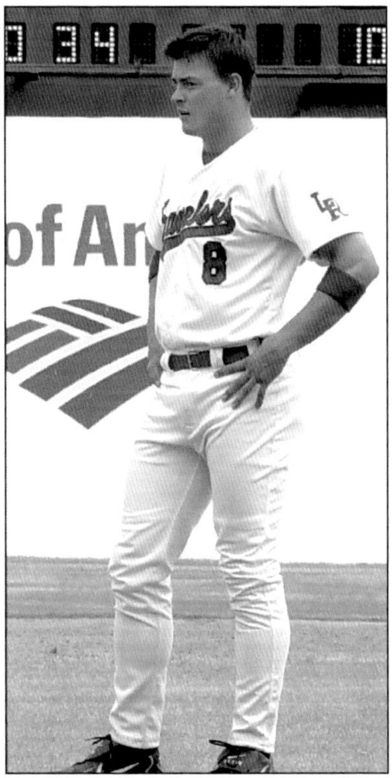

Traveler third baseman Dallas McPherson blasted one of the longest home runs ever seen at Ray Winder Field. In the second game of a double header against Midland, the 6-foot-4, 210-pound slugger arched a ball over the 55-foot screen in right field and into a nearby neighborhood. "John Young hit a home run in 1977 that cleared the freeway," said General Manager Bill Valentine. "This one probably matched it." Arkansas-Democrat sportswriter Jim Bailey, who has covered the team for over 30 years, said it "was almost beyond belief" to see McPherson hit three blasts over deep left center in one game. (Courtesy of Don Curdie.)

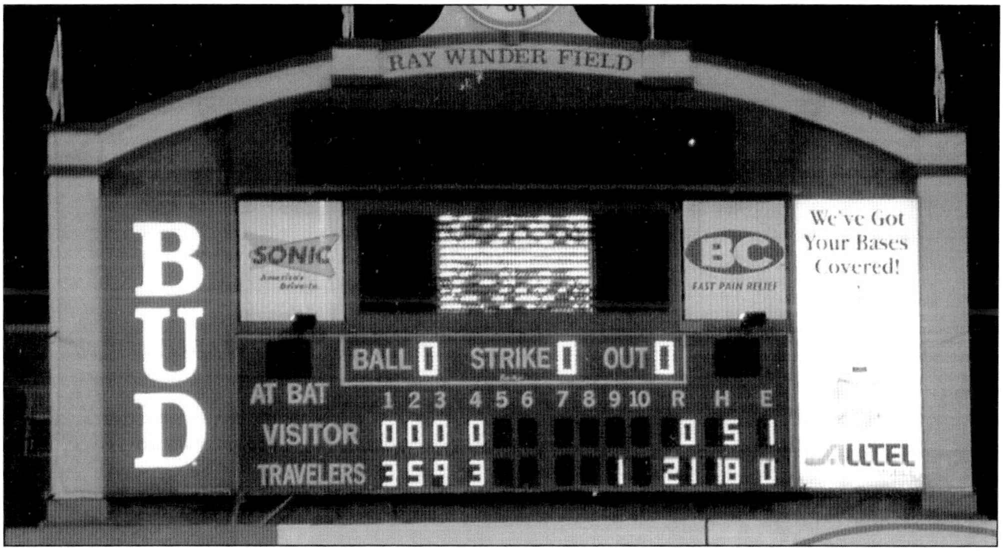

Twenty-one runs in the first four innings is an excellent way to start a game. The score was so dramatic that the Travelers scoreboard did not have space for double digits in an inning, so the extra run was placed in the bottom of the ninth. Midland was the August 16, 2003 victim. The Travelers 21-0 shutout win tied a 115-year-old Texas League record. The run total matched the team's previous high, achieved in a 21-20 win over Jackson on June 15, 1998. (Courtesy of Don Curdie.)

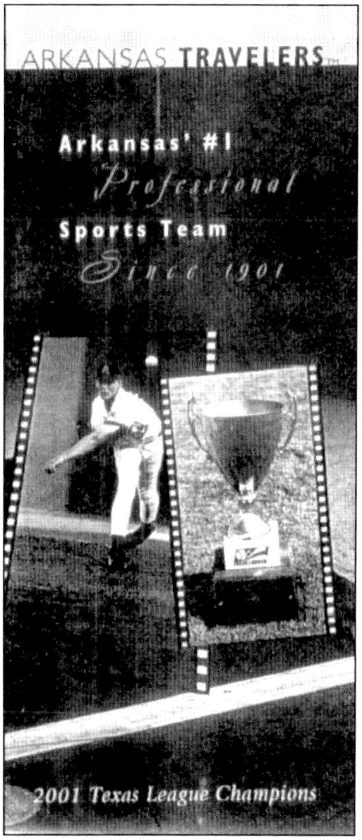

Scorebook coverboy Dusty Bergman touts the Travelers' hopes for the 2002 season. Bergman was a member of the 2001 Texas League champions led by Manager Mike Brumley. In the playoffs finals, Arkansas had a 2-0 lead over the Round Rock Express on the morning of September 11. All professional baseball was cancelled after the terrorist attacks in New York City, Pennsylvania and Washington, D.C. The Texas League voted to crown the Travelers as champions despite the protests of the Round Rock Express, the overall leader for the season. (courtesy of the Arkansas Travelers.)

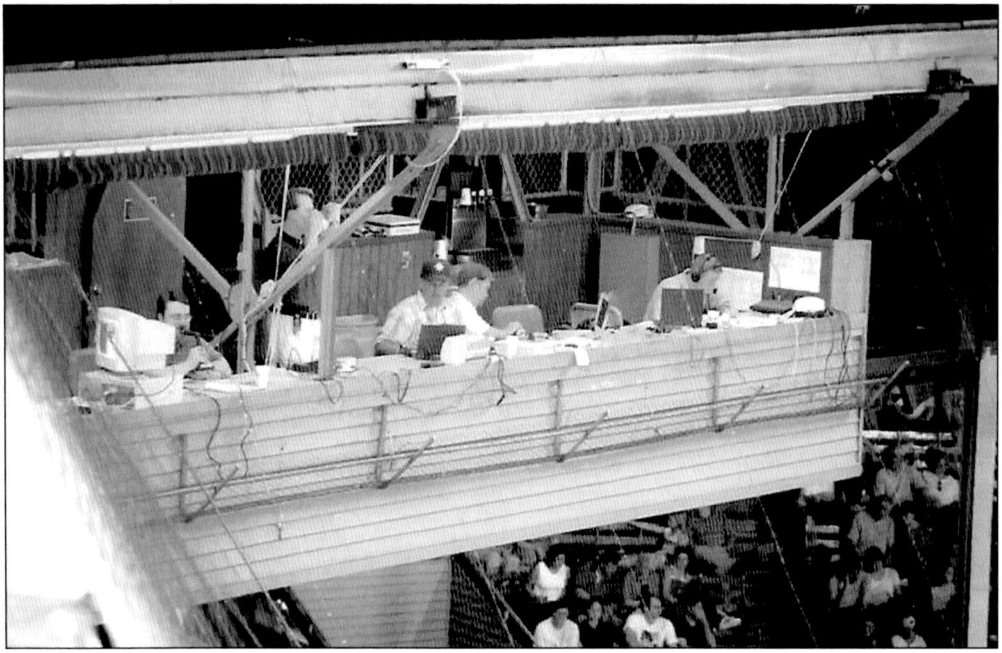

The "Jim Box" is what the press, media and scorekeepers call the press box at Ray Winder Field. It is named in honor of two "Jims"—longtime play-by-play man Jim Elder and Jim Bailey, an *Arkansas Democrat-Gazette* sportswriter. Both covered the team for over 30 years and Bailey still writes columns about the Travelers. (Courtesy of the Arkansas Travelers.)

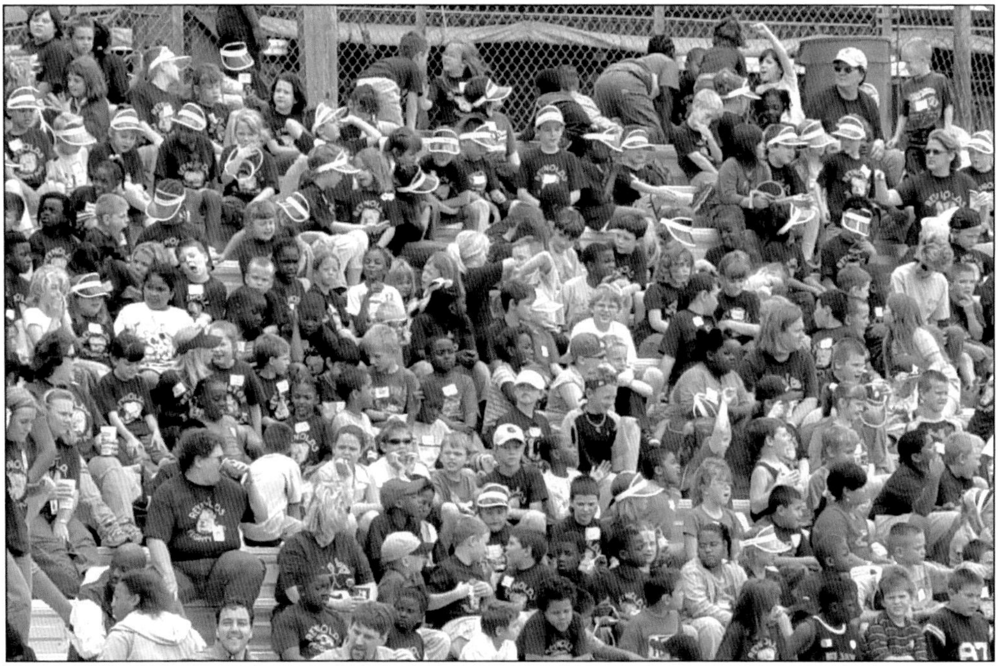

Over 6,000 school children attended a special morning game early in the 2004 season. School buses from all over Central Arkansas brought the students to Ray Winder Field where each received a free hot dog and soft drink. (Courtesy of Carl Enna.)

A young fan shows his dedication to the Travelers during a rain delay. Attendance at Arkansas games was terrific in 1980s and 1990s. The Travelers drew over 200,000 fans for 17 consecutive years. The team's switch to the St. Louis Cardinals led to the Texas League and larger crowds. After winning only four pennants in the Southern Association, the Travelers have won 11 league titles or half-championships since 1966 in the Texas league. (Courtesy of the Arkansas Travelers.)

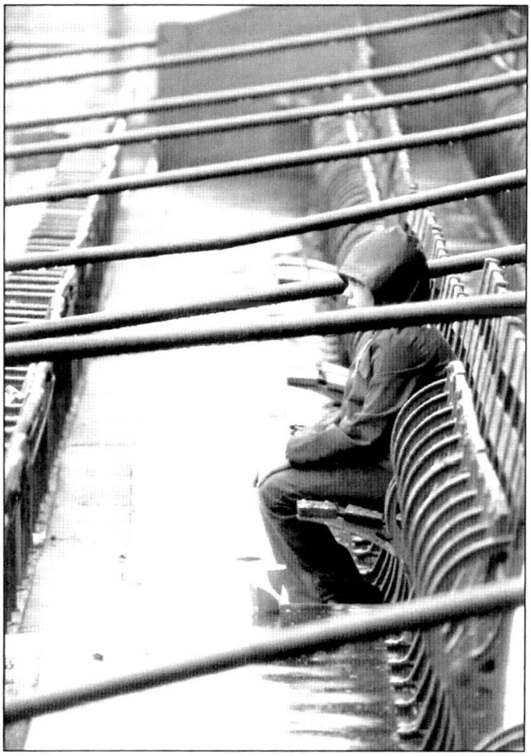

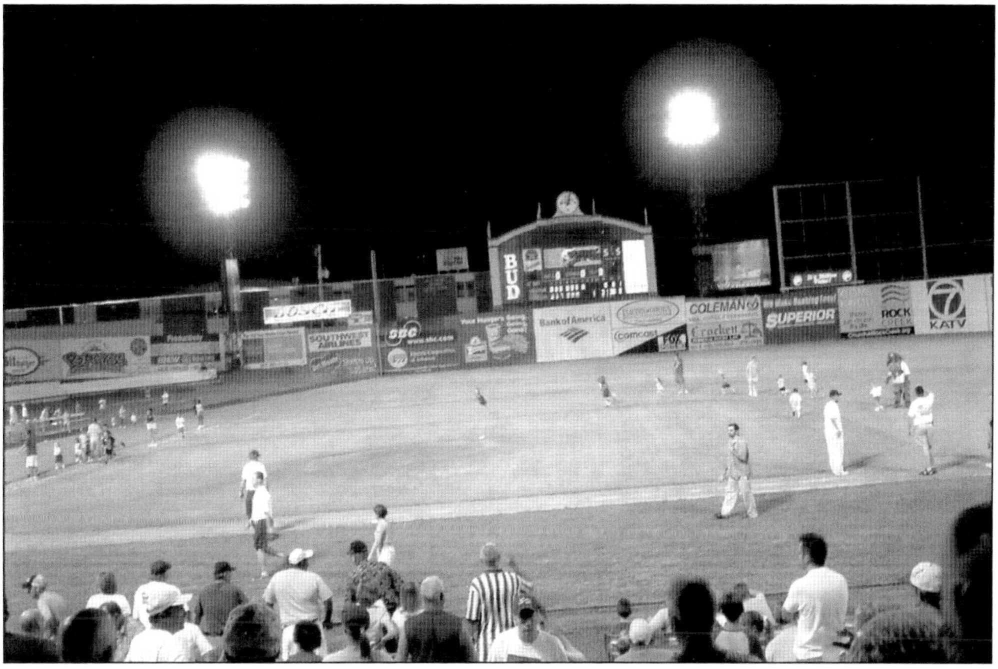

Following the end of each Travelers home game, children are invited to run the bases. Team personnel keep a careful eye on the "future" Travelers as they run the 360-foot route. (Courtesy of the Arkansas Travelers.)

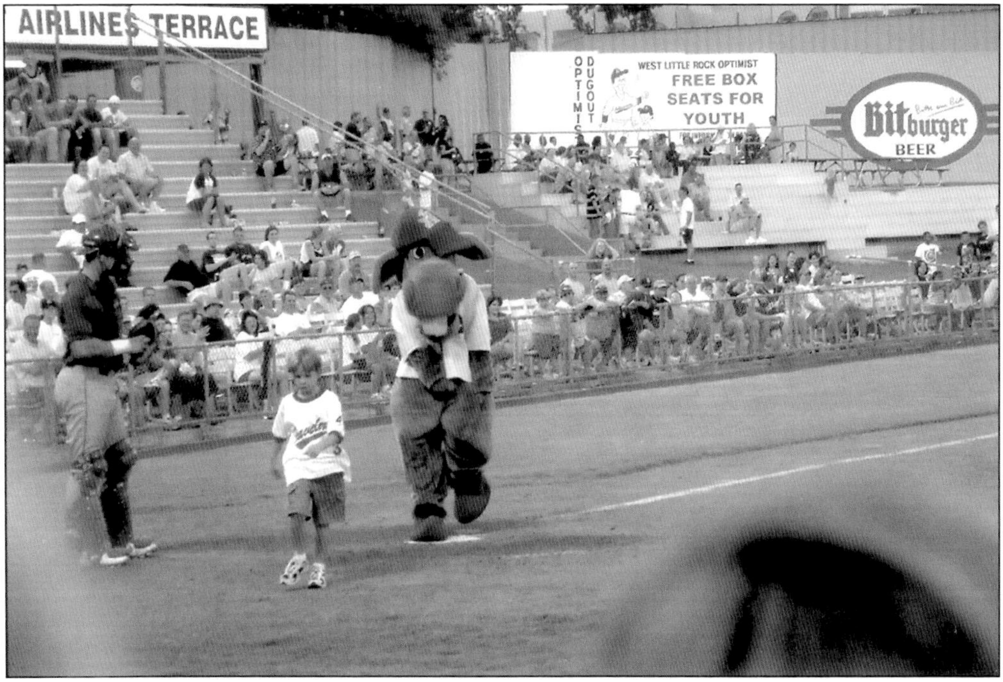

"Shelly," who represents the horse in the team's logo, loses another race to a young Travelers fan. Shelly had a two-base headstart on the youngster and still lost. (Courtesy of Don Curdie.)

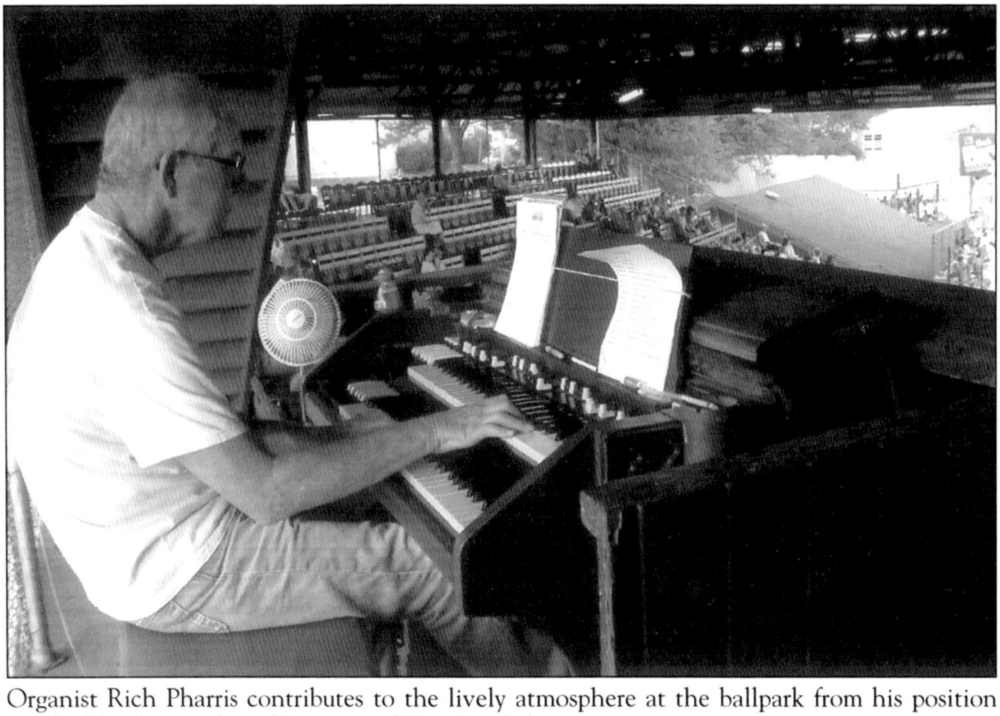
Organist Rich Pharris contributes to the lively atmosphere at the ballpark from his position overlooking home plate. (Courtesy of Don Curdie)

Since 1997, mascot Shelly has entertained Travelers fans with visits to the grandstands and the playing field. In this photo, Shelly performs as "Shellvis." Five individuals have donned the Shelly outfit. Kevin Thomas, Jason Benbrook, Bobby Reed, Tye Herring, and Kyle Hamsher were featured as the hospitable horse. (Courtesy of the Arkansas Travelers.)

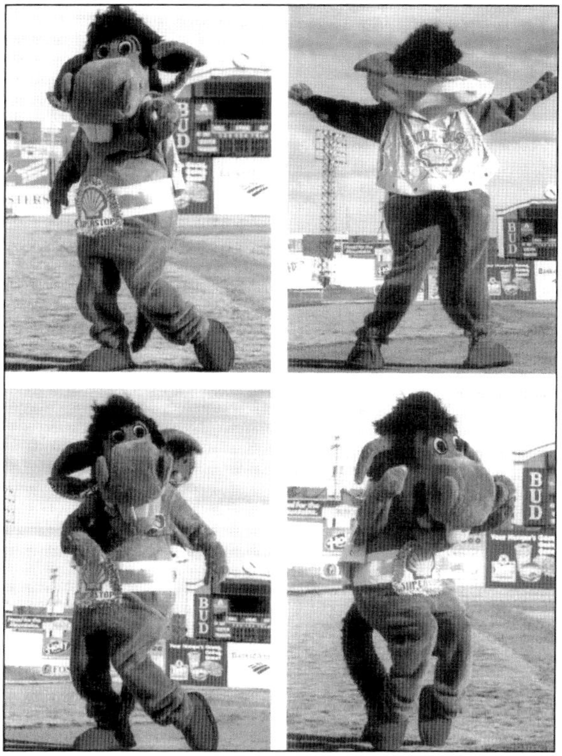

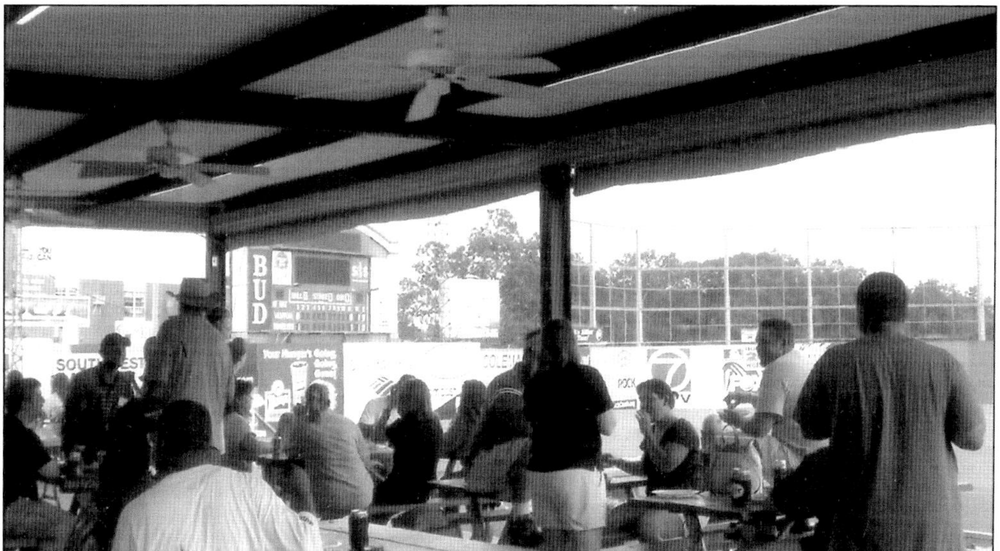

Ray Winder Field has both character and its characters. Two fan favorites were "Willie" and "Hookslide." Willie was a guest of a nearby hospital that brought patients to the game. He became such a fixture that he was provided with a uniform, helped with promotions, and was an employee of Ray Winder for $1 a day. Hook Slide was a vociferous fan. One day he did not approve of a player's hook slide. "I'll show you a hook slide," he yelled. He placed a popcorn box near the bleachers, took a running start and executed a proper hook slide. He won the fans' approval and a new nickname. (Courtesy of the Arkansas Travelers.)

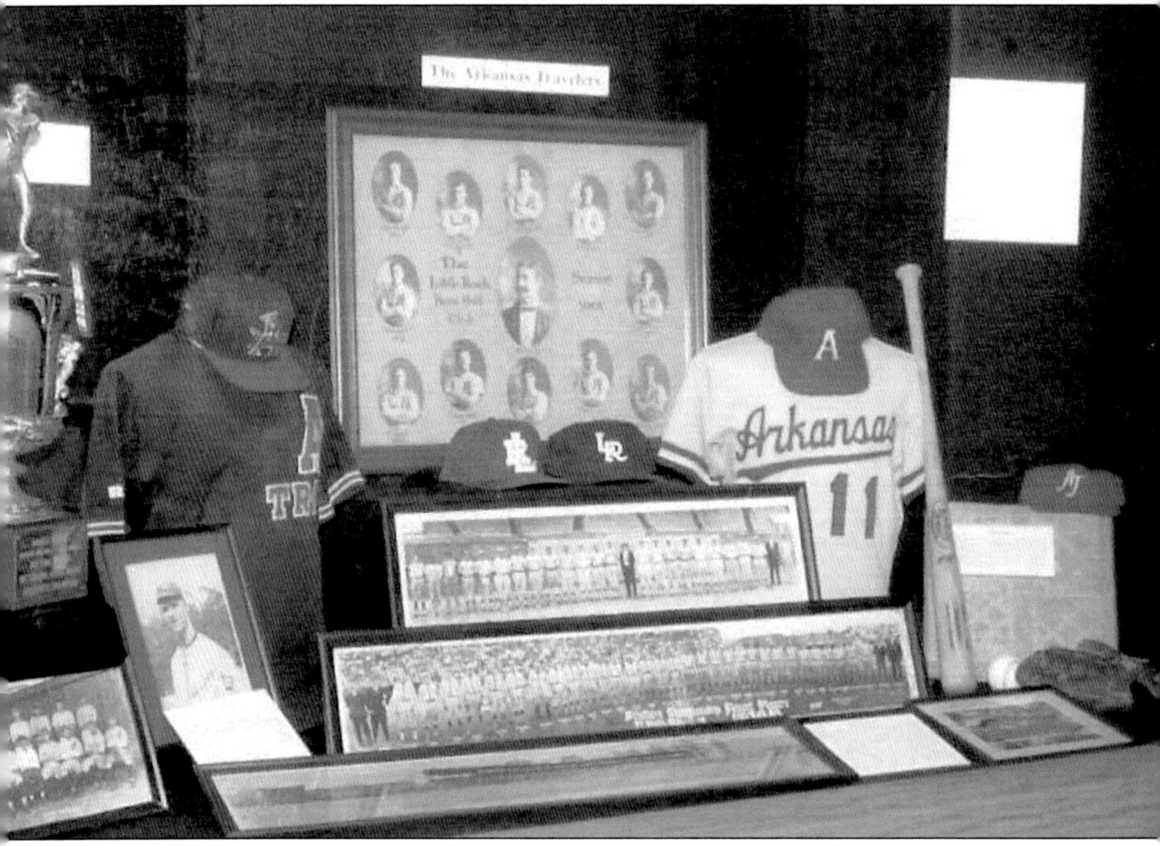

Little Rock and Arkansas Traveler baseball history were highlighted during a recent display at the Arkansas State Capitol. Featured are a picture of the 1901 Travelers of the Southern Association, the 1920 league champions, and more recent caps and uniforms. The Secretary of State's office organized the display. (Courtesy of the Arkansas Travelers.)

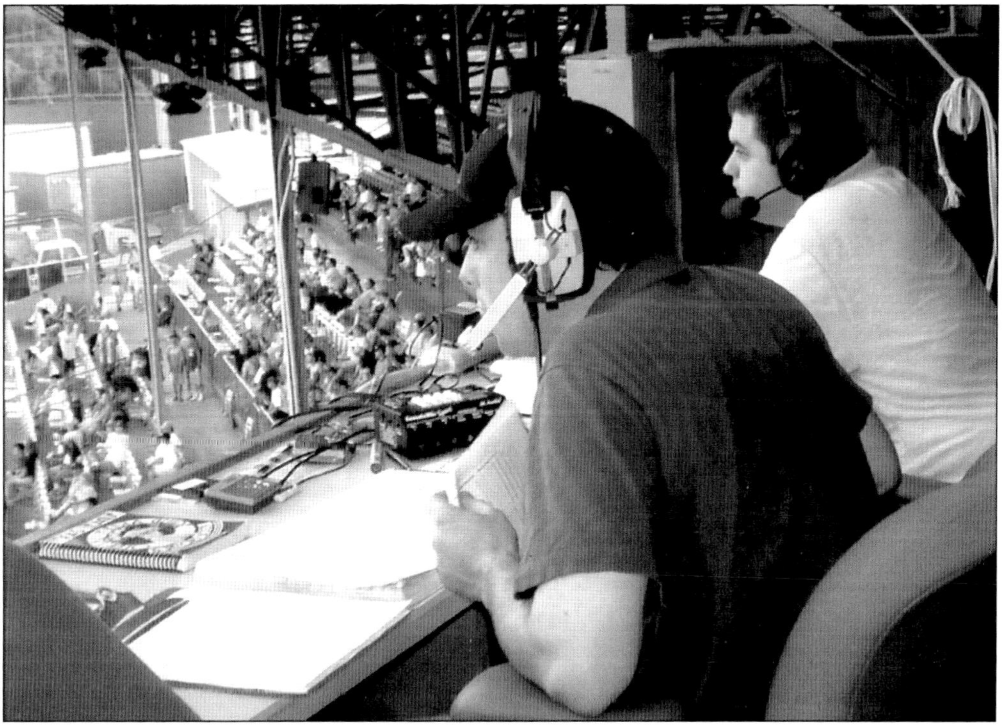

Phil Elson and Steve Marston manned the headsets for the Travelers' 2003 season. Elson began announcing minor league games at the age of 17. In 2004, he began his fourth year as play-by-play man. Marston started with the team in 2002. (Courtesy of Don Curdie.)

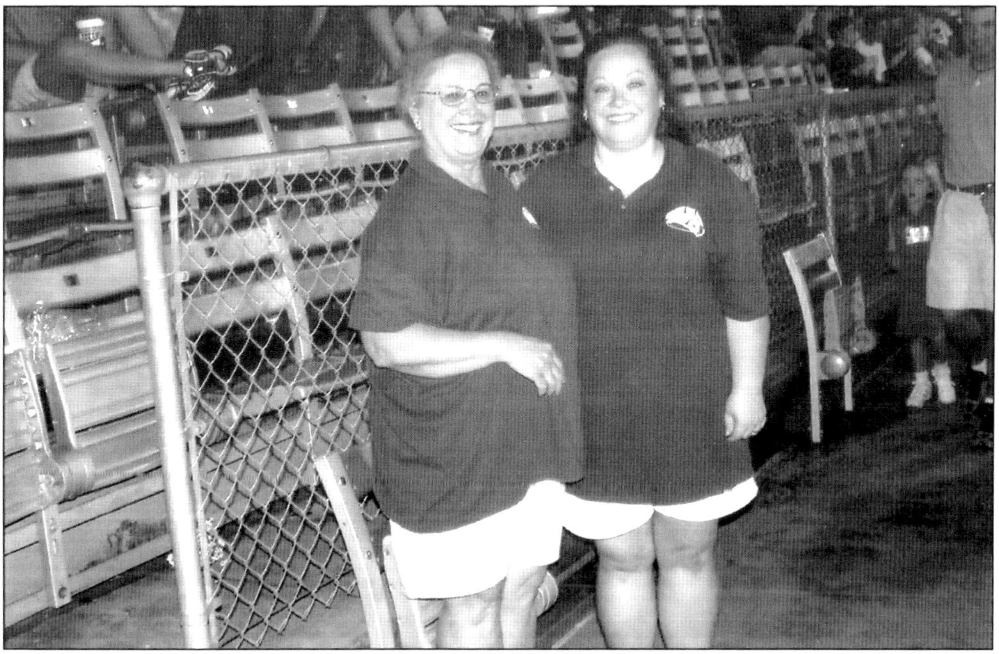

Usherettes Kathy Duncan (right) and Paula Benson assist Travelers fans to their seats along the first base line. Ray Winder Field and its employees reflect the friendliness found around the state.

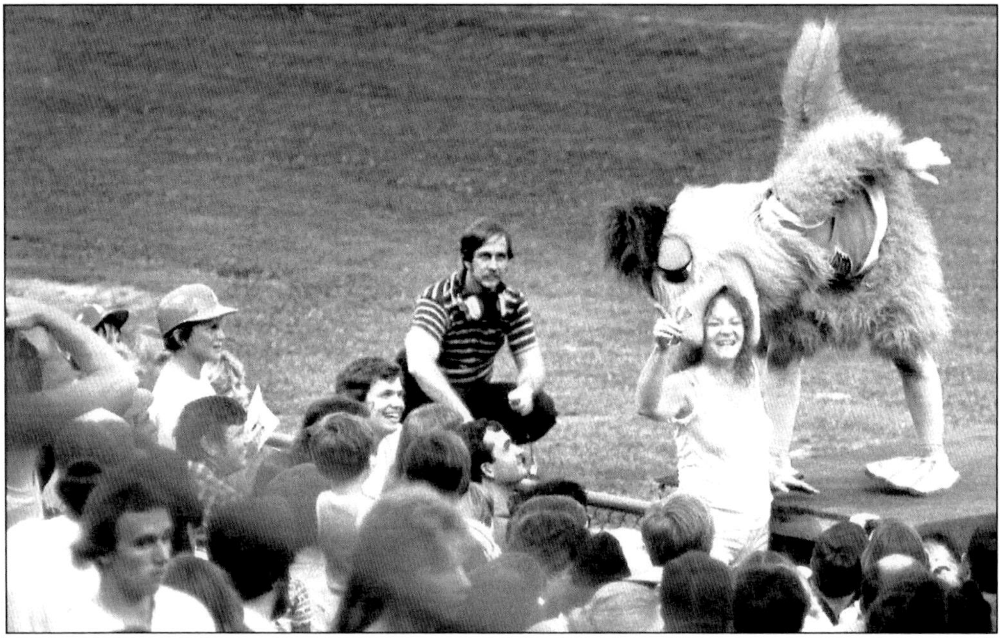

The San Diego Chicken plants a full-blown kiss on an unsuspecting Travelers fan. The "Chicken" made annual visits to Ray Winder Field as well as other minor and major league parks. In addition to good baseball, special promotions like the antics of the San Diego Chicken, Kar Klunker Night, or an appearance by Fernando Valenzuela on the mound draw the crowds. (Courtesy of the Arkansas Travelers.)

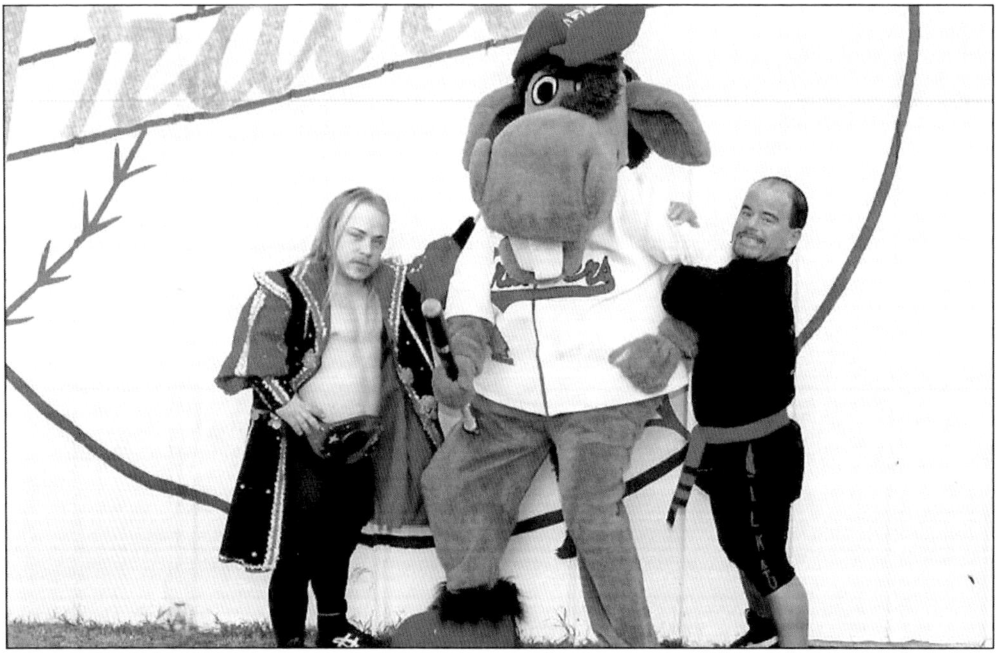

Beautiful Bobby (left), Shelly and L'il Kato advertise the next Midget Wrestling Night at Ray Winder Field. The tiny wrestlers have been one of the most popular acts signed by general manager Bill Valentine. (Courtesy of the Arkansas Travelers.)

The 2003 scorecard for the Arkansas Travelers promotes their association with the World Champion Anaheim Angels. The text also lists the former Travelers who played on the World Series: Adam Kennedy, John Lackey, Brendan Donnelly, Francisco Rodriguez and Chone Figgins. Kennedy was American League Championship Series MVP with a .357 average in four games and a three-homer game. Lackey was the first rookie in 93 years to win the seventh game of the Series. Donnelly limited San Francisco to one hit in seven and a half innings. Rodriquez earned the "K-Rod" nickname in 11 games with five post-season wins. Figgins was a valuable pinch runner with four runs scored in six games plus the Game Five clinching run in the ALCS. (Courtesy of the Arkansas Travelers.)

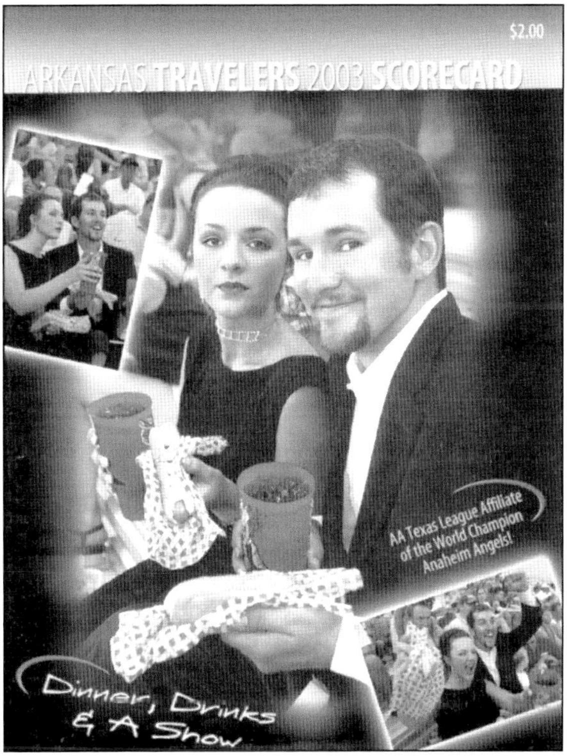

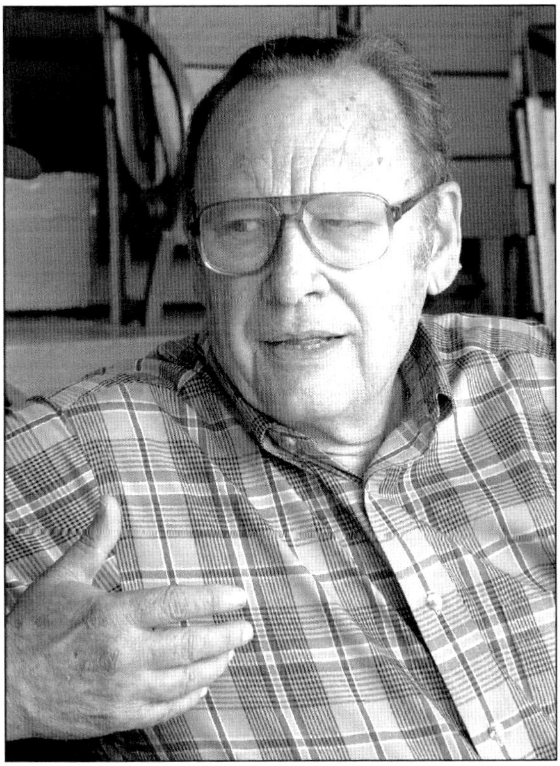

Jim Bailey covered the Arkansas Travelers from 1958 through 1987 as a sportwriter in Little Rock. He currently writes a sports column for the *Arkansas Democrat-Gazette* and remains a loyal Travelers fan. (Courtesy of Carl Enna.)

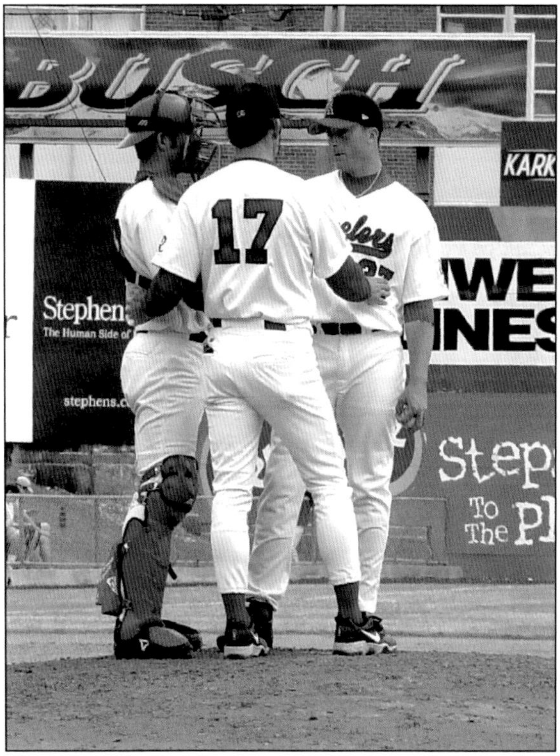

Pitching coach Kernan Ronan (No. 17) confers with pitcher Dan Mozingo (right) and catcher Jeff Mathis. Mozingo took control and the Travelers and won 10-5 on April 19, 2004. (Courtesy of Carl Enna.)

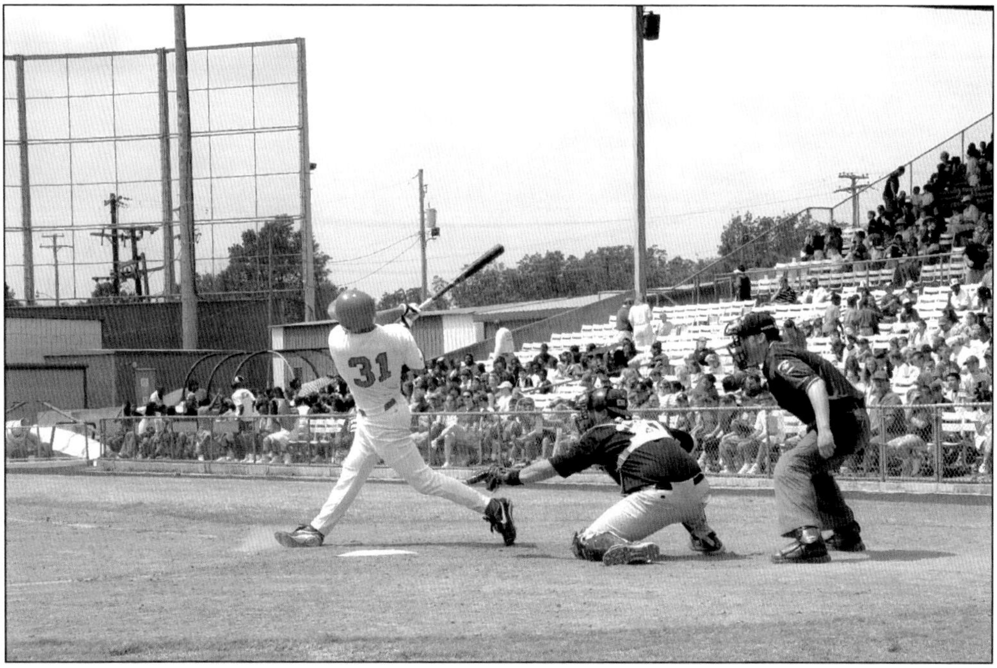

Casey Kotchman, 6-foot-3 and 210 pounds, was a number one draft choice of the Anaheim Angels. Kotchman, blessed with a classic southpaw swing, signed for the third highest bonus—$2,075,000—in Angels' history. He was hitting .378 when he made the jump from AA Little Rock to the Angels in early May of 2004. (Courtesy of Carl Enna.)

Four

The VIPs of the Arkansas Travelers

From Baseball Hall of Famers to beloved team officials to famous politicians, the Arkansas Travelers have hosted many celebrities. Five players enshrined in the National Baseball Hall of Fame have played for the Travelers: Tris Speaker, Travis Jackson, Bill Dickey, Jim Bunning and Ferguson Jenkins.

It is ironic that a Texan would be the first Hall of Famer to play for the Arkansas Travelers. As a 20-year-old outfielder in 1908 for Little Rock, Tris Speaker hit .350 and led the Southern Association in batting. He also led the league in runs and hits. He played 22 years and holds the all-time doubles record with 792. Speaker amassed 3,514 hits for a career average of .345 and played on three World Series champions. Nicknamed "The Grey Eagle," he played a very shallow centerfield and was involved in many double plays. Eight times he led the American League in doubles and five times he had 50 or more. Speaker struck out only 220 times in 10,195 at bats. He had 432 stolen bases.

Travis Jackson, born in Waldo, was the first Arkansas native to make the Hall of Fame after playing with the Travelers. The 18-year-old shortstop played 39 games in 1921 and 147 in 1922. In the latter season he batted .280 while being managed by Kid Elberfield. The New York Giants called him to the major leagues late in the 1922 season. In 1924, he became the starting shortstop for the legendary John McGraw. Batting over .300 six times, Jackson had a career average of .291. Twice he led the National League in fielding. He played in the only all-Hall of Fame infield. First baseman Bill Terry, second baseman Frankie Frisch and third baseman Fred Lindstrom rounded out the stellar unit.

Bill Dickey was born in Bastrop, Louisiana, in 1907, but moved to Kensett, Arkansas when he was seven. As an 18-year-old catcher, Dickey batted .375 in 21 games for the Travelers. Two years later, he played 60 games and batted .300. At the end of the 1928 season, the Yankees signed him and he played in 10 games. The following year he became New York's starting backstop. Famous New York sportswriter Dan Daniel said of Dickey, "Dickey isn't just a catcher. He's a ballclub. He isn't just a player. He's an influence." He led the American League catchers in fielding four times. The even-tempered Dickey composed a .313 career batting average. He played 13 consecutive seasons of 100 games or more. He was a roommate of Lou Gehrig and a teammate of Babe Ruth, Joe DiMaggio and Mickey Mantle. Gehrig and Dickey personified the class of the Yankees. After retirement in 1947, Dickey managed the Travelers for one season and had a 51-103 record. The Yankees and Casey Stengel asked him back to coach young Yogi Berra in 1949. Berra became a Hall of Famer like his coach. Dickey stayed on as a coach for Stengel until 1957. Dickey made the Hall in Fame in 1954. Dickey and Berra's number 8 uniforms were retired in a Yankee Stadium ceremony in 1972. Following his retirement from baseball, Dickey worked for Stephens, Inc. of Little Rock and remained active in the company until 1972.

Hall of Famer Jim Bunning did not record Hall of Fame numbers in two years with the Travelers. He was 5-12 with a 4.56 ERA in 1953, but improved to 13-11 and 4.29 in 1954. The 6-foot-3 right-hander took two years to catch on to American League hitters as a Detroit pitcher. He then won 20 games in 1957. Traded to Philadelphia in 1964, Bunning won 19 games that year and also threw a perfect game on Father's Day. He was the first pitcher to win 100 games in both the American and the National League.

Ferguson Jenkins was a 6-foot-5, 210-pound fastball pitcher for the Travelers. Pitching in 1964 and 1965, the future Hall of Famer compiled a 13-11 record over two years. The native of Ontario, Canada, was called up to Philadelphia on September 10, 1965. Twice he led the National League in wins and four times he led his league in complete games. In 1971, Jenkins won the National League's Cy Young Award. Along with fellow Travelers pitcher Jim Bunning, he is one of the few pitchers to win over 100 games in both the National and American Leagues.

Three colorful characters—William Kavanaugh, Ray Winder, Bill Valentine—have been instrumental to the Travelers and each has been credited with "saving" the team at a point in its history.

William Marmaduke Kavanaugh was the most influential man in the Travelers' early years of 1895 to 1915. Born in Alabama, educated in Kentucky, he came to Arkansas to seek his fame and fortune in 1886. Kavanaugh was a born leader. After only two years at the Arkansas Gazette, he became the City Editor and later was appointed sheriff of Pulaski County. During this time, the Little Rock Travelers were organized and he was elected team president. Eight years later in 1903, Kavanaugh was elected the Southern Association president. He was also chosen to the prestigious National Association of Professional Baseball Leagues. One of the perks of that job was an invitation to the opening of an oddly shaped ballpark in New York City—The Polo Grounds—in 1905. A few years later, he received a similar invitation to Ebbets Field, the stylish new ballpark in Brooklyn.

His presidency of the Southern Association brought a high standard of organization to the league. Kavanaugh served as league president despite the fact that Little Rock did not have a team in the league from 1910 through 1915. Judge Kavanaugh was elected to the United States Senate in 1913 by the Arkansas legislature to succeed the late Senator Jeff Davis.

The Little Rock Travelers had been absent from the Southern Association since 1909. Judge Kavanaugh presided at the spring meeting of the league on Saturday, February 20, 1915, hosted a banquet for the league presidents and managers that evening. Kavanaugh died the next day and the beloved judge was honored a week later by a crowd of 5,000 at a memorial service. The city, county and state saluted the public benefactor. At the time of his death he was either president, director or treasurer of 13 different organizations.

During the 1915 season, West End Park was renamed Kavanaugh Field and in 1936, Kavanaugh Boulevard was named in honor of the man who had helped build the street and helped develop the Pulaski Heights area.

Ray Winder began his career with the Travelers in 1915. He had just closed the last livery stable in Little Rock when he was hired by R.G. "Bob" Allen to be a ticket taker at the ballgame. In 1931, when Allen sold the team, Winder became business manager. That year was the Travelers' last one at Kavanaugh Field. By 1946, Winder was general manager. The post-war crowds were over 100,000 for seven of eight years. In 1959, Arkansas fielded no team and Winder had to scramble to gather a team for the 1960 season. He used all his contacts in baseball to amass a motley team of veterans and young players. Winder put together a third place team that won the Southern Association playoffs. Winder garnered honors from *The Sporting News* as Minor League Executive of the Year for his efforts.

According to Travelers historian Jim Bailey, the "single most important factor in the club's history was the rigid determination of Ray Winder" to keep the franchise afloat. "I'm a Little Rock man," said Winder. At the age of 75, he moved the Travelers for the second time from out of town back to Little Rock. A public stock drive was held to raise money for the team.

On August 26, 1966, at the ballpark, Hall of Famer Stan Musial crowned Winder "King of Baseball" and that night Travelers' Field was renamed Ray Winder Field.

Bill Valentine, the Travelers' current "savior," was born near the ballpark and as a youth, he was asked to umpire many kid baseball games. After graduation from high school, Valentine attended umpire school in Florida. At 18, he became the youngest man to umpire a professional baseball game. After an 18-year umpiring career, six in the major leagues, he took over the general manager's job for the Arkansas Travelers in 1976. In the words of Texas League President Tom Kayser, "Ray Winder Field became a hopping happening place." In his first year, Valentine attracted 90,255 fans to see a third-place team, a 34 percent increase in attendance.

Good teams brought in the crowds, but Valentine used his imagination, too. His first year as general manager, he told the press in a pre-season news conference that he would send a smaller player than Bill Veeck's midget to the plate to lead off the season. Sportswriters wanted to know who the player was and how short he was. Valentine said, "You'll have to be in the park to know." Actually, Valentine did not yet have the player and did not where he would come from. Just before opening day, tiny Roscoe Stidman dropped by Valentine's office and announced, "I'm your leadoff batter!" Stidman and a 6-foot-4 umpire named "Slick" Slickenmeier made quite a show and wowed the crowd.

"It never rains at Ray Winder Field" became a well-known saying because of Valentine. During the 1976 Travelers season, several times rain fell all around Little Rock, but not at Ray Winder Field. "It might be raining at University Avenue, on Kavanaugh Boulevard, but it would not be raining at Ray Winder Field," Valentine said. When concerned fans would inquire during a downpour in downtown Little Rock, Valentine would answer the ballpark phone: "It never rains at Ray Winder Field."

Valentine, ever the showman, also coined the phrase "The Greatest Show on Dirt." Barnum and Bailey sued him and the phrase was changed to "The Greatest Game on Dirt." With Kar Klunker Night, Dynamite Lady, Baseball Bingo, and Midget Wrestling and some championship baseball in 1977, the Travelers pulled in their second highest attendance in 13 years. Valentine was just beginning. He continues to host his "Greatest Game on Dirt" at Ray Winder Field.

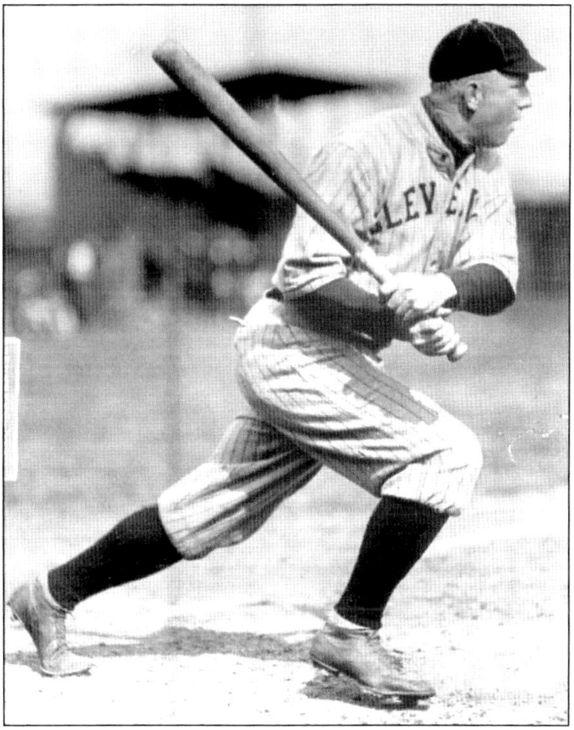

Tris Speaker led the Southern Association in hitting with a.350 average in 1908 as a Little Rock Traveler. Speaker was sold to Boston in 1909 and started a Hall of Fame career with the Red Sox. He was a fantastic defensive outfielder and teamed with Harry Hooper and Duffy Lewis to form one of the greatest outfields of all time, contributing to the the Red Sox's four World Series wins between 1912 and 1918. (Courtesy of the National Baseball Hall of Fame and Library, Cooperstown, New York.)

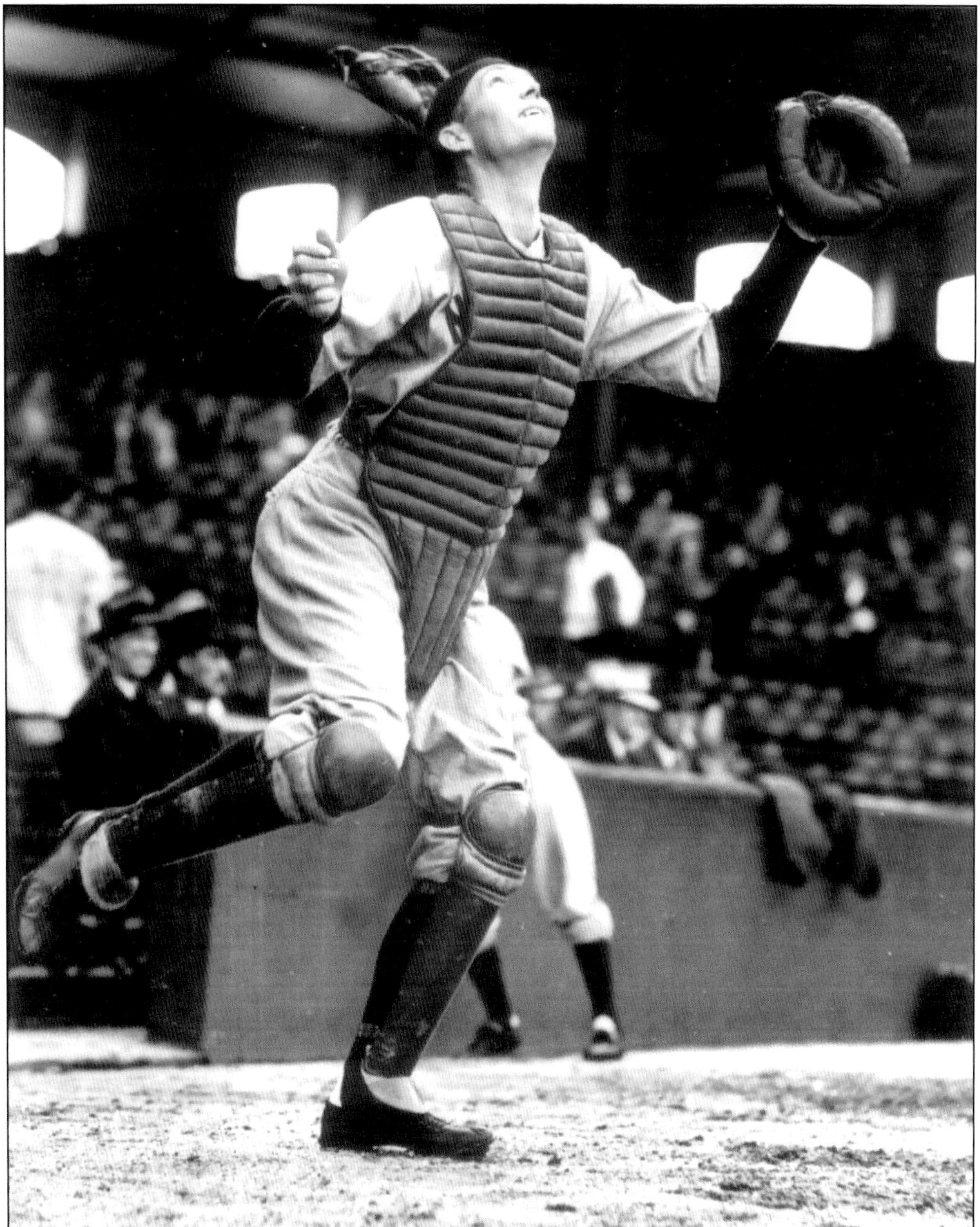

Bill Dickey, a beloved Arkansas Traveler and the Hall of Fame Yankee catcher, played in eight All Star Games and was a member of eight Yankee World Series Champions. Dickey retired to Little Rock. He was avid fisherman on the lakes of Arkansas. (Courtesy of the National Baseball Hall of Fame and Library, Cooperstown, New York.)

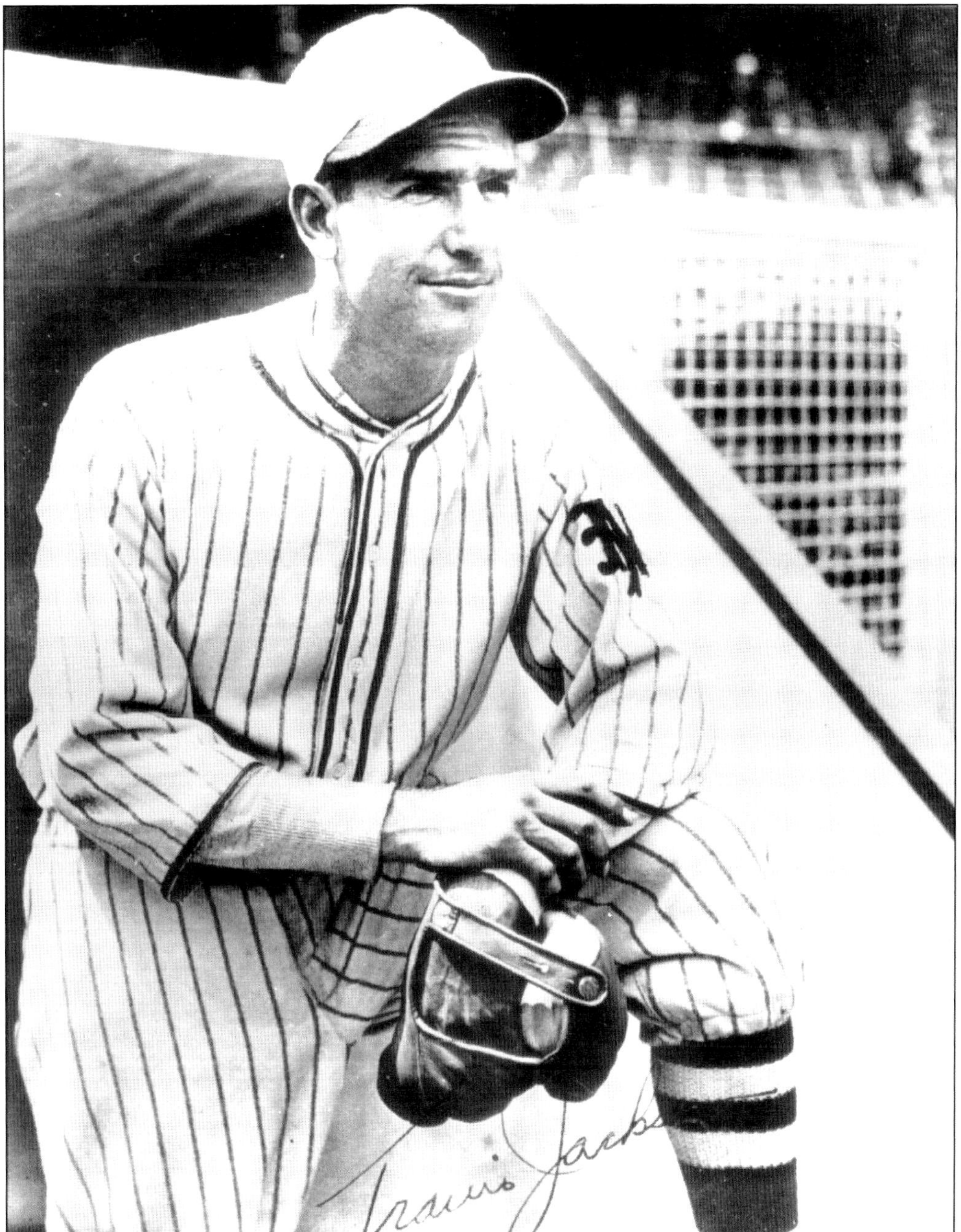

Travis Jackson played in the only "All-Hall of Fame" infield in baseball history. New York Giants Manager John McGraw, a Hall of Famer himself, put Bill Terry at first base, Frankie Frisch at second, Jackson at short, and Fred Lindstrom at third base. All four made the Hall with Jackson being inducted in 1982. Jackson played on the 1933 World Champion New York Giants. (Courtesy of the National Baseball Hall of Fame and Library, Cooperstown, New York.)

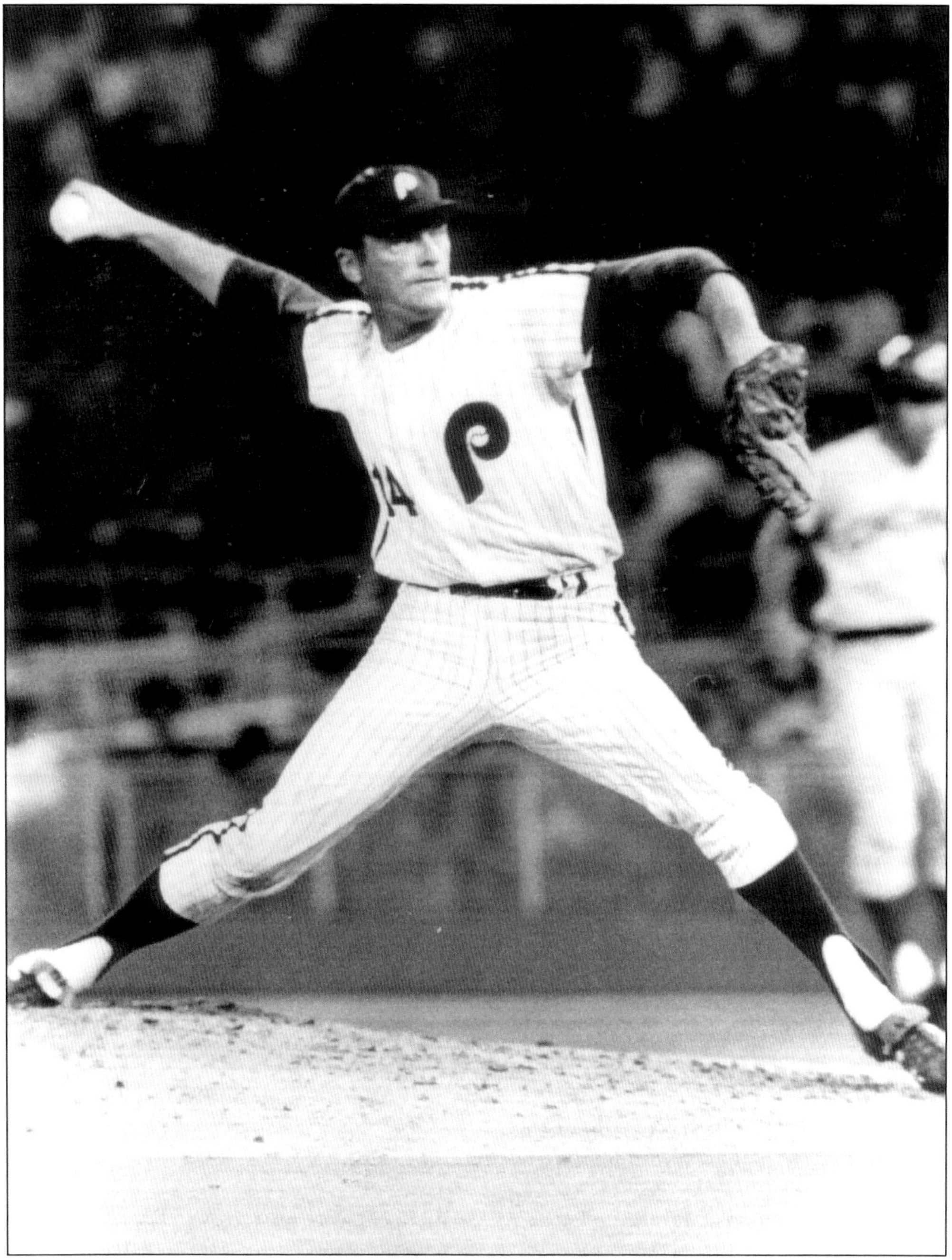

Jim Bunning proved he could win in both leagues. He won over 100 games with Detroit from 1953 to 1963 and then 100 with Philadelphia from 1964 to 1971. He was also the first pitcher to throw no-hitters in both leagues. The Kentucky native was elected to the Hall of Fame in 1996. He was also elected to the United States House of Representatives and the United States Senate. (Courtesy of the National Baseball Hall of Fame and Library, Cooperstown, New York.)

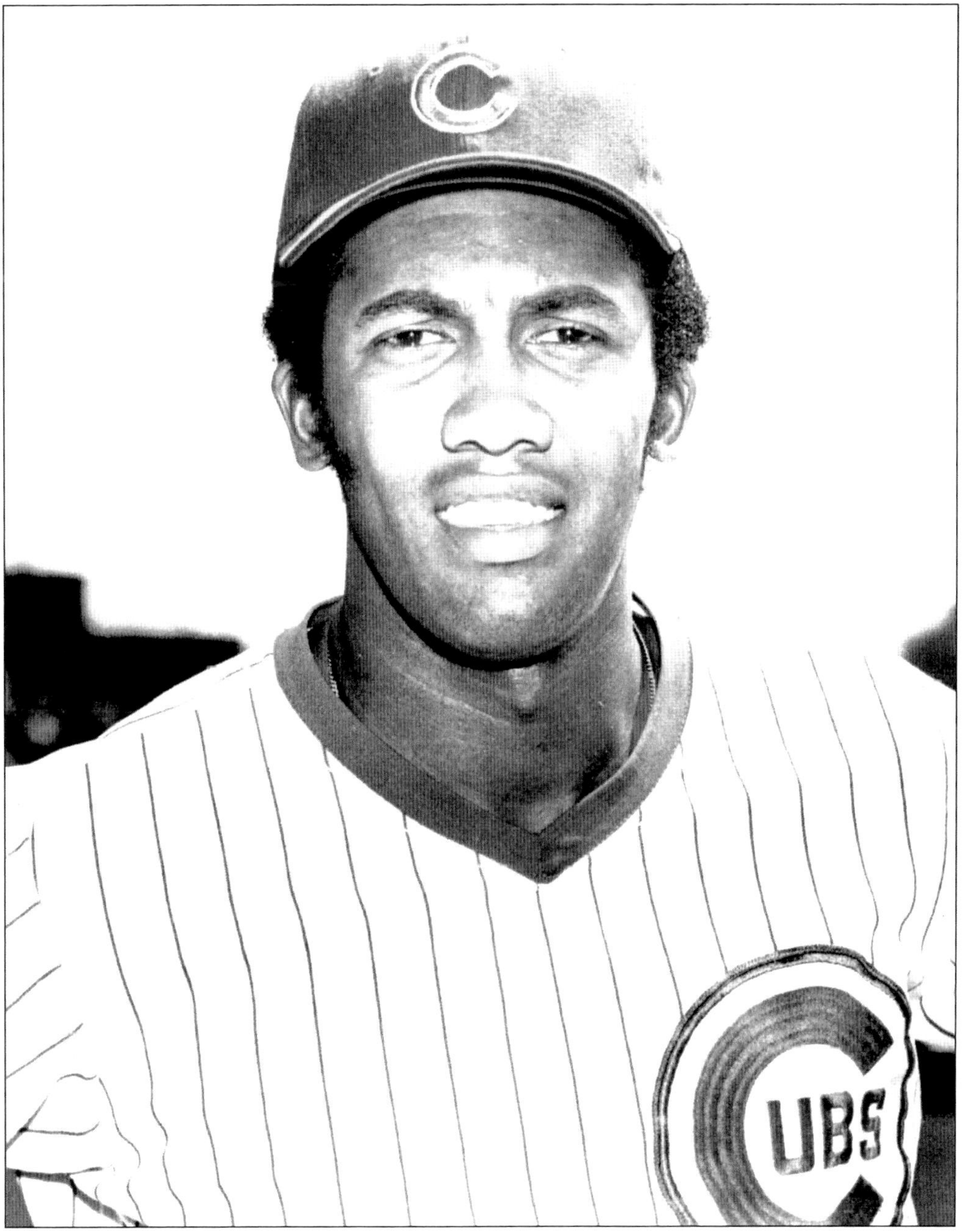

Ferguson Jenkins compiled a 13-11 record pitching for the Travelers in 1964 and 1965. The Canadian native twice led the National League in wins. Four times he led his league in complete games. In 1971, he won the National League's Cy Young Award. Along with fellow Travelers pitcher Jim Bunning, he is one of the few pitchers to win over 100 games in both the National and American Leagues. He was honored in a return to Ray Winder Field in 2003. (Courtesy of the National Baseball Hall of Fame and Library, Cooperstown, New York.)

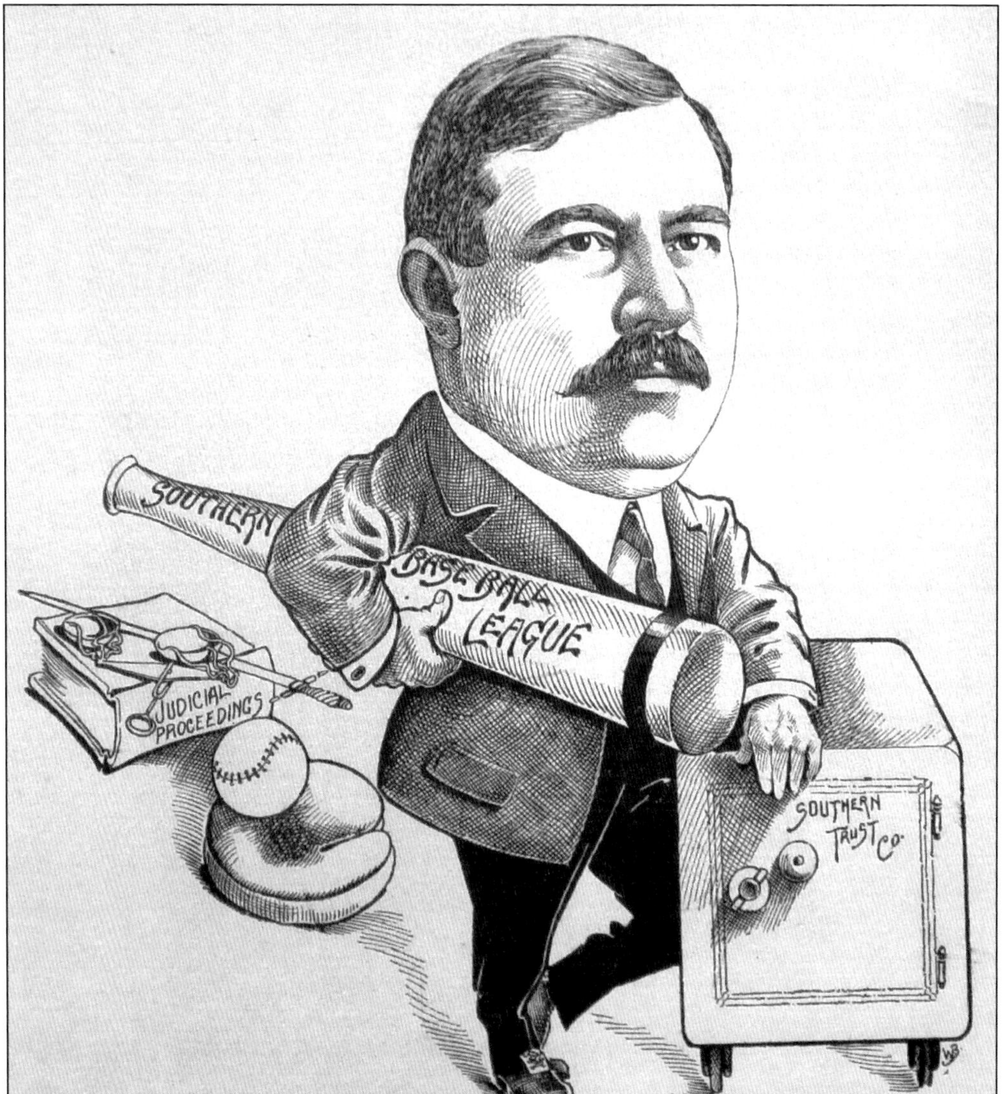

Judge William M. Kavanaugh was the Southern Association's "go to guy" in 1903. The Southern Association elected him to the league presidency in 1903. He had proven his capabilities as an Arkansas Gazette city editor, a county judge, and later a United States senator. Kavanaugh brought professionalism to the Southern Association as well as a calming influence. (Courtesy of Louise Atkinson Isgrig.)

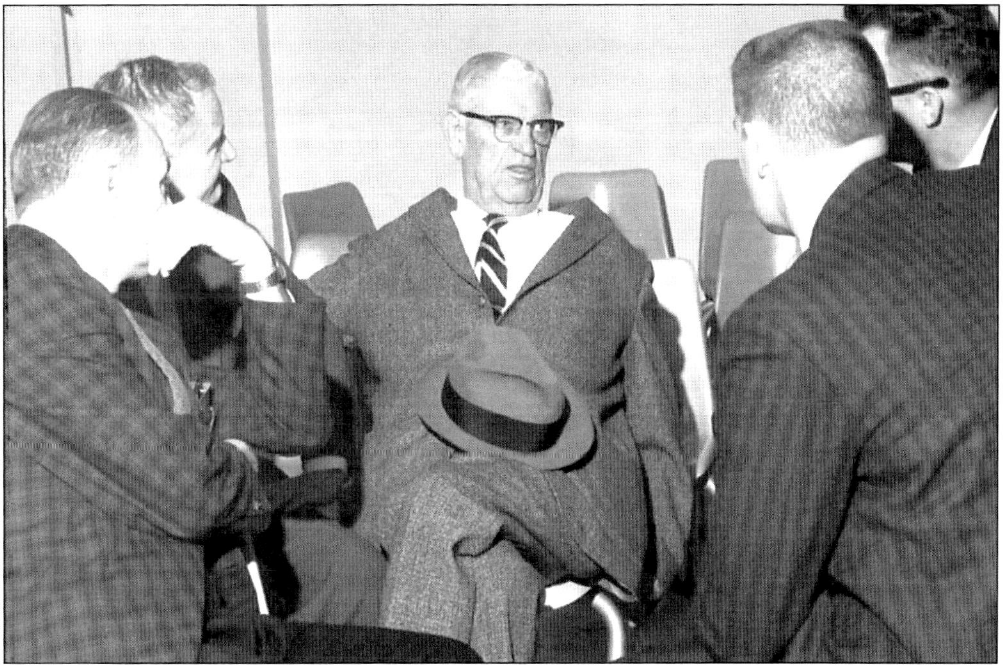

Travelers General Manager Ray Winder, center, engages in a conversation with Lee Rogers, Mel Geho and Len Monhaimer. Rogers and Geho were former Traveler players and Monhaimer replaced Winder as general manager. (Courtesy of the Arkansas Travelers.)

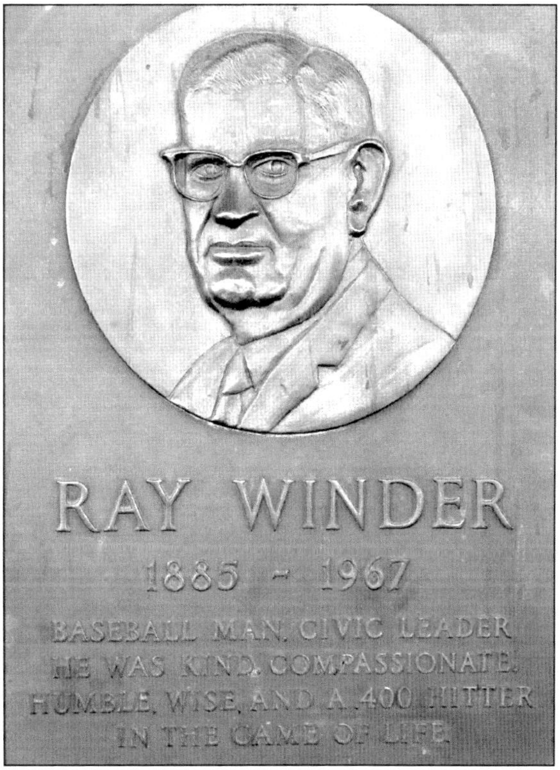

Ray Winder seemed to be a one-man committee at keeping the Little Rock franchise in minor league baseball. Twice he led efforts to bring the Travelers back into the Southern Association. He was doubly honored in 1966 when *The Sporting News* named him "King of Baseball" and Travelers Field was renamed in his honor. (Courtesy of Carl Enna.)

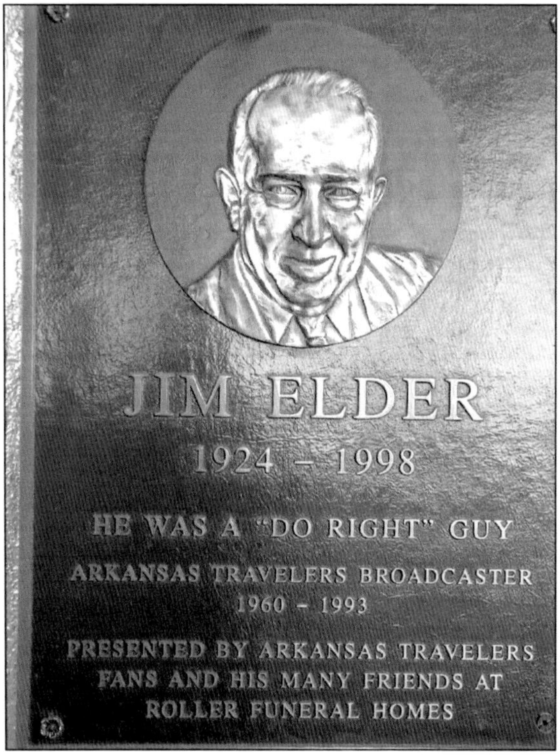

Jim Elder was a much-admired Travelers baseball announcer for 33 years. Bud Campbell, the team's play-by-play man, thought Elder's career as a former umpire would make him ideal as a color man. The pair clicked. When Campbell was killed in a car wreck, Elder became the play-by-play man and broadcast during the Travelers time in the International League, Pacific Coast League and the Texas League. (Courtesy of Carl Enna.)

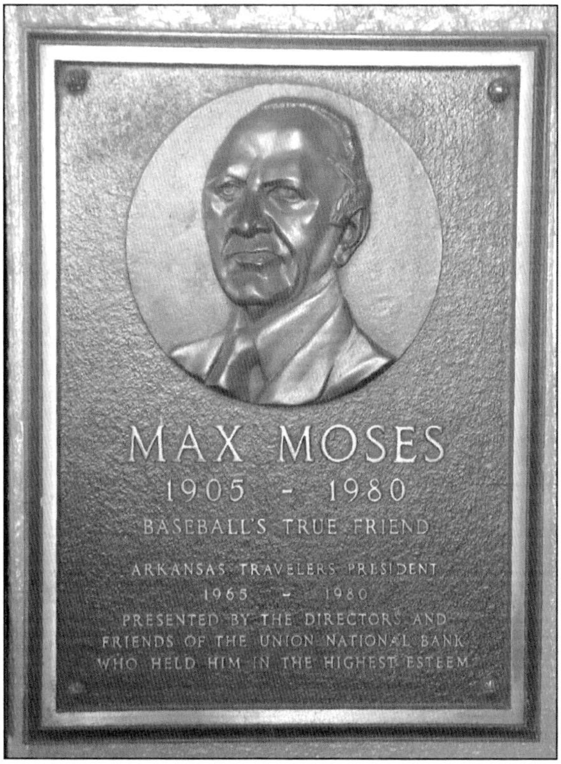

Max Moses was a Little Rock jeweler who led the campaign to get the Travelers in Double-A ball with the Cardinals. Because of his efforts, the Travelers' Board elected him team president. (Courtesy of the Arkansas Travelers.)

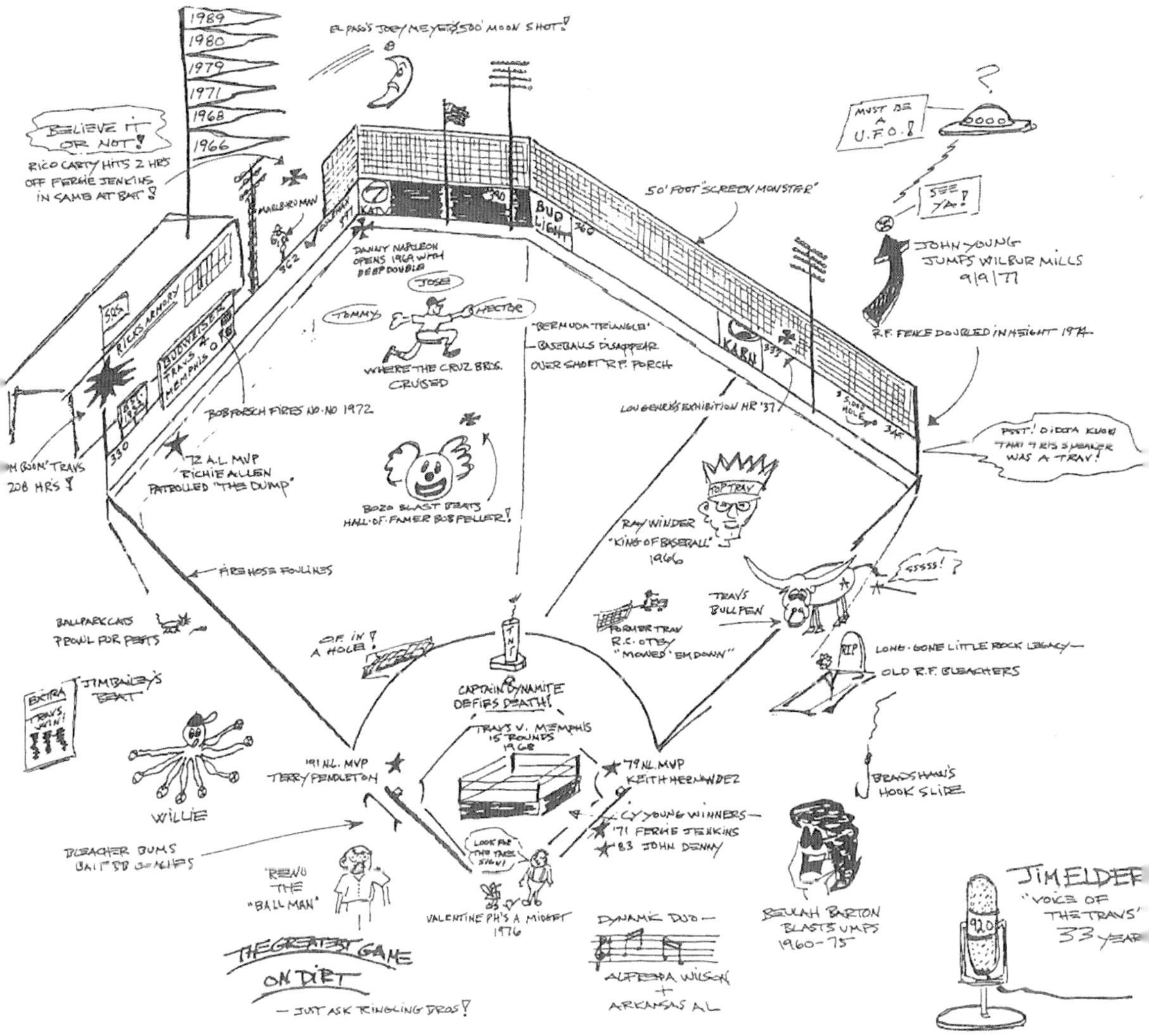

Jim Elder's radio career spanned 30 years at Travelers Field/Ray Winder Field. Elder had been an umpire and later became Bud Campbell's radio color man. On Jim Elder Night, June 30, 1990, cartoonist Bob Harrison recalled highlights of Elder's career.

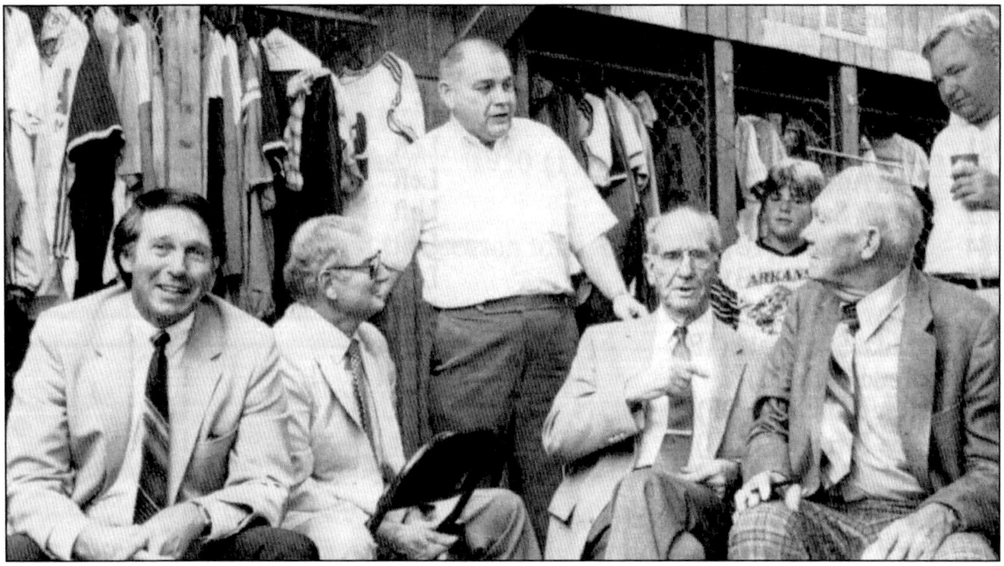

General Manager Bill Valentine, a former Major League umpire, visits with several Hall of Famers in the Travelers locker room. Little Rock-born Brooks Robinson, George Kell of Swifton, Waldo's Travis Jackson, and Little Rock resident Bill Dickey join the Travelers batboy, Ashton Jones, and Travelers President Bert Parke. Robinson spent his career with Baltimore. Kell starred with the Tigers before joining Robinson at Baltimore. Jackson was a star with John McGraw's New York Giants. Dickey caught a stable of great pitchers with the Yankees. (Courtesy of the Arkansas Travelers.)

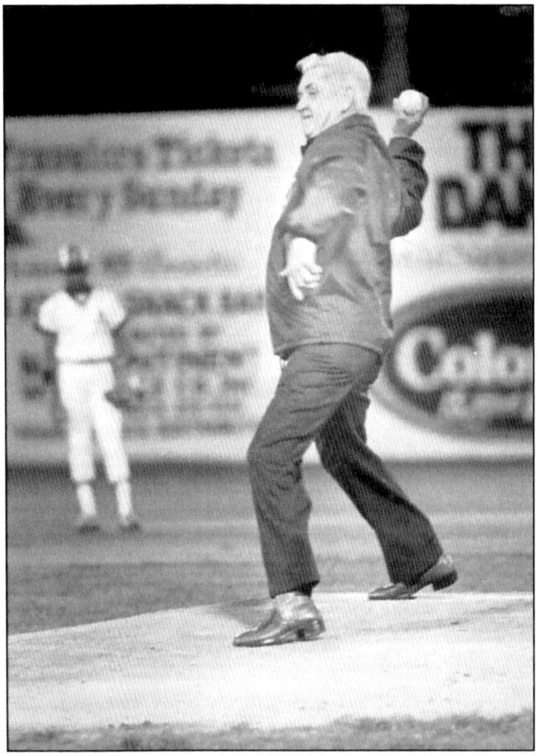

Veteran Travelers second baseman R.C. Otey throws out the first pitch on April 14, 1983. Otey was a popular member of the Little Rock team during a 10-year playing career. In his retirement, Otey served 30 years as groundskeeper at the Travelers ballpark. (Courtesy of the Arkansas Travelers.)

In 1966, Jack Pickens played a big part in getting the Travelers back in Double-A ball. He was a close friend of St. Louis Cardinals owner Gussie Busch and helped orchestrate the shift from AAA to AA in the Texas League. (Courtesy of the Arkansas Travelers.)

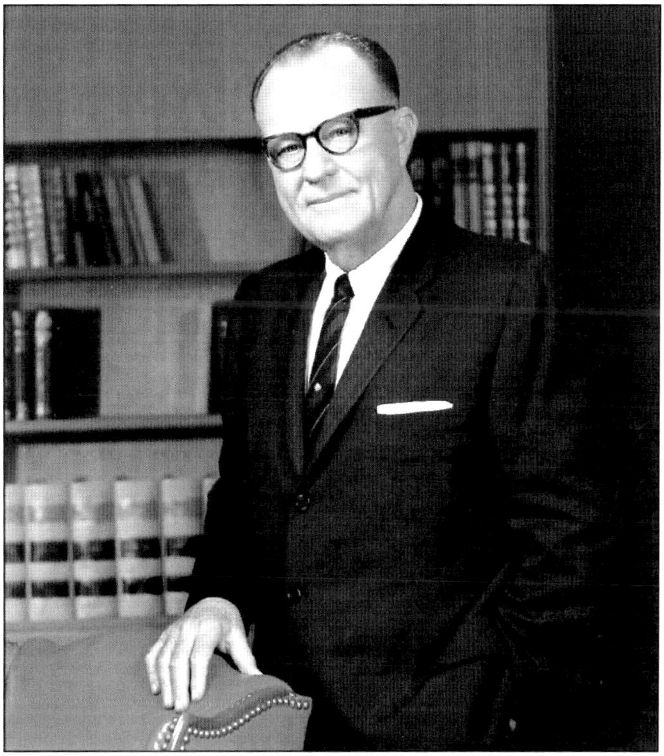

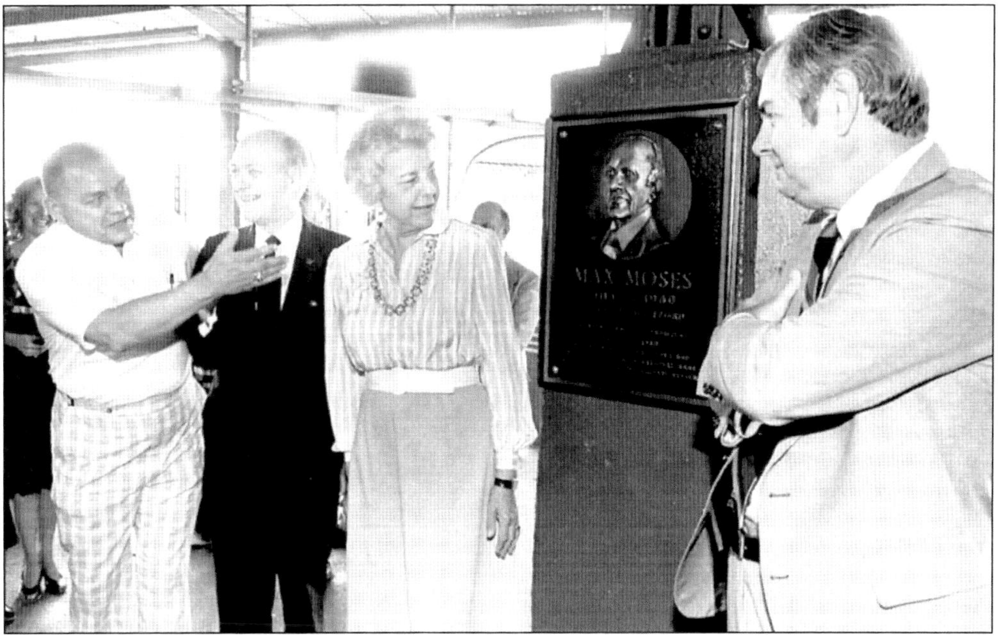

Traveler General Manager Bill Valentine points to the memorial plaque of former Arkansas team president Max Moses. Pictured from left to right are Valentine, Gene Smith, vice chairman of Union National Bank, Mrs. Hannah Moses and Gene Barlow, senior vice-president of UNB. (Courtesy of the Arkansas Travelers.)

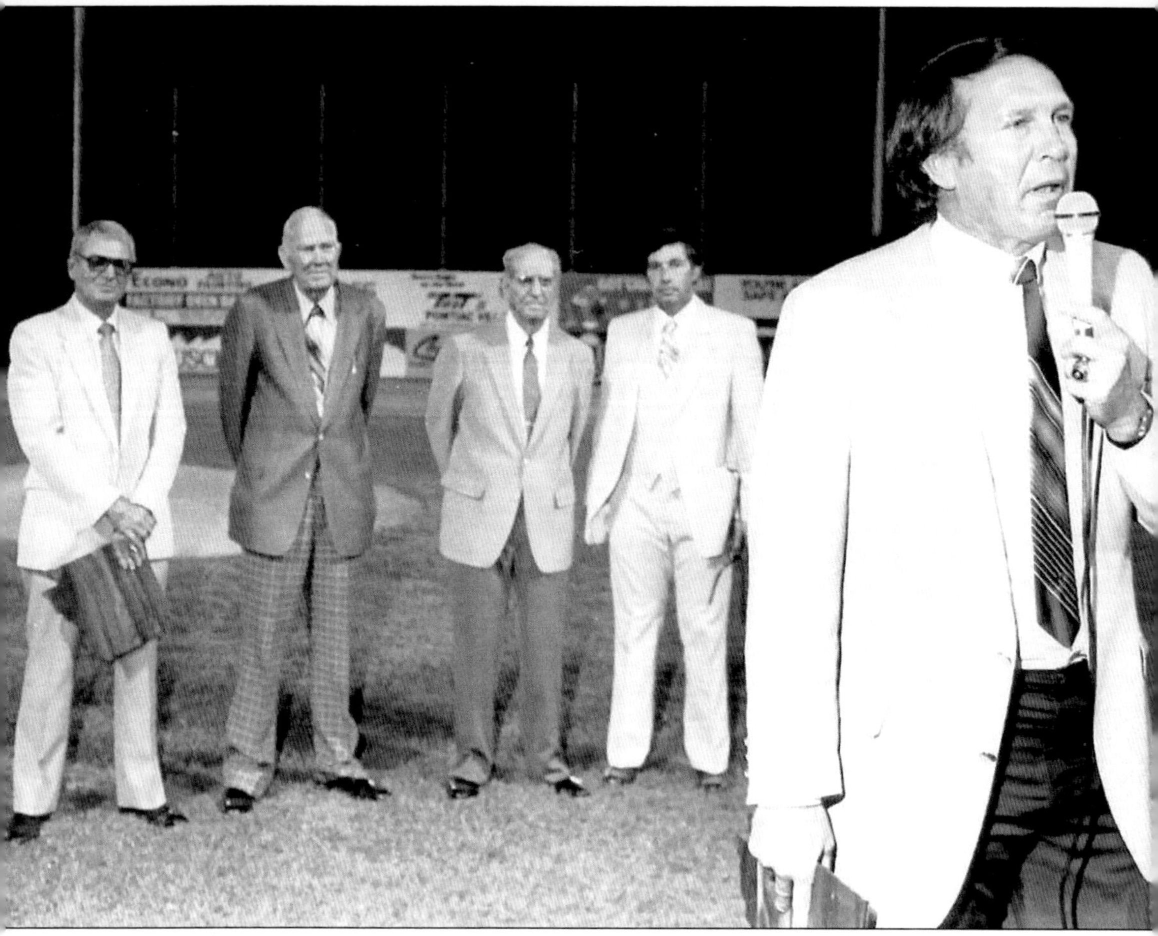

Brooks Robinson emcees a ceremony honoring Arkansans in the Baseball Hall of Fame. A native of Little Rock, Robinson played both high school and American Legion baseball in Central Arkansas. Pictured from left to right, behind Robinson, are Hall of Famers George Kell, Bill Dickey and Travis Jackson. (Courtesy of the Arkansas Travelers.)

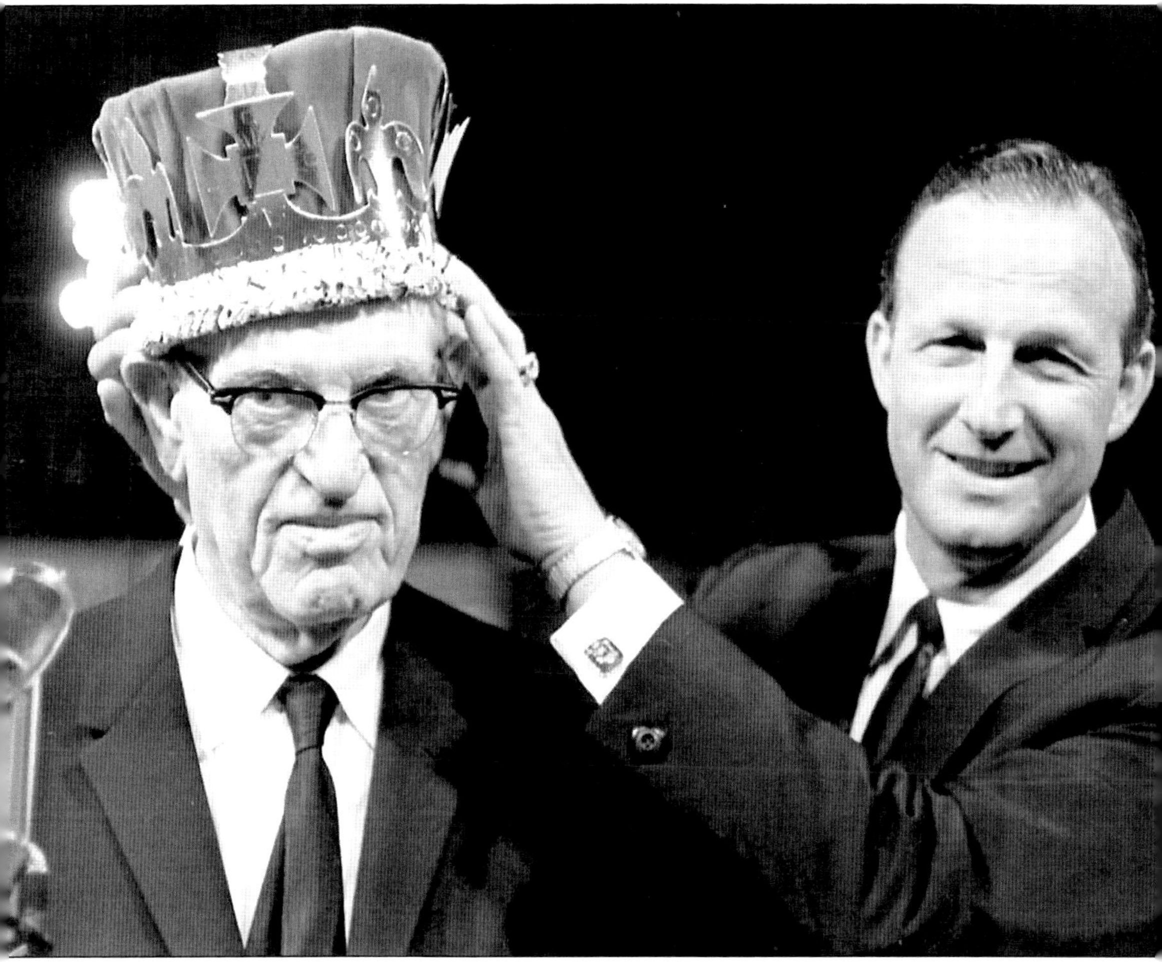

Stan Musial, Cardinals Hall of Famer, crowned Ray Winder "King of Baseball" on August 26, 1966, in a ceremony renaming Travelers' Field to Ray Winder Field. Winder's greatest moments may have come in 1960. At the age of 75, he, for the second time, moved the Travelers back to Little Rock. A public stock drive was held and the team became fan-owned. Winder garnered honors from *The Sporting News* as "Minor League Executive of the Year" for his efforts. (Courtesy of the Arkansas Travelers.)

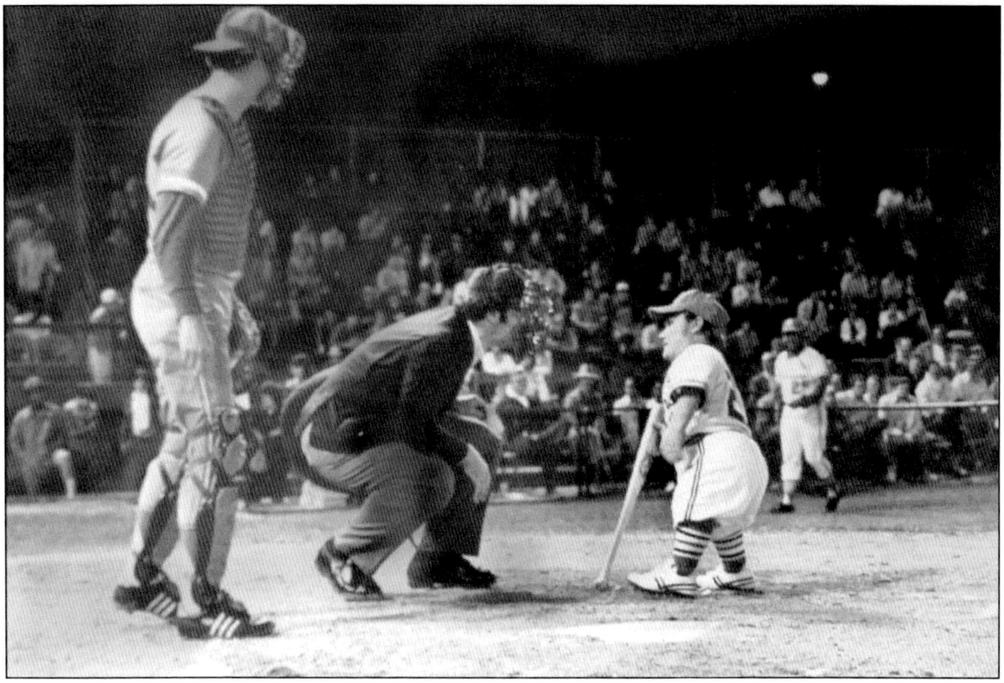

In 1976, Roscoe Stidman was the first hitter in the Bill Valentine era for the Arkansas Travelers. The tiny Traveler was called out on strikes, Stidman argued the call and was thrown out of the game. (Courtesy of the Arkansas Travelers.)

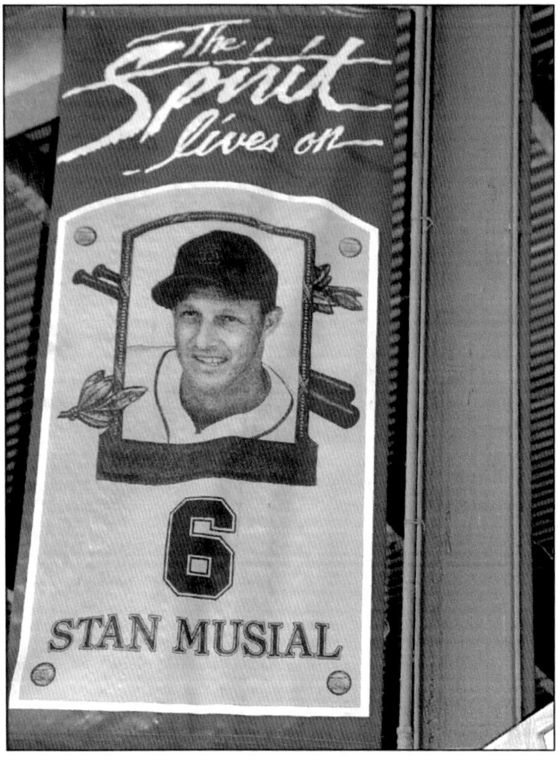

Even though the St. Louis Cardinals and the Travelers cut their ties after the 2000 season, Hall of Famer Stan Musial still has a large following in the state. (Courtesy of Carl Enna.)

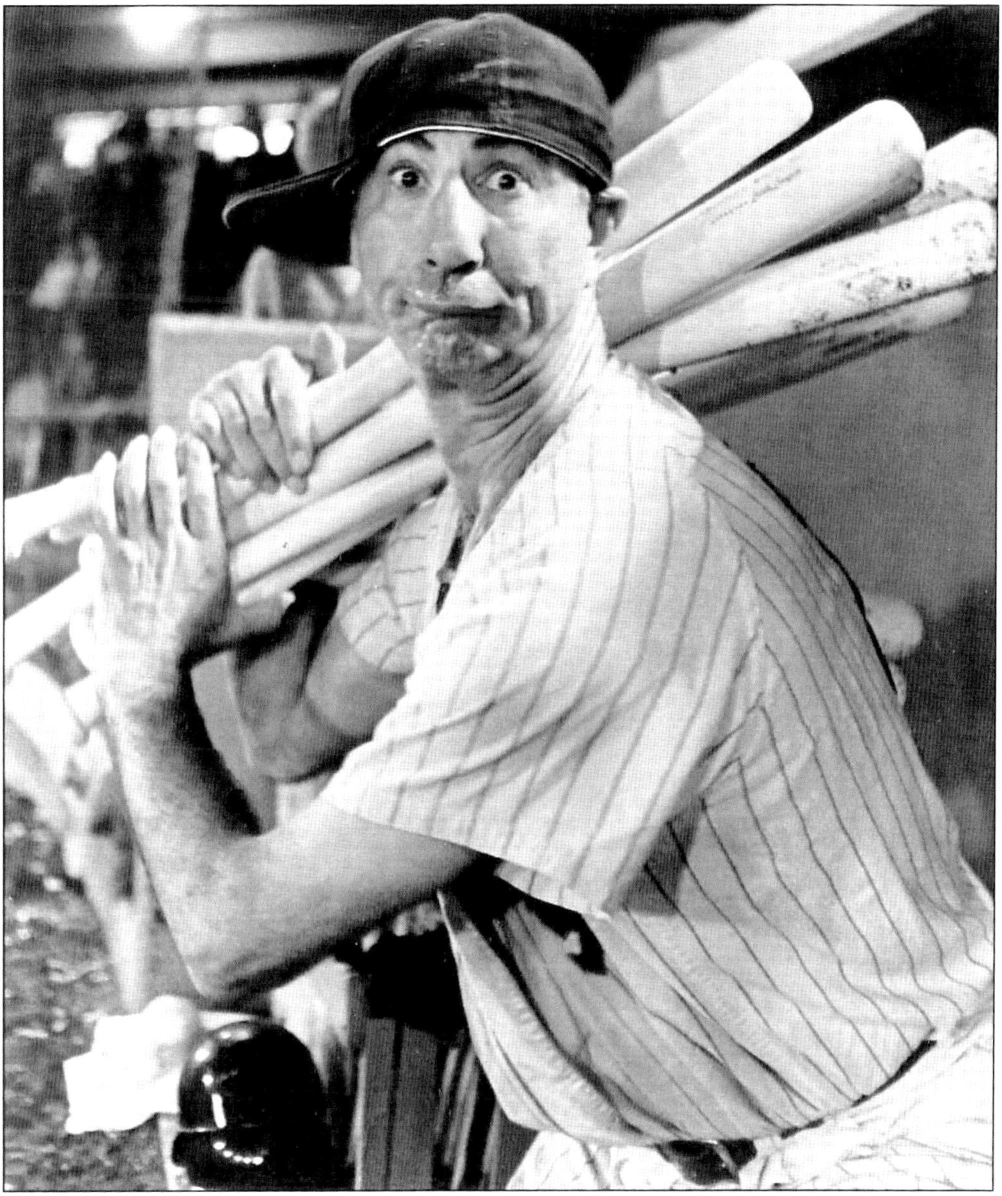

Rubber-faced Max Patkin entertained baseball fans coast-to-coast for five decades. Bill Veeck first hired Patkin as a pitching coach, but Patkin's antics were perfect for public relations and promotions. Patkin became more well known playing himself in the popular baseball movie "Bull Durham." Patkin entertained at Ray Winder Field as well as major-league parks. (Courtesy of the Arkansas Travelers.)

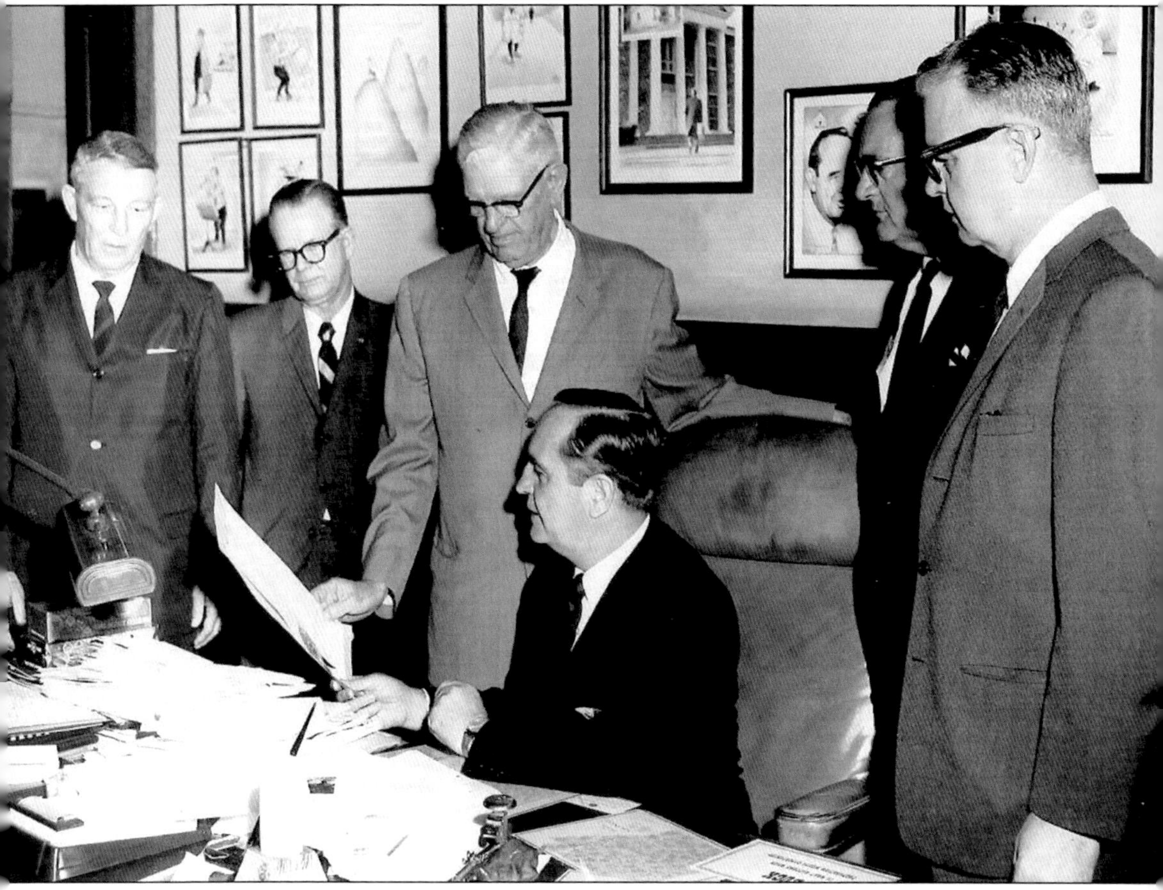

Ray Winder reviews a proclamation observing opening day for the team from Arkansas Governor Orval Faubus. Pictured from left are Allan Berry, Hal Totter, Winder, Governor of Arkansas Faubus, Harold May and Ike Murry. Traditionally, Arkansas governors support the state's baseball team in various ways: throwing out the first pitch, issuing commemorative proclamations or calling a few innings on the radio. (Courtesy of the Arkansas Travelers.)

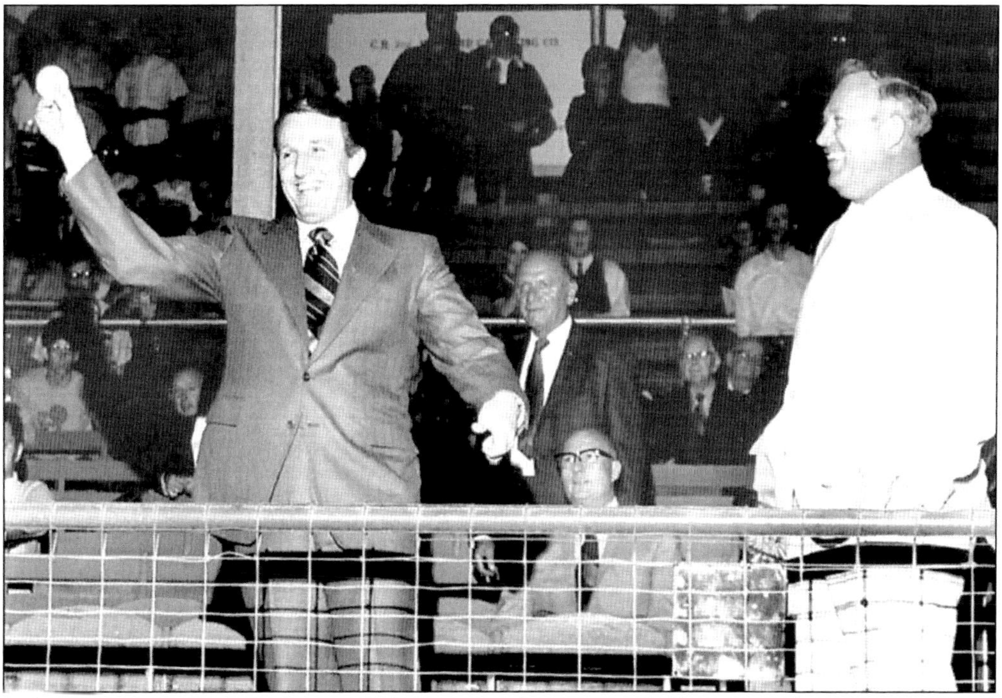

Arkansas Governor Dale Bumpers throws out the first pitch for a Travelers game. General manager Carl Sawatski is at right. Local celebrities and politicians are often involved in pre-game activities. (Courtesy of the Arkansas Travelers.)

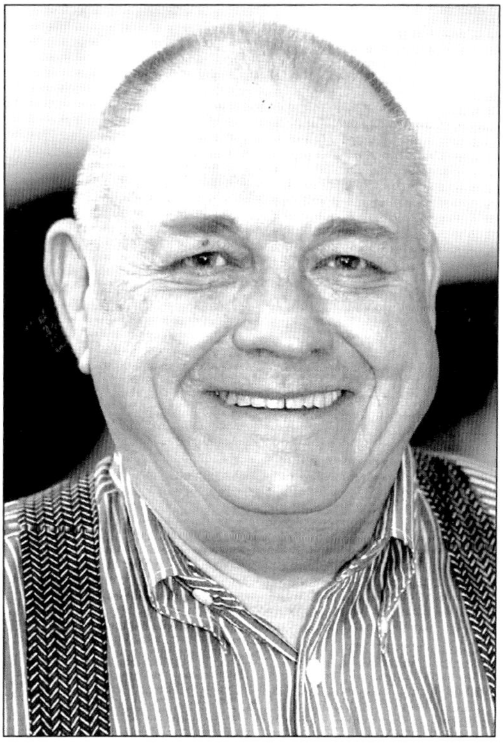

Bill Valentine's presence can be felt across the ballpark. Fans hear his recorded voice as they enter Ray Winder Field and his reserved bleacher seat is on the first base side, right around the corner from his office. As executive vice president and general manager, Valentine has received numerous professional and civic awards. In 1983, he won the Professional Baseball Lee McPhail Award. In 1988, Valentine was chosen *The Sporting News* Minor League Executive of the Year. Five times he has been named Texas League Executive of the Year. In 2004, he was inducted into the Arkansas Sports Hall of Fame. (Courtesy of the Arkansas Travelers.)

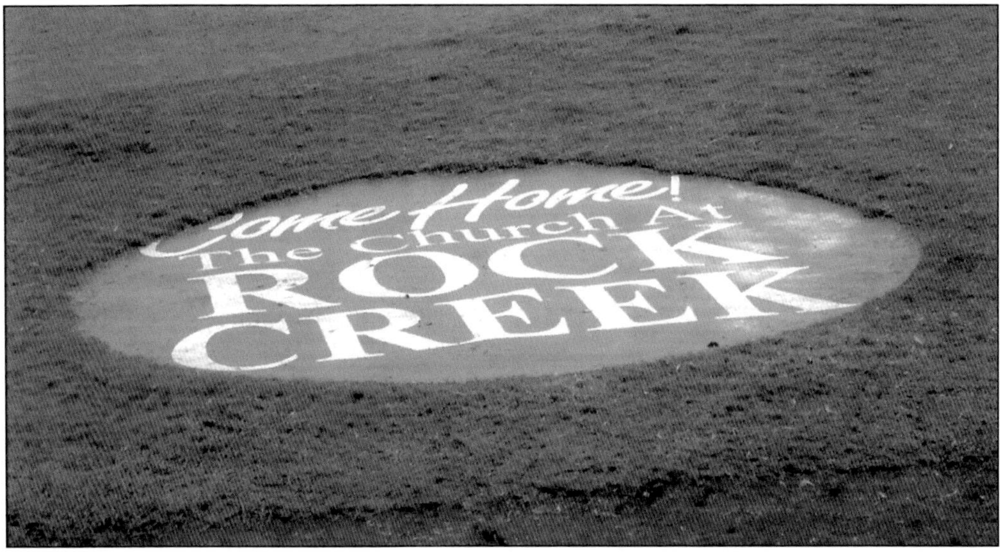

The Church at Rock Creek sponsors two batting circles at Ray Winder Field. The Rock Creek pastor, Mark Evans, is a season ticket holder and still holds close ties to the team since his service as a batboy and clubhouse manager. (Courtesy of Don Curdie.)

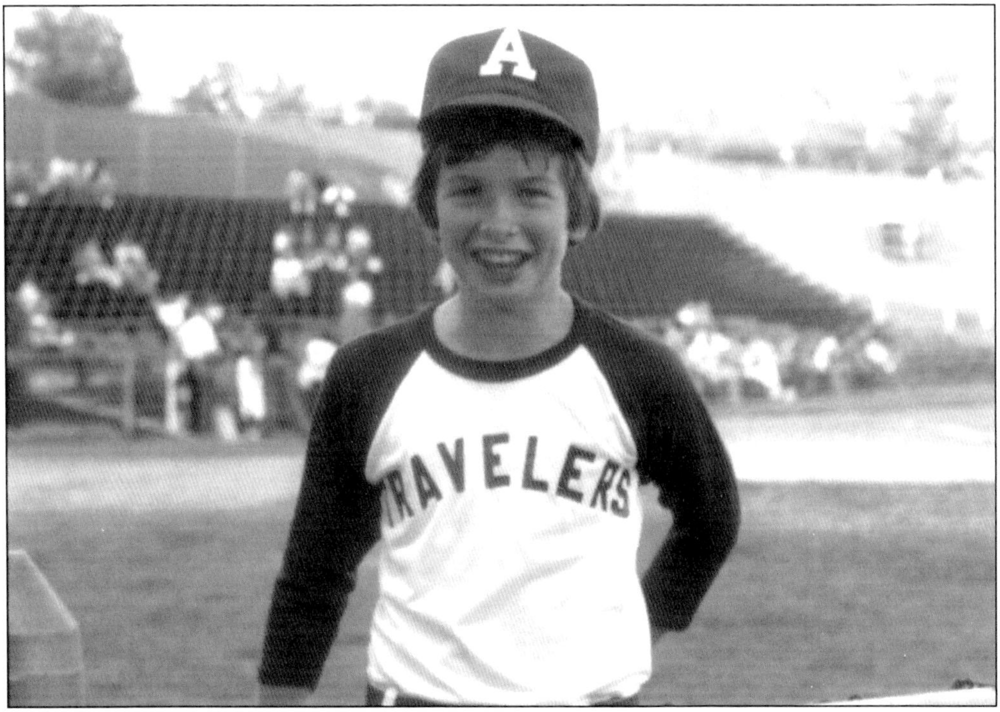

Eleven-year-old Mark Evans's love of baseball led to a dream job. Travelers' GM Bill Valentine noticed that young Evans was a frequent visitor to Ray Winder Field in 1977, so he asked him to be the Travelers batboy. Evans performed the job with the same evangelical flair that he would use as minister at The Church at Rock Creek in Little Rock. Evans became clubhouse manager and traveled with the team on road trips. He was employed during the heyday of the Travelers three pennants in four years (1977–1980). (Courtesy of Shirley Rieve.)

Forty-six years' worth of season tickets are displayed by Arkansas fan Shirley Rieve. Rieve had home tickets for the Travelers since 1958. Her seat is adjacent to the Travelers' dugout and she has kept score of games since the 1950s. (Courtesy of Don Curdie.)

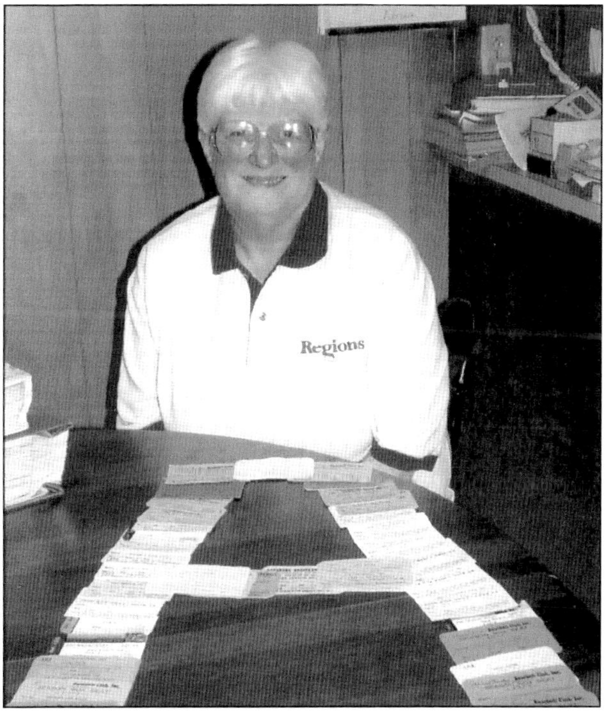

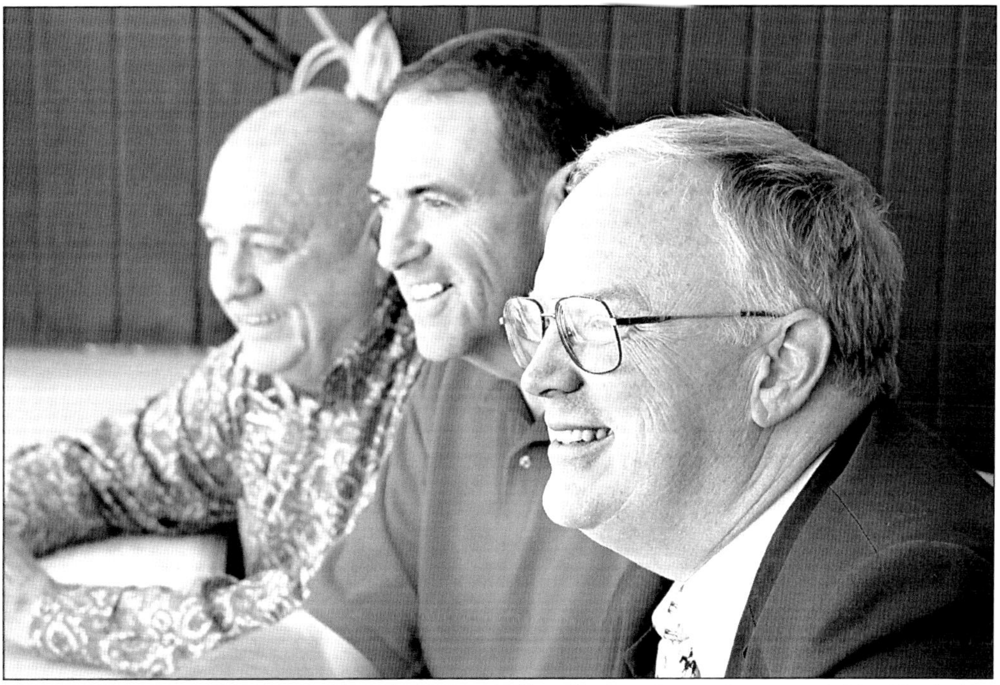

General Manager and "Baseball Ambassador" Bill Valentine hosts Governor Mike Huckabee and Rex Nelson in the press box at Ray Winder Field. The governor is committed to increasing tourism in the state and the Travelers are an excellent draw for Little Rock and the surrounding area. The three men share a love for Arkansas, baseball and broadcasting. All three have announced baseball games on the radio in their varied careers. (Courtesy of Carl Enna)

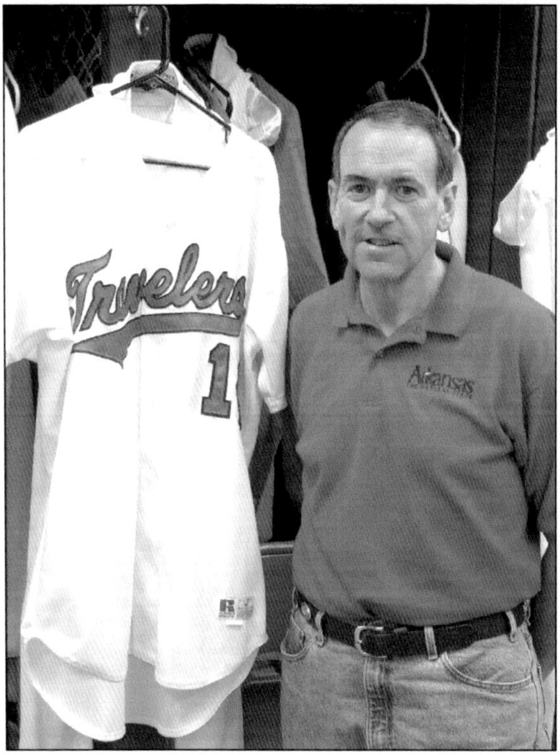

A former Little League All Star catcher in his hometown of Hope, Arkansas, Governor Mike Huckabee remains a baseball enthusiast. He started broadcasting games over the radio at the age of 14 and has announced Travelers games as a guest play-by-play man. (Courtesy of Carl Enna.)

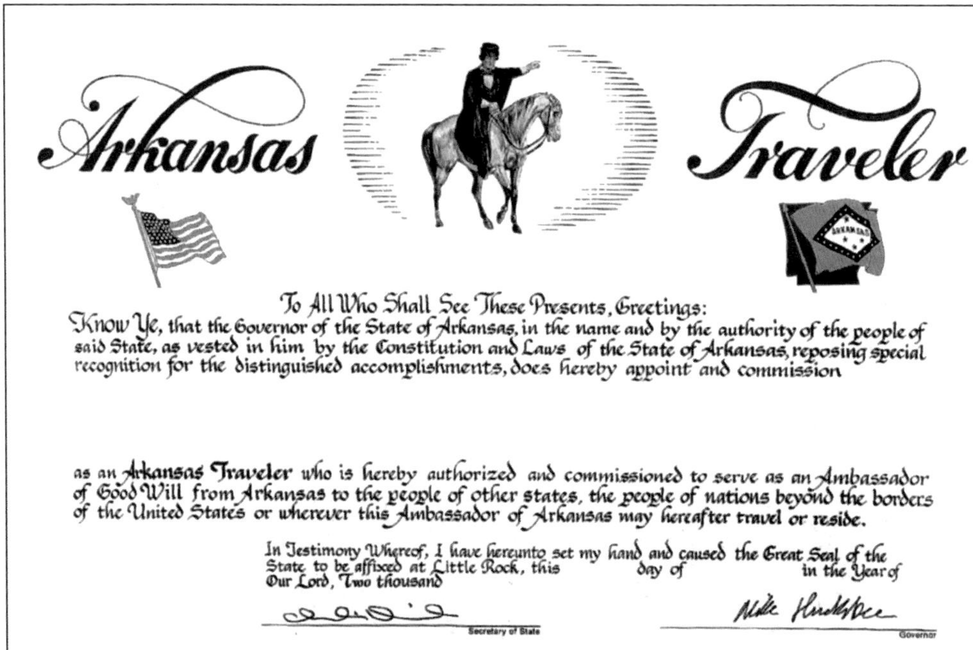

Arkansas Traveler

To All Who Shall See These Presents, Greetings:

Know Ye, that the Governor of the State of Arkansas, in the name and by the authority of the people of said State, as vested in him by the Constitution and Laws of the State of Arkansas, reposing special recognition for the distinguished accomplishments, does hereby appoint and commission

as an Arkansas Traveler who is hereby authorized and commissioned to serve as an Ambassador of Good Will from Arkansas to the people of other states, the people of nations beyond the borders of the United States or wherever this Ambassador of Arkansas may hereafter travel or reside.

In Testimony Whereof, I have hereunto set my hand and caused the Great Seal of the State to be affixed at Little Rock, this day of in the Year of Our Lord, Two thousand

Secretary of State

Governor

The Travelers baseball name and logo represents more than just a team's mascot. The entire state is proud of the "Arkansas Traveler" and as a salute to the folk song legend, special visitors to the state may receive an official certificate from the governor naming them as honorary "Arkansas Travelers." (Courtesy of the Office of the Governor, State of Arkansas.)

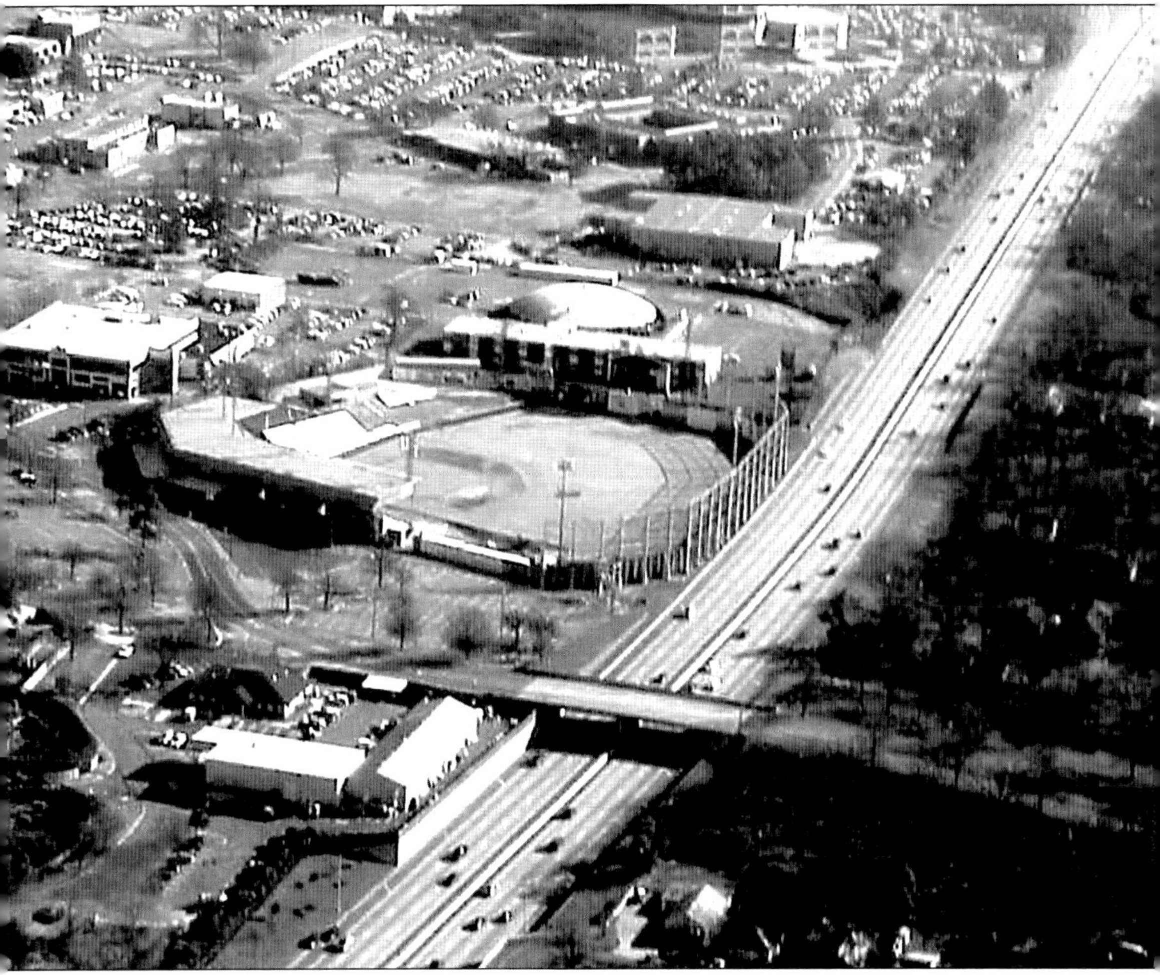

For over a century, Arkansans have loved baseball in Little Rock. Fans today still go to the ballpark to root for the home (state) team. Despite the long years of pennant droughts in the Southern Association, the Traveler fan of today can readily remember Arkansas's last Texas League title in 2001. Ray Winder Field is the fifth oldest ballpark in professional baseball. The changes in appearance at Ray Winder Field have been largely cosmetic. When it started life in 1932, a dusty road skirted around the right field fence. Today, over 70 years later, bustling Interstate Highway 630, a six-lane freeway, connects west Little Rock to downtown. The freeway tightly borders rightfield and occasionally, a long homer flies over the 55-foot high fence to startle motorists. Centrally located in the city, the ballpark is located in an area now known as War Memorial Park and includes an 18-hole public golf course, tennis courts, the Little Rock Zoo, and a few blocks from revered War Memorial Stadium. (Courtesy of John Knight.)

Photo Credits

Arkansas History Commission
Betty Baird
Don Curdie
Carl Enna
Kirk Jordan
John Knight
National Baseball Hall of Fame and Library, Cooperstown, N.Y.
Shirley Rieve
Texas League Archives
Jim Vasaldua

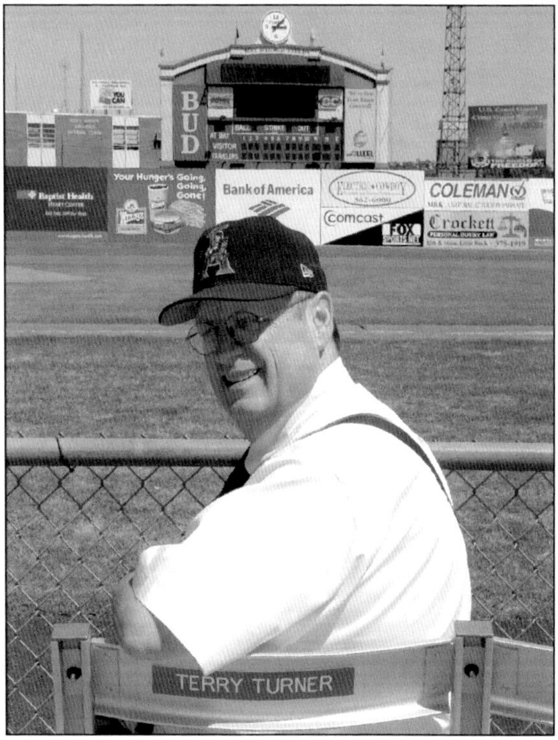

Author Terry Turner, a season ticket holder of the Arkansas Travelers, watches the "Greatest Game on Dirt" at Ray Winder Field. (Courtesy of Carl Enna.)

In Appreciation

Arkansas History Commission
Arkansas Travelers Baseball Inc.
Jim Bailey
Betty Baird
Marynell Branch
Brooks Robinson-George Kell Chapter of SABR
Bill Burdick
Don Curdie
Mike Dugan
Phil Elson
Carl Enna
Mark Evans
John R. Husman
Louise Atkinson Isgrig
Greg Johnston
Kirk Jordan
Tom Kayser
John Knight
Pete Laven
Madison McEntire
Kathy McQueen
W. Lloyd Mobley at Curran Hall
National Baseball Hall of Fame and Library, Cooperstown, N.Y.
Rex Nelson
R. C. Otey
Jim Rasco
Shirley Rieve
Jeff Ruetsche
Kerry Rodtnick
Troy Russell
Texas League Archives
Brenda Turner
Bill Valentine
Jim Vasaldua
David Ware, Arkansas Secretary of State Office

Bibliography

Appel, Martin and Burt Golblatt. *Baseball's Best: The Hall of Fame Gallery*. New York: McGraw-Hill Book Company, 1977.

Bailey, Jim. *90 Years of Travelers Baseball*. Little Rock: Arkansas Travelers Baseball Club, Inc., 1997.

Johnson, Lloyd and Miles Wolff. *The Encyclopedia of Minor League Baseball*. Durham, NC,: Baseball America, Inc., 1997.

Kayser, Tom and Scott Hanzelka. *The Texas League 2003 Official Media Guide and Record Book*, San Antonio, TX: The Texas League of Professional Baseball Clubs, 2003.

Murnane, T. H. *Official Guide: National Association of Professional Baseball Leagues*. New York:A. G. Spalding and Sons, 1905.

O'Neal, Bill. *Texas League 1888–1987: A Century of Baseball*. Austin, TX: Eakin Press, 1987.

Patten, William and J. Walker McSpadden. *The Book of Baseball: The National Game from the Earliest Days to the Present Season*, Collier and Son, Publishers, New York, NY, 1911

Robinson, Brooks. *Third Base is My Home*. Waco, TX: Word Books, 1974.

Spalding's Official Baseball Guide. New York: American Sports Publishing, 1908.

The Arkansas Democrat

The Arkansas Gazette

Thorn, John, Pete Palmer, Michael Gershman, and David Pietrusza. *Total Baseball V: The Official Encyclopedia of Major League Baseball*. New York: Viking, 1997.

Wright, Marshall D. *The Southern Association of Baseball 1885–1961*. Jefferson, NC: McFarland & Company, Inc., 2002.